"Frank Bender is one of the unsung heroes of crime detection . . . In an original and highly readable nonfiction thriller, this book brims with authenticity and the complexities of crime-solving procedurals . . . [A] fascinating story of a brilliant forensic artist's quest to solve some of the most baffling murder cases ever. It is exceptional crime writing that is timely and informative."                                              —*Tucson Citizen*

"Action-packed . . . Botha's work relays Bender's surprising conclusions about the case and imparts more information about reconstructing the faces of the dead than most readers will expect."                                                        —*Booklist*

"[A] crackling account of a quirky, maverick forensics artist, Frank Bender, and his largely successful efforts in facial reconstruction of murder victims . . . What is extraordinary is Botha's writing, with his unerring depiction of Bender's painstaking work and the eventual unraveling of the brutal crimes it solves . . . The tales in this book accurately capture the dark motives and complexities of senseless murder, and even the most savvy true crime reader will not be able to resist the author's insightful storytelling."                    —*Publishers Weekly*

## ALSO BY TED BOTHA

*The Animal Lover*

*Mongo: Adventures in Trash*

*Apartheid in My Rucksack*

*The Expat Confessions* (with Jenni Baxter)

# THE GIRL WITH THE CROOKED NOSE

A Tale of Murder, Obsession,
and Forensic Artistry

## TED BOTHA

BERKLEY BOOKS, NEW YORK

**THE BERKLEY PUBLISHING GROUP**
**Published by the Penguin Group**
**Penguin Group (USA) Inc.**
**375 Hudson Street, New York, New York 10014, USA**
Penguin Group (Canada), 90 Eglinton Avenue East, Suite 700, Toronto, Ontario M4P 2Y3, Canada
(a division of Pearson Penguin Canada Inc.)
Penguin Books Ltd., 80 Strand, London WC2R 0RL, England
Penguin Group Ireland, 25 St. Stephen's Green, Dublin 2, Ireland (a division of Penguin Books Ltd.)
Penguin Group (Australia), 250 Camberwell Road, Camberwell, Victoria 3124, Australia
(a division of Pearson Australia Group Pty. Ltd.)
Penguin Books India Pvt. Ltd., 11 Community Centre, Panchsheel Park, New Delhi—110 017, India
Penguin Group (NZ), 67 Apollo Drive, Rosedale, Auckland 0632, New Zealand
(a division of Pearson New Zealand Ltd.)
Penguin Books (South Africa) (Pty.) Ltd., 24 Sturdee Avenue, Rosebank, Johannesburg 2196,
South Africa

Penguin Books Ltd., Registered Offices: 80 Strand, London WC2R 0RL, England

The publisher does not have any control over and does not assume any responsibility for author or third-party websites or their content.

PRINTING HISTORY
Random House hardcover edition / May 2008
Berkley trade paperback edition / January 2012

Library of Congress Cataloging-in-Publication Data

Botha, Ted.
   The girl with the crooked nose / Ted Botha.—Berkley trade pbk. ed.
      p.  cm.
   ISBN  978-0-425-24683-2
   1. Bender, Frank, 1941-2011.  2. Police artists—United States—Biography.  3. Criminals—Identification.  4. Composite drawing.  I. Title.
   HV8073.4.B67   2012
   363. 25'8—dc23
   [B]
                                                                                    2011037750

PRINTED IN THE UNITED STATES OF AMERICA

10  9  8  7  6  5  4  3  2  1

*For Jan Bender*

# CONTENTS

# INTRODUCTION

*The poster on the side of the bus shelter at Villelobos Ocho was frayed and faded from the sun and the sandstorms that blew through town every afternoon, whipping up dust and trash left behind by the day's travelers. The poster had probably been put up a few years earlier, but when it wore out, no one bothered to come back and replace it with something new. The words written across the bottom of the torn ad, as far as she could make out, read ¿Qué pasa, hermoso?*

*Her guess was that it advertised a men's fragrance, although it was hard to tell. The only clues she had to go on were the lower section of a stubbled chin, three well-manicured male fingers clasping what looked like a bottle, and the word "Gabbana." Perhaps it was liquor, but she preferred the idea of cologne.*

*She stared at the ad whenever she was standing at the bus shelter, which was often. She stood there for at least an hour every day, seven days a week. First she took a bus from her home in Puerto Anapra that dropped her at Villelobos Ocho, where she waited for another bus to the maquiladora on the eastern side of the city. At night she made the same trip in reverse, stopping once again at the bus shelter, where the man from Gabbana would be waiting with his truncated bottle of cologne.*

*After a few moments she would find herself staring at it once again, all the while imagining. She wondered who could afford such an expensive-looking fragrance. Maybe some of those businessmen she had passed as they went into the Hotel Lucerna or Maria Chuchena's. Everyone else who wanted to smell good used soap or rosewater.* Agua de rosa. *She knew* agua de rosa *well because her mother wore it on special occasions, like her nephew's baptism and funerals. That was also where she'd gotten her name from.*

*The incongruity of a cologne decorating a decrepit bus shelter that reeked of old urine didn't matter to her. It gave her all the more reason to immerse herself in this other life, this poster life. The ad for Gabbana, as well as the others for Toyota Hilux and Kelvinator T2000 refrigerators (at Villelobos Siete and Nueve), transported her to another place, making life just that little bit more exciting. And she took what little excitement she could find with open arms.*

*Today, for what seemed like the millionth time, she imagined what it must be like to have all the things from the world of the posters. El mundo del fotografía, she called it. She pictured herself in that world. Yes, she would live in a house across the border, in El Paso, and she would have not one refrigerator but three, which she would stock with beef and cheese and those candies whose wrappers she saw floating around the bus depot when the wind came up, the ones with words written on them that she didn't understand. American words. She would have a husband who drove a Toyota Hilux, and when he took her out in it, for dinner at the McDonald's in downtown El Paso, he would dab himself with Gabbana. The manicured fingers would hold her face, the stubble would brush her as he kissed—*

"Hola, linda!"

*A car pulled up in a rush of noise and dust, frightening her out of her reverie. It was dark, and she had been standing at Villelobos Ocho* for over an hour. *The bus was later than usual. She was annoyed that she'd been taken away from* el mundo del fotografía, *but then she saw the vehicle was a Toyota Hilux—at least it looked like one in the poor light—and that was comforting.*

"¿Qué pasa, linda?"

*She could feel herself blushing, surprised and embarrassed at the same time. The driver's words were exactly the same as those in the Gabbana ad, and one of them was a word that people seldom used for her,* linda, *causing her to instinctively bring her hand up to her face. But everything else about him was wrong. She didn't know what the man in the ad looked like above his chin, but she certainly didn't think he looked like the Toyota driver. The stranger was pudgy, and his oily hair was pulled back so you could see a scar across his right brow. He also had much more stubble than the man in the poster, thick dark facial hair. She couldn't see his eyes because he was wearing dark glasses.*

"You want a ride?" he called out.

*She looked at the ground.* Don't talk to strangers, *her mother had warned her ever since that first time she'd left their small house in Candelaria to walk the four miles to school on her own. Well, not always alone—sometimes Agnes had been with her.*

Never talk to men whose eyes you cannot see.

*She cursed under her breath. Why weren't there other people around now? Why weren't there lights at the bus stop? She suddenly regretted having worked an extra hour, putting herself in this predicament of having to deal with the man in his shiny pickup. If only she had been in time for the earlier bus. Then she wouldn't be standing here on her own, with no one to help her get rid of the stranger. Having other women around her helped, even if she didn't know them. They all knew about the killings.*

*And yet, curiously enough, she was secretly thrilled by his advances. Her! He was coming on to her.*

*The man in the dark glasses got out of the pickup and sidled over. Even though she was looking down, she could see he was short and bowlegged. She wondered what he did that he could afford to buy such a big car.*

*"Where are you from,* bonita*?"*

*There it was again—*linda, bonita.

Arrows in your heart, *her mother said.* Men will use them to catch you and reel you in like a fish.

Sí, Mamá. But what a fish I'd be!

*He was wearing cologne, although the smell of it made her want to cough. He had been talking all the time, but she'd taken in only pieces of what he said. She had caught phrases like* linda *and* bonita, *of course, and "Ride with me" and "Do you have a boyfriend?" Was that really what he'd said, or was it one of those conversations she'd had with Agnes about how they imagined their first date with a man would go?*

*Before she knew it, she was standing close to his pickup. She put her hand on the silver medallion and the letters GM, and he reached across the hood, and his finger touched her. She quickly pulled away, and he laughed. It wasn't a bad touch. Rough but not bad. Still, she had already decided that she would only talk to him, nothing more. She wouldn't get in his pickup.*

*"Don't you want to ride with me?" he asked again, as if reading her mind. "I can take you anywhere. Why wait for the bus? It will never come."*

*Looking at the road that the bus usually came down, she wondered how long she would be here still. Alone. The night getting darker, chillier. She wanted to go home, eat, go to bed. She had to wake up in time to catch the bus back for tomorrow's shift. She hated that, getting up at four* A.M. *day after day. She was nineteen, and she wanted more than those early mornings followed by nights at the bus stop with the man from Gabbana her only company.*

*The stranger was suddenly next to her, and he put his arm around her. She didn't like it, but she struggled only a little. She had seen other girls do it, put up with strange men flirting with them. And if they could, she could. It meant nothing. At least he can take me home, she thought. Then, quite unintentionally, that crazy idea crossed her mind again. Could he become my boyfriend? she wondered.*

*The inside of the cab reeked of a combination of his searing cologne, cigarette smoke, and something she at first couldn't figure out. It was like a pine tree but also like something you'd use to clean the kitchen. She knew that she would figure it out—she always did.*

You can pick up the scent of anything a mile away.

*She winced as she recalled those words. They offended her every time her mother used them, not because they were untrue or were meant to hurt her, but because they made her think about the one feature of her face that stood out most.*

*The clashing smells in the vehicle made her feel nauseated, and for a moment she thought she might vomit. But then she caught sight of something in the front of the cab that she knew must be the source of the unidentified smell—a small cardboard cutout of a tree hanging from the rearview mirror to make the cab smell better. As he began driving, she concentrated on its swaying motion, which made her feel better.*

*He looked at her every now and then. She turned her head away so he couldn't see her face. In a way, she was glad the cab was so dark, the way the bus shelter had been. With strangers, she felt best in the shadows. He turned his music up so loud that she could barely hear him.*

*"Come for a drink," he shouted.*

*Once again she was scared and thrilled at the same time. "No." Her voice felt small to her, constricted.*

*"It's close by."*

*It was as if he hadn't heard her. He turned down Calle Duarte, and they passed the open-air market; most of the stalls had closed down for the night. Knowing that other people were nearby somehow comforted her, even though she could see no more than shifting shapes. The faces of the merchants were hidden behind the boxes they carried on their shoulders, the same way the people in the cars around them were masked by their black windshields.*

*"Agnes!" she called out. She tried to roll down her window, but it was locked. "There's my friend Agnes. Can I get out to say hello to her?"*

*It was a lie. She hadn't seen anyone she knew.*

*"Ay, bonita," he said, somehow charged by her sudden show of spirit. He kept on driving, and as she looked back at the market, he leaned closer to her. She froze, but he only wanted to retrieve a bottle from the cubbyhole. He unscrewed the top and took a few sips, then offered it to her. Before she could shake her head, he pulled it back.*

*"We're going to Lucy's," he said.*

*She began to feel a sense of urgency about leaving the pickup and escaping the smells and getting away from him. She needed to go home, make it an early night. She touched her face. It was something she did whenever she got nervous, embarrassed, even hungry.*

*"Why do you touch your face so much, linda?" the driver said.*

*She turned away. "My nose," she said, and immediately regretted saying it.*

*"What about your nose? It's beautiful."*

*"No," she said, and hesitated. "It's different."*

They were approaching a Mobil gas station, and he pulled in. The fluorescent lights were bright and glaring; all at once she felt naked. No more shadows to hide behind. She turned away from him as much as possible, but she could feel him looking at her.

"That's not true," he said before getting out. She lifted her head slowly, watched him walk away, and then chuckled. Even if he was lying, his words somehow made her feel better.

Alone now, she realized that nothing lay between her and Calle Duarte. All she had to do was open the door and leave. This was her chance. But she was miles from anywhere, miles from the bus depot, miles from Puerto Anapra. She had missed her bus and would have to wait two hours for the next one. And she was sure the stranger would never agree to take her back to Villelobos Ocho, so she'd have to walk.

Beneath her, she felt the soft leather seat. It was truly wonderful after a day of standing at the factory.

Just a few more moments resting, she thought. Just go with him to Lucy's and then get a lift home. You will probably get home before the bus—and in comfort and style.

She eased herself farther back into the soft seat. When the stranger returned, he said, "Still there, beautiful nose?"

She smiled shyly, but he didn't notice.

"I'll come to Lucy's with you."

"Eh?"

She said it again, but her voice was lost in the noise of his door slamming. He lit a cigarette and revved the pickup back onto Calle Duarte. She concentrated on the pine tree swinging from the rearview mirror.

"What is that?" she asked, pointing at the bottle between his legs. He held it out to her.

*"Tequila, bonita."*

*She reached for the bottle hesitantly, the vapors of the alcohol reaching her before she took a sip. She coughed and almost dropped the bottle. He slapped her on the back, and once she had stopped coughing, he laughed.*

*"You're a fine one. Never drunk before?"*

*She blushed and reached for her face, but he caught her hand before it could reach its goal.*

*"Don't," he said, then added, "it's beautiful."*

*She saw something in his face at that moment. But as soon as she saw it, it was gone. One moment he was showing warmth and care, the next moment he was drawing back.*

There are two men in life—the man you first meet and the man you get to know.

*She took another sip of tequila to drown out thoughts of her mother, her face, her life working at the* maquiladora. *The liquor was less abrasive the second time, not so difficult to swallow. And she felt like laughing with him when he smiled at her. The liquor was good for that. It warmed her up, inside and out.*

*They pulled into an alley at the back of Lucy's, and she looked at him expectantly.*

*"We go in the back," he said.*

*There was a heavy metal door with a man standing guard next to it. A big sign next to the door read* NO SE PERMITE PISTOLAS. *Good, she thought, no guns. She almost fell over when she got out of the pickup. Now that she was standing, she grew light-headed. It struck her only then that she was in her factory smock, covered in dust from work and the bus shelter. She was about to bring her hand to her face, but she laughed instead.*

"It's okay if I go in like this?" she asked.

"Of course," he said. "Come with me, linda. You're perfect as you are."

It didn't take more than three or four more drinks. She was so unsteady on her feet he had to help her back to the pickup. As he drove out to Guadalupe Victoria, he had to stop and vomit. He couldn't think properly, and he didn't know whether it was the liquor or what he was about to do. Looking down at his hands, he wondered what she would feel like.

# MEXICO

# THE NIGHTMARE

Frank was used to the bad dreams. They came with the strange hours and the heads. It was a trio that he had learned to live with ever since the murder of Anna Duval.

The dreams returned at random, like old acquaintances—the man hanging in the tree, the boy tied up and strangled and burnt and shot through the temple, the man cut in half by a train—especially when he was working on a new case.

It was very early. He had come to bed only at two A.M., after working on a skull that he had just gotten from the New York police. He could hear Jan breathing faintly next to him. Boy lay at his feet while Guy, black and haughty, was barely visible on top of the video recorder in the corner, his eyes the only thing that gave him away.

Frank knocked his knee against the side table as he got up. Boy shifted slightly and then settled back into place. Frank turned to see if he had woken Jan, but she hadn't moved.

He pulled on a pair of boxer shorts. He looked good for a man who had just turned sixty-two—a flat hard stomach from years of exercising his abs by hanging off the sofa, skin tanned from cycling along the banks of the Schuylkill River, an eagle tattoo on his sinewy left forearm that he'd gotten in the navy. He resembled the English actor Patrick Stewart with a goatee, or, in his more serious moments, Vladimir Ilyich Lenin.

Over the years he had cultivated a habit of trying to appear mysterious by bending his head forward slightly so that he looked at a person through his eyebrows. If it worked on men, it made women uncomfortable. But as soon as he smiled, the jig was up. His mischievous grin was infectious, and most people couldn't help liking him.

He had immortalized the grin in a life-size self-portrait that he'd painted several years earlier. Anyone standing close enough to it would see the silver tooth near his upper right incisor—that is, if they weren't first struck by another part of his anatomy. Not only was Frank naked, but he had done his penis in 3-D.

The unframed painting was propped up against a wall near the entrance to his studio door, which meant that anyone who came in—friends, FBI agents, artists, journalists, policemen, criminal profilers, U.S. Marshals, even his grandchildren—had no choice but to see Frank and his penis. It was as much a joke as his statement to the world: *Here I am. Take me or leave me.*

Cocked head, wide grin, upper right incisor glinting.

Frank walked from the bedroom into the studio, which was flooded by a full moon shining through the skylight. The luminescence lit up the rows of heads that either looked down from several shelves along the eastern wall or stared up from the floor, at least three dozen bodyless saints and devils.

Yvonne Davi took up a corner near Rosella Atkinson, who was next to James Kilgore, the last member of the Symbionese Liberation

Army. Ira Einhorn was situated comfortably far from Brad Bishop and the 5,300-year-old man. Near the front of the studio was the icy-eyed Hans Vorhauer, a version of whom Frank had done in concrete to show off the man's pitted skin. John List hid behind Anna Duval, who looked slightly shocked under her ten-dollar wig, as if Frank had sculpted her a split second before the bullets had entered the back of her head.

Some of the busts were unpainted, identified even before Frank had a chance to add their skin tone or the color of their corneas. Other busts had almost too much color, like the girl with green eyes, sculpted when *National Geographic* was trying to track down the peasant from Afghanistan who had become one of its most famous cover girls.

The heads that hadn't been identified—at least not yet, or not that Frank knew of—were usually known by an epithet that he or the police had given them, one that came with the manner or location of their death. The Boy in the Bag. The Girl in the Sewer. The Burnt Boy. The Girl in the Well. The Man in the Dumpster.

The victim Frank had dreamed about tonight, the Girl in the Steamer Trunk, was inconspicuous between all the others on the shelves, smaller, darker. She had braids that Vanessa had helped him with. Her body had been found dumped under a Philadelphia bridge in the winter of 1982.

# BRAIDS

February 1982

Detective Ellis Verb was on the other end of the phone. The police had a body that needed to be identified.

"She's a young girl," he said, "maybe five years old—or younger. You want to come down and take a look."

Frank's heart sank. It was never easy seeing someone who had not only died violently but also, after having decomposed for several weeks, had skin like leather or bits of flesh left on exposed bone, and was sometimes covered in maggots. But at least they were adults. Now it would be a child. His own children, Lisa and Vanessa, were seventeen and nine.

It was nighttime, and Philadelphia was in the middle of a harsh winter, although Frank hardly felt the cold as he got on his Harley-Davidson and headed down to the Philadelphia medical examiner's office.

The smell of the place no longer had an effect on him. He had stopped noticing it almost right after he saw his first corpse there five years earlier. Who knew that he would get to know this ugly building so well?

Ellis Verb was waiting at the end of the corridor. The detective was of medium height and friendly, although his smile was absent now. Behind him was the door that led to the storage room, which he opened.

There were gurneys in various parts of the room, each one holding a body, but Frank noticed the one with the little girl immediately. It stood apart and was slightly rusted, the tiny corpse covered in a sterile sheet. The walls were a dirty yellow, either from age or from the dim light, and the floor, after years of old blood being washed away, had turned a russet color. Not for the first time did Frank recall a song that he'd learned as a child: *Red and yellow, black and white, they are precious in His sight.*

Verb lifted the sheet. Frank wanted to turn away at the sight— dirty bone; hair with no scalp; jaw missing several teeth, some of which had fallen into the skull; eyeless sockets—but he didn't. He had made a pact with himself on his very first trip to the medical examiner's office never to get involved. If he did, he wouldn't be able to do the job. He was here to see a skull and to put a face on it. That would hopefully lead to an ID, which might let the victim's family get some closure. It could even help find the killer. (When Frank was called in, there usually was a killer.)

The child had been left in a rusted steamer trunk under the George C. Platt Memorial Bridge. The two workers from the transportation authority who'd found the trunk had first rummaged through it to see if there was anything of value inside. Only afterward did they report the body, which was wrapped in a sheet and plastic trash bags, a delay that somehow made her death even more inhuman.

She had been dead about seven months and had probably been beaten to death.

"It's often by the parents," Verb said across the gurney.

By the following night, the head had been detached and cleaned by one of the assistants. Frank put it in a box that he tied to the side of his Harley with a bungee cord. Instead of going home, he rode across the Schuylkill River to his studio on South Street. He wanted to start on the head right away—his first bust of a child and his first bust in his new studio.

The building was a narrow one-story that had once been a meat market. Frank had bought it a few months earlier, and it was still in pretty bad shape. The windows were boarded up, floorboards were missing, and there were cracks and holes in the roof. Because Philadelphia had imposed a moratorium on new gas hookups, there was no heat, and stalactites of ice hung from the ceiling.

For his workspace he had chosen the smallest room, an old meat freezer in the back. Snow and rain came through the roof in places, so he set up three umbrellas to protect him and the bust. The cold clay was like rock between his fingers, so he moved a small electric heater closer.

The nightmares about the Girl in the Steamer Trunk began several nights later, and they were always the same. He was in a long hallway with gurneys all around him when two corpses suddenly got up and started chasing him. But each time a little girl came to his rescue—he knew she was the Girl in the Steamer Trunk—and she would call out, "It's going to be all right."

On the weekend, he brought Vanessa to the studio with him. She sat nearby as he added bits of clay to the bust, cut into facial crevices, peeled away excess clay, refined the nose and the cheeks. Sometimes he let her touch the clay with a small flat stick.

After making the plaster mold of the bust and painting it, he gave it to the police, who had a photograph of it broadcast on the local news within twenty-four hours. That same night Frank had another nightmare. The girl was in it again, but her face was rounder, she was wearing a different-colored dress, and her hair was slightly altered. Instead of pigtails she had braids. For the first time—and what would be the last—he made a decision to redo a head he had already finished. The next day he called Verb.

"I want the bust back," he said.

Verb had already seen what Frank had done with Anna Duval and Linda Keyes, so he trusted him. With the bust back in the studio, Frank reconstructed a new one, making the cheeks fuller and adding short braids, just like in the dream. On painting it, he also made the skin tone lighter.

Vanessa watched from her stool. "Wait," she said. She went to her schoolbag, reached in, and came back with two scrunchies. "For her hair," she said.

The new bust was shown on television, but there wasn't a response to this version, either. Frank made a copy of the second bust and placed it on a shelf in the South Street studio. There she would remain, unnamed and unclaimed until the day she might be identified, known by everyone who saw her simply as the Girl in the Steamer Trunk.

## THE MEAT MARKET

### June 2003

More than twenty years later, the meat market still wasn't much to look at: single-story, flat roof, fifteen feet wide and almost ninety feet long, its sunflower exterior faded and peeling. Two bay windows were positioned on either side of a recessed front door that had a heavy brass knocker whose sound reverberated throughout the high-ceilinged, cavernous space.

The three main sections—the front room, the studio, and the living quarters—were situated one behind the other, divided by eight-foot walls of Sheetrock or cinder block. Privacy was nonexistent, although no one seemed to mind, a point made quite clear by Frank's nude self-portrait and another he'd done of his friend Caroline. He had done her breasts in 3-D.

The front room, or entrance area, was packed with bric-a-brac, leaving barely enough space to move around once you'd closed the front door. A large chest that was low enough to sit on was covered in books, magazines, an old camera, and a box just the right size to hold a skull. Parked in a nook behind the door was a heavy Schwinn cruiser bicycle.

Unframed paintings hung on the walls or were propped up against them. In one of the bay windows was an installation, an old grandfather clock whose face had been removed and replaced with the image of a human one. A very strange image. It was the plaster cast not of a bust Frank had created but of what the clay looked like once the rubber had been pulled off. He wanted to show the deformation of a decomposed face without giving away the identity of whose it was.

What little information there was about the victim filled the rest of the clock. In place of the pendulum, there were photographs of the murder scene—a barren lot surrounded by yellow police tape, as well as the police station's phone number, with the words "Anyone with information, please contact"—which Frank had taken off the television news. The photographs were in frames that would have held baby pictures, to emphasize the fact that the victim's life had been cut short. Younger than the Girl in the Steamer Trunk, the child was only four years old when his body was found in a duffel bag on May 27, 1994.

On the doorknob of the clock, Frank had tied a ticket that looked like it came from a piece of luggage but was the boy's toe tag from the medical examiner's office—case number 2599. But before long, he became known as the Boy in the Bag.

The middle room, the largest by far, was Frank's studio. A combination of an atelier and a junk store, it was the kind of richly textured, fantastic place that a set designer on a motion picture might have put together, with something to focus on in every nook and cranny.

A black leather love seat was almost covered in slides and photographs of body parts. Shelves were loaded down with art books, candles, and countless oddments, from souvenirs (a pair of castanets) to memorabilia (a contraption his father had once used to make a faux wood grain). There were also two more bicycles, nine 8mm film projectors, and an aluminum sculpting armature, all twists and curves, that was speckled with dried clay. Stuck haphazardly on the walls were photographs—Frank in a muscle shirt sitting astride his Harley 1200; Jan at age twenty, her wide-set eyes smoldering; an old girlfriend in a bikini on the beach; the actress Kim Delaney from *CSI: Miami,* whom Frank had once photographed—and newspaper stories about the fugitive John List and the man who had been murdered and buried in a cornfield, Edward Myers. Set off on its own, as much a gag (because his taste ran more to Ingmar Bergman and art-house movies) as an indication of the macabre world he worked in, was a poster of the movie *Bride of Chucky*. Random items—coins or a postcard of the drag artist Lypsinka—had been stuck on the floor and then polyurethaned. On a ledge two thirds of the way up to the ceiling was an enormous fiberglass dinglehead he had sculpted for the model to wear at a photographic shoot; a toy sailboat; a giant corroded 7UP sign found on the street; and part of a cow's skeleton.

The art on the vast walls seemed to be by someone who couldn't make up his mind what style he wanted to follow. Not far from a massive oil of a topless young woman in Daisy Dukes and high heels, bending suggestively in front of a hot rod, was a death mask that resembled Charles Laughton as Quasimodo in *The Hunchback of Notre Dame*. A series of five landscapes took up a wall behind a sculpture of a naked lady, her right hand draped over a bent knee as she sat on the edge of the table.

Scattered everywhere were small watercolors—what he called his downloads, his way of expunging the nightmares—splashed with primary colors that seemed too vibrant and bright to be about death. You couldn't tell by looking at them, but this one was of a woman found in a suitcase, that one of a corpse lying half on the bank of a river and half in the water. Sometimes he did a small sculpture, like the one of the Girl in the Steamer Trunk, her skeleton on the gurney downloaded as wood, wire mesh, red paint.

In the very middle of the studio, on three shelves you couldn't miss seeing as you walked by them to the back, were the sculpted heads.

On Frank's workbench was a skull that had arrived several days earlier from the New York police. The UPS package was taped with a green sticker that read REFRIGERATE UPON ARRIVAL, although he didn't pay much attention to the warning. If the flesh was removed, there wasn't much chance a skull would smell or need refrigeration. Most times, that is.

An opening in the floor in the middle of the studio led down to an area known as "the pit," where Frank kept his model trolley cars. They ran on rails that followed the perimeter of the room before disappearing through a tunnel in the wall and entering the basement. Along the trolley's route were a small town, a subway station, miniature cars and trucks and fire engines, park benches, trees, and little people, all of which he'd collected or made. He did it whenever he needed time away from the heads. Above them were several long shelves that sagged under the weight of files Jan diligently kept about Frank's work: THE WOMAN IN THE SUITCASE, FUGITIVES 1986–1996, LINDA KEYES, ALPHONSE "ALLIE BOY" PERSICO, THE VIDOCQ SOCIETY, THE EXHUMATION.

In the back of the pit was a low-ceilinged basement where he stored sculpting equipment and a stainless-steel case that he sometimes used for carrying heads. For several years there was also a body down there that the police had forgotten to collect. The floor was bare earth, and it gave off an odor that made the place smell like a newly dug grave.

The third and last section of the meat market, the living quarters, lay behind a wall at the back of the studio. Besides a compact bedroom, a living room, and a bathroom, there was the old meat freezer where he had sculpted the Girl in the Steamer Trunk. Now it was Jan's office.

The rudimentary kitchen, with its four-seat Formica-topped steel table, was a transition area between the studio and the living quarters, a place less to eat than to gather, drink, and talk late into the night with friends, police officers, pathologists, old and new girlfriends, artists, private investigators, FBI agents, and criminal profilers. The sink was the large metal kind you'd find in a restaurant, and there was a drain in the floor, so if Frank had to, he could clean heads there.

## THE MAN WHO LIVED IN THE MONSTER

The next morning Frank told Jan about the nightmare. She had to think for a moment about who the little girl from over two decades earlier was. So many heads had come through the front door—mostly women and girls—that she sometimes got them confused.

"Oh," she said, suddenly remembering, "the one with the pigtails."

"Braids," he corrected her.

"Oh, yes."

Her voice was not quite husky, and she spoke slowly, as if she had just woken up or was thinking about what she was going to say next. Eight years younger than Frank, Jan had always been beautiful. She rarely wore makeup and didn't need to. She lit up a cigarette while she dressed.

Frank went across the road to the café and bought her a latte, which he shared with her at the kitchen table. Before she left, she told him that there was a message on the machine for him.

"Who was it?" he asked.

"Bob," she said, then closed the front door behind her.

Jan smiled as she headed down South Street and then took Nineteenth Street toward Rittenhouse Square. She knew the kind of reaction Frank would have at the mention of Bob's name. A call from Bob always meant something was up. At the very least, he would want to talk about a case, but it also could mean that he had some work for Frank.

Bob Ressler was one of the most famous people in forensics, and his specialty was the serial killer, a term he himself had coined. He had interviewed every serial killer from Sirhan Sirhan to Jeffrey Dahmer, and had been the last person to talk to John Wayne Gacy before he went to the electric chair. An expert in criminal profiling who had worked for many years at the FBI's behavioral science unit in Quantico, Virginia, Ressler was said to have been a strong influence for the character Jack Crawford in *The Silence of the Lambs*.

Frank had met Ressler at a conference in Australia in the early 1990s. Now retired, Ressler had been writing books such as *I Have Lived in the Monster: Inside the Minds of the World's Most Notorious Serial Killers* and working as a consultant. One of his jobs for the past few years had been in Mexico, where he had been invited by the state government of Chihuahua.

At first Ressler's job had been to help train the police to deal with a case that possibly involved a serial killer. Since 1993 there had been a string of inexplicable murders of women, and almost all of them had taken place in Chihuahua's most populous city, Ciudad Juárez. The number of victims was put as high as four hundred.

After Ressler had been down to Chihuahua City several times, he was asked to put together a system of classification to try and distinguish how the women had died. Was it the result of spousal abuse, prostitution, drugs, or a serial killer? He estimated that fewer than one hundred had been murdered, but it was impossible to be accurate.

Once the classification was done, however, a further problem remained. As many as a quarter of the four hundred victims lacked identities because their bodies had decomposed by the time they had been found. Juárez being a town of itinerants looking for work, it was unlikely there would be any dental records to identify the dead—if they could afford a dentist, that is—or even someone to know they were missing in the first place. How could a killer be found when it wasn't even known who'd been murdered?

That was when Ressler thought of Frank. With faces on the skulls, perhaps the police could come up with some identities, which would give impetus to the stalled investigation.

The perfect opportunity to introduce Frank to Mexico, and the Mexicans to Frank, was coming up. Chihuahua was holding its first-ever forensics conference in August 2003. Ressler thought he could put forward Frank's name as a possible speaker and, once he was there, suggest that Frank be included in the investigation.

"How would you like to go to Mexico?" Ressler asked Frank on the phone.

Frank didn't even have to think. He was always ready for an adventure. "When are we going?"

## ■ THE *FEMINICIDIOS*

In January 1993 the body of a thirteen-year-old girl named Alma Chavira Farel was found in an empty lot in an area of Juárez called Campestre Virreyes. She had been raped both anally and vaginally, beaten, and strangled.

Two days after Chavira's discovery, a pregnant sixteen-year-old, Angelina Villalobos, was found strangled with a television cord. The killer turned out to be a man she and her husband knew. In May the fifth female victim of the year, a pregnant woman aged about thirty-five, was the first one to be classified NO IDENTIFICACIÓN, or UNKNOWN.

Alma Chavira's death was later taken as the start of the official count of what was to become known as the *feminicidios*. A local group, Casa Amiga, began monitoring the deaths, which vacillated between sixteen in 1993 and a high of thirty in 1998.

In 1994 a state criminologist advised officials that there could be a serial killer on the loose. A year later, an Egyptian named Abdel Latif Sharif, who had been deported from the United States and was living in Mexico, was arrested in connection with the killings. In spite of his incarceration, the murders continued, although one of the theories maintained that Sharif was using other people to carry out the killings while he was in jail. Some people said that Sharif was being turned into a scapegoat. Others said there wasn't one serial killer but several.

On Ressler's suggestion, a few FBI profilers were invited to Mexico in 1999 to investigate the murders, but Chihuahua government officials rejected the report, saying they believed that Sharif was guilty. In spite of his being in jail, the murders continued.

In November 2001 the bodies of eight women were found in an empty lot near a busy intersection of Juárez known as the cotton field, or *el algodonero*. Several days later, two bus drivers were arrested for the so-called cotton field murders, although they claimed they'd been tortured until they confessed. Death threats were sent to their lawyers, one of whom was killed the following year by the police, who said they mistook him for a fugitive. In 2002 the medical examiner, who earlier had said he believed the killings were part of an organized criminal effort, resigned instead of fabricating evidence against the bus drivers.

In early 2003 four more bodies were discovered northeast of the city, near a mountain called Cristo Negro, where two women had turned up only a few months earlier. Their arms were bound, their dresses pulled up over their heads, and large chunks of cement covered their bodies, all of which were in different stages of decomposition.

The people of Juárez were angry and frustrated. Why did the police seem to be doing nothing? Why wasn't the federal government in Mexico City becoming involved? Was there a link to drug trafficking?

Human rights groups claimed that whenever they tried to protest or publicize the murders, they were harassed and intimidated by the police. Amnesty International in particular became more vocal about the crimes.

The government of Vicente Fox, whose opposition National Action Party had won an unprecedented victory in the election of 2000, said it would make the *feminicidios,* sometimes know as *las muertas de Juárez,* a priority. But it wasn't that simple. The police force was not a single entity that could be controlled. The Chihuahua state police, or *judiciales,* were notoriously corrupt, badly paid, and inefficient, but they were responsible for dealing with crimes committed within the state. The more reliable federal police—the PGR, or *federales*—could get involved only if the case became a federal crime or if they were invited to.

In its most visible effort to do something about the *feminicidios,* the attorney general of Chihuahua had, in the late 1990s, created a task force called the Fiscalía Mixta, or Agencia Mixta. It was under the agency's banner that Bob Ressler had been brought into the investigation.

## CHIHUAHUA

Mexico's biggest state—about the size of Germany—Chihuahua borders Texas and New Mexico. The word *chihuahua* comes from a Nahuatl word that means "a dry sandy place," even though the state has two other distinct regions. Besides desert, there is a central plateau and a mountain range, the Sierra Madre.

Known mainly for the Copper Canyon, which is four times larger than the Grand Canyon and one and a half times as deep, Chihuahua has its capital in Chihuahua City. The more populous Ciudad Juárez lies on a river the Mexicans call the Rio Bravo del Norte, but to Americans it's the Rio Grande. Right across the river from Juárez is El Paso, Texas.

During the Mexican revolution, Pancho Villa fought in the region and became Chihuahua's provisional governor. Sixty years later, in the 1980s, the countryside turned into a battlefield of a different kind. Along the border with America, three major drug cartels each controlled a particular territory—the Tijuana cartel had California; the Sonora cartel had Arizona; and the Chihuahua cartel had Texas. The Chihuahua cartel was based in Juárez.

In 2000 the violent cross-border trade became better known throughout the world because of a movie called *Traffic*. By then the *feminicidios* had been going on for seven years.

## NEANDERTHAL

Frank and Ressler flew to Chihuahua on August 12, 2003. On the floor of the plane, next to Frank's feet, was his bust of the Girl in the Sewer.

Ressler briefly explained the setup to Frank. The attorney general's office was in Chihuahua City, but the office of the Fiscalía Mixta investigative team was in Juárez. There were several people he worked with, most notably a Mexican by the name of Manuel Esparza Navarrete. An American, Steve Slater, was also involved, but Ressler wasn't sure how and had hardly ever seen him.

Frank wanted more details. Did Ressler believe the murders had been committed by a serial killer? So far, no—or at least not by one serial killer. Did he believe that the Egyptian immigrant Sharif was the killer, or one of the killers? Possibly, but that too was growing more unlikely. What about the two bus drivers who had been arrested? Ressler didn't think they were guilty. Frank had more questions than Ressler had answers.

"But I'm glad you're here with me," the profiler said. "Other forensic people are scared to come down. Some of them even think they might be kidnapped or hurt. Maybe they're right."

Frank liked Ressler. He was like the medical examiner Doc Fillinger and the U.S. marshal Tom Rapone—he believed in Frank's work. And that was enough for Frank to get involved in a case. It didn't bother him that he understood little about Mexico or what was happening there. Those were usually the circumstances under which he joined an investigation, as an amateur and an outsider. That was the way it had always been.

At the airport outside Chihuahua City, they were met by Manuel Esparza, a friendly, stocky man in his early thirties who was dressed in civilian clothes. He was shorter than Frank, his hair jet black and his skin paler than that of most Mexicans. He spoke good English, and on the drive into the city, he told them that one of his first jobs after joining the police had been to investigate the drug cartel. He had been one of the local police used in the movie *Traffic*.

The Primer Congreso Internacional de Ciencias Forenses took place over three days. Besides a forensic biologist from Germany named Mark Benecke, Ressler and Frank were the only two non-Spanish speakers scheduled to address the conference. Ressler's talk on serial killers had the audience more rapt than usual, although that could have been because they'd read in the local newspapers like *El Diario* and *El Norte* about the very real possibility of a serial killer being on the loose in Chihuahua.

Frank was meant to have talked after a Cuban expert in neurophysiology, but his driver got him to the auditorium too late. He didn't mind too much, because no matter how many times he spoke to public gatherings, and had done so since the ID of Anna Duval in the 1970s, it still made him uncomfortable. In any case, he was here to learn about Mexico, not teach them anything—at least not yet.

Along with the other conference members, Frank and Ressler visited the local police academy, as well as an impressive state-of-the-art medical examiner's office that had been built with European aid. In front of the building stood a brand-new mobile laboratory where you could carry out an entire autopsy. In appearance, it was much better than anything Philadelphia and many other American cities had.

But as Ressler had warned Frank, there was little expertise to go with the equipment. The investigation didn't have an entomologist or even a forensic anthropologist. The facility was fantastic but only for show.

Knowing that Frank was famous for his facial reconstructions, Esparza showed them what one of their own artists had done. When Frank saw the bust, he was taken aback. Even though the artist had been working on it for a year, it looked like the effort of an amateur. The waxy face had no hair, no eyebrows, and the lips were pulled back tightly into a grimace. It resembled less a reconstruction than someone who had been burnt alive.

"It looks like a Neanderthal," Ressler whispered.

IIIIIIIIIIIIIIIIIIIIIIIIIIIIIIIIIIIIIIIIIIIIIIIIIIIIIII

The next day, the final day of the conference, Esparza drove the two men down to the attorney general's offices in central Chihuahua. It was for his presentation to the attorney general that Frank had brought along his bust of the Girl in the Sewer, as well as numerous slides.

On their way, they passed a memorial to the murdered women. About five hundred heavy, roughly hewn nails with pink ribbons attached had been driven into a huge ten-foot board. Each nail had a tag—Elizabeth Castro García, Viviano Areyano, Mireya Mendiz— but many said simply NO IDENTIFICACIÓN. Divided diagonally by a heavy chain, half the board was painted blue, half pink, with poems and drawings stuck between the nails. There was a large wooden cross centered by a sculpted white hand, and at the top was a sign: NI UNA MÁS. NOT ONE MORE.

On a smaller board behind it was written, in Spanish, "To all those who have died in Juárez, and around the world, due to violence, rest in peace. In Juárez there have been more than 300 women violated and killed. They have not been able to rest in peace, thanks to the inefficiency of the state government. No more crimes. No more impunities."

The attorney general was a tall, distinguished-looking man named Jesús Jose Solís Silva. After brief introductions, a projector was brought into the office, and Frank showed his slides, which were from some of his best-known cases, such as Linda Keyes and John List.

But it was the head in the box that fascinated Solís most. The victim had been found in a sewer on Twenty-first and Bellevue in Philadelphia in the early 1980s. Frank had given her reddish lips and had left her mouth slightly open to show the diastema, or gap, between her two front teeth.

Solís took the head and turned it over in his hands, whereupon the wig fell off and Frank bent down to pick it up. When Solís commented on how light the bust was, Frank explained that unlike most of the others, which were made of plaster, this one he'd done in fiberglass.

The fact that the Girl in the Sewer had never been identified didn't seem to bother the attorney general, who considered it for a few moments longer. Giving the bust back to Frank, he said he would like to show his visitors around the governor's palace.

The four men walked out of the building to the northern end of the Plaza Hidalgo, where they entered an ornate building dating back to 1892. The freshly painted courtyard was decorated with potted palms and huge wooden doors set in peach-colored walls. Behind the white balconies on the second floor were large murals depicting muscular Mayans, republican soldiers marching to the revolution, monks bent in prayer, and liberation leaders who defiantly held their fists in the air.

Walking between the rooms on the upper level, they saw a group of schoolchildren standing around a tall, well-dressed man. It was the governor, Patricio Martínez García.

"Let me introduce you," Solís said.

They waited to one side as the governor finished shaking hands with the children.

"Señor Martínez," Solís said, speaking in Spanish, "I would like you to meet Frank Bender. You already know Señor Ressler."

The governor smiled and shook their hands. Solís explained that Frank had come down for the forensics conference and was keen to work on the investigation into the murdered women.

"Señor Bender," Martínez said. "How are you? Tell me what it is you do exactly."

Frank instinctively bent his head slightly and looked through his eyebrows. "I put faces on the skulls of murdered people and get them identified," he said.

As Solís translated, the governor nodded. "We could do with your assistance down here, Señor Bender. Would you think about coming down to help us?"

Strangers were always fascinated by what Frank did, so he wasn't surprised by this warm reception. But he couldn't believe how fast things were happening. Ressler had suggested merely the possibility of his involvement, yet the governor seemed to have just made him a bona fide offer.

It was agreed that Frank's trip back to Philadelphia would be postponed for several days so the paperwork could be finalized and he could be taken up to Juárez to familiarize himself with the case.

"Maybe later on you could even take some heads back with you to work on in America," Martínez suggested.

Solís gave Esparza a quick look, and Frank could tell that the governor had spoken out of turn. The Chihuahua police were unlikely to let him take a single head out of the country.

## CITY OF PINK CROSSES

A policeman named Gus was their driver and interpreter. When he arrived at the hotel in his white police pickup to fetch Frank and Ressler, he was wearing clothes that made him look less like a cop than a cowboy.

Several miles outside of Chihuahua, and then again before Juárez, they passed a military checkpoint—PUESTO DE CONTROL MILITAR. The road went due south for two hundred miles, following the railway line, and Gus drove at about ninety miles an hour all the way.

"Trains are important to us in Chihuahua," he said. "Pancho Villa robbed trains to give money to the poor."

The dry countryside was marked by a few sites that the policeman pointed out: the Samalayuca sand dunes, where a woman's skeleton was found in June 2000, and the towns of Ojo Caliente, Moctezuma, and Candelaria.

In the desert before Juárez, Frank noticed the pink crosses planted at intervals next to the road. Gus said each one represented a dead woman who had been found nearby. The bare landscape made the markers look even more haunting, and Frank knew that he would paint them when he got home.

By the time they reached the center of Juárez, it was midafternoon, and the temperature had risen to 115 degrees. Unlike the capital, with its museums and art deco buildings and the mansion of Pancho Villa, Juárez was chaotic and the streets badly paved. The city had grown rapidly and with little planning, and its wide boulevards weren't suitable for pedestrians, running haphazardly from downtown and between empty lots and industrial parks, which created an archipelago of factories surrounded by unused land, shops, and dwellings. Long chain-link fences followed walls of cinder blocks. Weeds and long grass broke through the paving. The low-lying buildings stretched as far as the eye could see in the arid haze, and there were said to be as many as two million inhabitants.

Founded in the mid-seventeenth century by Spanish explorers, the town that grew on both sides of the Rio Grande was called El Paso del Norte, after the chasm between two mountain ranges. Following the Treaty of Guadalupe Hidalgo in 1848, the part of the city lying north of the Rio Grande became American and was named El Paso. Forty years later, the Mexican half was renamed after Benito Juárez, whose republican forces were headquartered there.

The two modern-day cities—linked by four bridges and a history—were so close that American teenagers used to drive into Mexico for a good time and be back home by midnight. Women came to have their hair done, and movie stars came for quickie divorces. Rich people had houses in both towns, and poor people crossed the river from Mexico every day to find work in El Paso (in fact, as many as 80 percent of its eight hundred thousand inhabitants came from Mexico). But while El Paso was one of the safest big cities in America, Juárez was one of the most unsafe in Mexico. El Paso's tall office blocks topped with huge signs for Chase and Wells Fargo overshadowed downtown Juárez, where the first area one reached on crossing the Stanton Street Bridge was the red-light district. The view from El Paso's luxurious houses, which were situated off of Mesa Street and in the foothills of the Franklin Mountains, at the end of the Rockies, was not only of downtown Juárez but also of the sprawling shantytown Anapra. People sometimes joked that the cars that had started new on the I-10 and the roads of El Paso were sold secondhand in Juárez, where they finally ended up on the huge junk heaps, called *jonkes,* that now dotted the city.

From the early 1960s, assembly plants, or *maquiladores* (for short, *maquilas*), were erected along the border that stretched from the Pacific to the Gulf of Mexico. Parts that had been manufactured elsewhere in the world were brought to Mexico to be put together and then shipped out.

In 1993, the same year that the official count of the murders in Mexico commenced, the North American Free Trade Agreement was signed. There were two significant effects on Mexicans. Not only did NAFTA give American farmers incentives that helped put Mexicans out of business—causing them to flock to cities like Juárez in search of jobs—but major American corporations started taking advantage of the low wages and tax incentives by erecting *maquilas.* Of the four thousand assembly plants along the two-thousand-mile *frontera,* four hundred were located around Juárez, 20 percent of which belonged to Fortune 500 companies like General Electric, Thomson, Tyco, Ford, and DuPont. Many of the *maquila* executives lived in El Paso.

The factories were known to employ mostly women, who were viewed as more agile with their hands and were less likely to create problems. Many of them had migrated from as far away as the states of Oaxaca and Chiapas in the south. If they didn't find a job in the *maquilas,* they worked in stores or the informal sector, or they walked the streets. They lived in places like Anapra and Puerto Anapra, where homes were often made of scraps of wood, Styrofoam, and plastic; there was no running water and car batteries were used to generate light. Looming above both shantytowns, even though it was in El Paso, was the disused Asarco copper refinery.

Besides the start of NAFTA, the year 1993 saw another significant shift in the region. Control of the Juárez drug cartel changed hands, which set off an unprecedented wave of violence and crime in the city, where people were gunned down in restaurants and public places.

As Gus drove down Avenida de los Insurgentes and turned onto López Mateos, Frank made a point of studying the women walking alongside the roads. Their skin was different from the shades he was used to working with, the hairstyles fairly uniform.

At the corner of Triunfo de la República, a woman stood begging below a billboard advertising a new casino that was situated on the road to Mexico City. Gus said she was a member of the Tarahumara Indians, who lived on a bare hillside that he pointed out. The blatant clash of new and old worlds, rich and poor, reminded Frank of Philadelphia—a bit like Rittenhouse Square versus North Philly—only much worse. One of the beacons of prosperity in Juárez was the hotel where Frank and Ressler were staying, the 140-room Lucerna.

Once they had dropped off their bags and checked in, they were driven to the cotton field where eight bodies had been found in 2001. The name suggested a place in the midst of farmland, but it was a plot of unused land in the middle of Juárez. In fact, it was within sight of a Wal-Mart. Half a dozen large pink crosses stood where the eight bodies had been found. More crosses were erected along a nearby railway line.

Gus kept the pickup moving all the time, so they never got out or walked around. On the way back to the Lucerna, he drove them through an area with expensive houses partially hidden behind high walls.

"This is the area where the drug cartel lives," he said. "It is called the Golden Zone."

He sounded almost deferential.

|||||||||||||||||||||||||||||||||||||||||||||||||||||||||||

In the lobby of the hotel, they were met by Esparza, who had driven up from Chihuahua after them. He was in a good mood and wanted to give them a night on the town. Ressler was tired, so Frank and the Mexican went out alone to eat at a popular restaurant called Maria Chuchena's.

"This is going to be great," Esparza told Frank. "You are going to come down and help us."

The next morning Esparza took them to the main police station in Juárez. Afterward they drove out on Eje Vial Juan Gabriel to Barranca Azul, where they turned right. On their left was the huge Cereso prison, with its own church and hotel, and where some of the suspects in the *feminicidios* were being held.

The team investigating the murders, the Fiscalía Mixta, had recently moved offices to a building beyond the prison that had once been a police academy. It was an unobtrusive setting, considering the enormity of the crime being investigated. There were only a few people in the offices, the walls needed painting, and the floors were cracked. Stray dogs wandered in and out of the building.

The medical examiner's office was located in a single-story structure nearby. Even though it was newer than the building they had just come from, it was much less showy than the facility in Chihuahua. The coroner, Maria Carmen Sánchez, was an attractive, friendly woman of about forty, with a nice smile and long dark hair.

She didn't speak much English, but she showed them around and took them into a room where some bones were arranged on an autopsy table and about a dozen skulls were lined up on a stainless-steel shelf. The heads had all been cleaned, although not one of them had an identity.

For the first time, the reality of the *feminicidios* hit Frank. These dozen skulls were the women he had read and heard so much about over the past months. Even though he'd worked on more than forty heads over the years, most of them belonging to people killed in the most horrific ways, there was something about Juárez that made it different, more heartbreaking. Maybe it was the sheer scale and atrocity of the crime. Or the fact that there could be a serial killer involved.

Esparza's cell phone rang. After a short conversation, he told them that Solís wanted them back in Chihuahua. He had lined up a private plane, a small eight-seater, for the journey. When they met with Solís, he was finalizing the contract for Frank. They spoke briefly about his doing five heads to start with. If all went well, maybe he could return later on to do another five.

Before they left the office, Solís gave them several books about Mexico as souvenirs. They had almost reached the airport to fly back to Juárez when Esparza's phone went off again. Solís wanted them to return to the office immediately. Esparza swung the car around, and the two passengers thought something had gone wrong. When they got to Solís's office, he said he'd forgotten to give them another book, a paperback, also about Mexico. With that, he let them go. It was a small, forgettable incident, and yet it stuck with Frank.

|||||||||||||||||||||||||||||||||||||||||||||||||||||||

The same month that Frank was in Chihuahua, Amnesty International released a scathing report about Mexico titled "Intolerable Killings: Ten Years of Abductions and Murders of Women in Ciudad Juárez and Chihuahua." The organization's London-based secretary-general, Irene Khan, condemned the Mexican government for ignoring the murders.

The report claimed that many of the victims had been abducted, held captive for several days, and subjected to humiliation, torture, and the most horrific sexual violence before being strangled or beaten to death. Almost all of them were young, poor women working in the *maquilas* or the informal sector—women, it added pointedly, "with no power and whose deaths have no potential cost for the local authorities."

Shoddy investigative work and bad documentation kept by the police from the start of the murders had left gaping holes and made it almost impossible to establish potential motives or patterns behind the killings. The police were focusing on crimes that involved abduction and rape—almost one hundred, according to Amnesty's count—and not on those involving less clear sexual elements or nonsexual domestic violence. So while Ressler's classification system suggested that only a quarter of the women were "real" victims, Amnesty believed all four hundred were. The police, Amnesty said, also often implied that the murdered women were prostitutes or women of loose morals and therefore somehow deserved their fate.

It was a damning report and did nothing to endear Amnesty to the Chihuahua government or to the police in Juárez. Amnesty said it was merely speaking for the mothers and families of the murdered women who, for years, had been campaigning in vain to bring attention to the killings.

Pressure increased on Governor Martínez and Attorney General Solís, neither of whom took the accusations well. Solís told *El Heraldo* that the authorities were being unjustly victimized, while Martínez took out an advertisement in local papers attacking Amnesty.

Several weeks after returning to Philadelphia, Frank got a call from Mexico. It was Esparza, and his voice was urgent.

"You have to come down right now!" he said. "They have found another woman. This time it was in Chihuahua. You must get down here at once."

Frank had been waiting for a call from the Mexicans. "I can come down today if you want me to," he told Esparza, "but that wouldn't help. It will take ten days to get my equipment shipped down there."

"Then you must start organizing today."

"I will," Frank said. "Believe me, I want to do this job more than any job I've ever done."

As soon as he hung up the phone, Frank began making arrangements. He ordered three hundred pounds of non-hardening clay and another three hundred of plaster. He called Polytek for synthetic rubber and cans of releasing agent, and his art supply store for more brushes and varnish. At the hardware store he picked up epoxy, putty knives, plastic buckets, and dozens of rolls of duct tape. He packed everything except a change of clothes and a few toiletries, which he put in an overnight bag. Esparza told him to ship it all to a retired Mexican policeman in El Paso—just to be safe—and he would pick it up there and drive it across the border.

Frank called Jan at work to give her an update. She was scared and excited for him. From the very first time she'd heard about Mexico, she'd known it was the perfect case for him. Not only was he good at getting skulls identified, but he was especially good with murdered women.

# THE BEGINNING

# AN ANATOMY LESSON

Almost every weekday after Frank finished work at his photographic studio on Arch Street in downtown Philadelphia, he took night classes at the Pennsylvania Academy of the Fine Arts.

He had studied art off and on for almost as long as he could remember. He first took classes when he was five, painted and drew in high school, and won a local competition when he was fifteen. In the navy, he sketched guys who worked with him in the engine room. On Arch Street, he asked the prostitutes standing outside the Apollo Hotel to come up and pose for him.

When he heard that the Veterans Administration had a program that would allow him to take free night classes at the academy, he started going once a week, then twice, then whenever he could. He took painting with Oliver Grimley and drawing with Arthur De Costa, who suggested he also do some sculpting.

"You'll learn a lot about form," De Costa said. "You're already a photographer, and you can see how highlight and shadows work. But sculpting will help you with your painting."

Little though it interested him, Frank thought a semester of classes wouldn't hurt. Besides, he liked the teacher, a large man named Tony Greenwood, who had a deep voice, long hair, and a gray beard and wore a chicken-bone necklace. Greenwood also didn't care for the gallery scene, a characteristic that made Frank like him even more.

As a sculpting teacher, Greenwood never said much and didn't spend much time in class, just long enough to walk around and comment on each student's work before going up to his own studio. At the end of the night, he came back and had another walk around.

"Fraaaank," he said in his deep voice one night as they were finishing up, "you need to take another look at the model. Look at the proportion. She's got a more rounded face."

With a caliper, Greenwood measured Frank's half-finished bust from forehead to chin and then took it up to the model in the center of the room to show Frank what he meant. He made Frank stand up close to the model.

"Look. And then look. And then look again," Greenwood said.

Frank had never taken an anatomy class before, and he knew it would help him. The academy didn't give anatomy classes at night, and Frank couldn't afford to pay for them, so he tried to find an alternative, one that wouldn't cost anything. An opportunity finally presented itself with Bart Zandel, who took fingerprints off bodies at the Philadelphia medical examiner's office.

When Zandel, who sometimes went to the city's go-go clubs, wanted some photographs taken of one of the girls, a friend suggested he approach Frank. On hearing where Zandel worked, Frank proposed that instead of payment he might take him down to the medical examiner's office sometime to see the bodies. They set a time to meet up the following week.

||||||||||||||||||||||||||||||||||||||||||||||||||||

The Philadelphia medical examiner's office was on University Avenue, less than a mile from Thirtieth Street Station and a few blocks from the Schuylkill River. The severe-looking two-story structure had been built with lots of gray concrete and not enough windows, and the loading bays where the corpses got dropped off were separated by thick walls. Its appearance alone screamed "morgue."

A body bag, once it had been off-loaded, was taken through one of two doors to the autopsy section on the left or, if it was especially decayed, to the smaller decomposition room on the right. In the first room of the main section, the body was weighed and fingerprints were taken, and all the available information about the victim was logged. In a room off to the right were the investigators, who gathered evidence at the scene and tried to find out anything they could about the victims and how they had died. Out of the dozen investigators, Frank met two, Gerry White and a new recruit, a heavy, jovial young man named Gene Suplee.

Typically, Zandel explained, the medical examiner investigated a death that was unexpected, sudden, or unusual. The police handled the scene of a crime, but the medical examiner was responsible for the body. Investigators like White and Suplee went to the scene, checked it out, collected any belongings, and talked to friends, family, and witnesses.

"There are three things we're looking for," Suplee added. "We call them the mortis brothers—rigor, livor, and alvor: stiffening, coloring, cooling."

Zandel introduced Frank to two of the assistant medical examiners walking by, Robert Segal and Robert Catherman, before their conversation was interrupted by someone pushing a gurney with a body bag past them.

Behind double doors at the end of the hallway was an autopsy room containing two tables, with an extra table in an adjoining room. On the wall in between were stainless-steel shelves lined with jars containing internal organs—hearts, livers, brains—from autopsies done over the years.

A corpse lay on each autopsy table. The one closest to Frank was a man, maybe twenty years old, maybe fifty, it was hard to tell. A rubber body block had been placed under his lower back to lift his chest. The assistants had made a Y-shaped incision that ran from his shoulders down to the pubis; then they'd cut the ribs and collarbone with a Stryker saw and removed the breastplate.

"The internal organs are taken out and weighed," Zandel whispered to Frank, "and sometimes the blood and fluid in the eyes get sent for a toxicology test."

An incision had also been made from behind one ear over the top of the head to the other ear so that the scalp could be peeled forward and the front half of the skull removed. The brain would be taken out and examined by the neuropathologist, Lucy Rorke.

A pathologist whom Frank hadn't met, a man in his early fifties and of medium height, walked up to the table on the left. He examined the body briefly and then stuck his bare hand into the chest cavity and moved around inside as if searching for something he'd dropped in there by mistake. He kept muttering softly to himself, and it took Frank a while to realize he was talking into a tape recorder in his top pocket. Seeing Frank watching him, the pathologist winked.

Frank had seen corpses before, but at funerals on North Leithgow

Street, where he'd grown up. If a neighbor died, the body was embalmed and laid out in the family's front room for people to come by and pay their respects. Unlike those bodies, which had been made to look good, these were naked, cold, and had odd expressions—sometimes fright or horror, but mostly nothing at all, as if the people had died right in the middle of doing something quite forgettable, like mowing the lawn.

A large white man hit by a train had been severed through his thighs and lay in two pieces on a gurney to one side of the autopsy room. Each time Frank passed him in the next hour, he noticed a change in the man's appearance. First he'd been covered in blood, then he'd been hosed down, and finally, someone had pushed the two pieces together.

Behind a big steel door in the hallway was the storage room, where most of the bodies were kept. As soon as Zandel opened it, they were met by a rush of cold air from a giant air-conditioning unit.

"The bodies need to be kept cool, but not too cool that they freeze and it damages the skin," Zandel said.

The smell of formaldehyde, which hung over the medical examiner's office from the moment you entered, was now mixed with a sweet-sour smell so thick you could almost taste it, like garbage on a humid day.

The storage area could hold about sixty gurneys, and there were collapsible racks on the wall to hold more bodies if necessary.

"New York has drawers," Zandel added. "We have racks."

All the bodies were covered in sterile sheets that had to be lifted to see the toe tags. Zandel pointed to several gurneys on the right, explaining that the small bodies were babies who had probably died from sudden infant death syndrome but still had to be examined. Farther into the room, Zandel lifted a sheet to expose not a corpse but three suitcases that contained the body parts of a woman who had been cut up and dumped near the New Jersey Turnpike.

Shaking his head in disbelief, Frank said more to himself than to Zandel, "This sure isn't an anatomy lesson."

The bodies were often bludgeoned, shot, knifed, swollen, or rotting, sometimes in combination. This was death in the raw, instant and permanent. The medical examiner's office was the last place to study the human form, Frank realized, and yet he was fascinated.

Zandel led the way through the main entrance and down to the left, where the decomposition room was. The stench there was more overpowering than in the storage room, even though the air-conditioning was on and there were only two bodies. Suplee came by to see how they were doing.

"They can decompose fast," he said. "A nice cool house, it happens a lot slower. Also depends on animal life and insect activity. But after a couple of hot days, they're not recognizable." He shook his head. "We had a guy worked here, died in his house. If you had asked me after a week, I wouldn't have known who it was. And he was someone I saw every day."

By the time they returned to the storage room, they weren't alone anymore. The pathologist who had winked at Frank earlier was there with two assistants, collecting a body to autopsy.

Zandel led Frank to a body they were finished working on. Her toe tag identified her as number 5233. Her skin hadn't decayed too much, although far enough that someone who knew her probably wouldn't have recognized her. Her bloody hair had dried against her head, part of which had been blown away by several gunshots.

"She's white, about fifty," Zandel said. "She was found in a field near the airport with a man's jacket wrapped around her head. There were three bullets in her head."

Frank was surprised by his reaction to being right next to the corpse—he didn't feel any nausea—so he took the opportunity to have a closer look at her.

"The police sent out multistate alerts, checked her fingerprints. She had no ID on her, and we have no idea what she might have looked like. That's one of the biggest problems here."

Frank studied the woman's face. There was a calmness around her eyes. Her face was a bit fleshy, her nose narrow, her lips thin. He knew that what he said next to Zandel sounded crazy for a man who had never been in a medical examiner's office before, although it made absolute sense to him.

"I do know," he said. "I know what she looks like."

The pathologist came up. "Excuse me," he said, "but I couldn't help overhearing. You say you know what this woman looks like?" Frank nodded. "Well, she happens to be my case, and I'd like to know who she is."

Zandel introduced Frank to Halbert Fillinger, another assistant medical examiner.

"Do you know anything about forensics?" Fillinger asked.

Frank shook his head. "I don't even know what the word means."

Fillinger led the way out of the storage room. "Things are wrapped up neatly in the movies—even on TV shows—these days." The show *Quincy, M.E.* had been on television for two seasons, starring Jack Klugman as an assistant medical examiner working in Los Angeles. "But I see countless cases that go nowhere. Sometimes what we do as pathologists and investigators isn't enough. Like the woman

on the gurney. We've done all we can, but we cannot get her identified. Yet you believe you can?"

"I really think so," Frank said. He told Fillinger that he had
drawn his whole life and had always studied people and what they
looked like, their faces especially. Looking at people was his hobby.

Fillinger hesitated. He had seen his share of wiseacres at the
medical examiner's office before, but there was something about
Frank's cockiness and naïveté that he was ready to take a chance
on. Plus, he needed to identify the woman.

"If we find out who she is," Fillinger said, "we could possibly also
find her killer. Would you like to help us do that?"

Frank said he would.

"We can't pay you anything."

"That's fine."

"Okay, so do what you have to do, and show me what she looks
like," Fillinger said before walking out.

Out of his satchel Frank took some sketching paper, a caliper he
used in his art classes, and a ruler. He went back into the storage
room with Zandel, and they pulled the gurney holding number
5233 out into the hallway. He drew a rough outline of a face and
took random measurements of the woman's head with his ruler.
From the top of the cranium to the bottom of the chin he measured
9¾ inches; her forehead was 6¹⁄₁₆ inches broad. The space between
her orbits measured 2⅝ inches. Her right ear was 2⅝ inches long, her
mouth 2¼ inches wide, and there were 1¹¹⁄₁₆ inches between her mouth
and her chin.

Even though the woman's facial skin was sagging, the more Frank
looked at it, the more he saw someone taking shape. Members of

the staff came by to see what he was doing, as if he were painting a canvas in the park. When one started chuckling, Frank asked him what was wrong.

Pointing at Frank's ruler, the assistant said, "We use millimeters around here."

Before Frank left, he asked Fillinger if there was anything he should know about the woman that might help him make a face. The pathologist said she had been wearing a herringbone suit and a white blouse at the time of her death. She was healthy and didn't smoke. She had painted fingernails, and her hair was dyed dark blond but was graying at the roots.

Frank said he would like to come back to the medical examiner's office later that week to carry on with the sketches he'd begun.

"Midnight on Friday is good," Fillinger said. "That's when I do the graveyard shift."

## WOMAN FROM ARIZONA

By the time Frank got home, he was exhausted. Jan met him at the door of their house on Palmetto Street in the suburb of Lawndale.

"Jesus Christ!" she said. "You stink!"

She knew he had been at the medical examiner's office, so she could guess where the smell came from. His heavy shirt had soaked up the odors. She told him to take off his clothes outside the house and put them in a garbage bag while she got him something to change into.

There was plenty of photographic work to keep Frank occupied until Friday, but he kept thinking about the murdered woman. He had decided to make a sculpture of her. Fillinger had said he could do any kind of artistic representation he wanted, and even though Frank drew and painted a lot better—he'd been sculpting for barely a month—a life-size three-dimensional bust made more sense.

Late on Friday, he went back to the medical examiner's office to finish his sketches and to take some photographs of the corpse. Hardly anyone was around except Fillinger, who was talking into his Dictaphone as he walked around a body on the autopsy table. Frank tried to get his attention.

"I'm busy here," Fillinger said. "Why don't you go into the storage room by yourself. You know where the body is."

Frank went back down the hall to the steel door. On opening it, he was met by the deafening sound of the air-conditioning unit and the familiar sweet-sour smell, but everything else about the room had changed. The gurneys had been shifted around, and the woman wasn't where he remembered seeing her. All he had to go on was her toe tag number, 5233. He went back outside and saw an assistant.

"Do you know where this body is?" he asked, showing the assistant the toe tag number.

The assistant shook his head. "Just keep looking in there and you'll find it."

Frank went back inside and began lifting the sheets in search of the toe tags. Often the body was the wrong way around, so instead of the feet, he found the head. Under the first sheet was the man who had been sliced in half by a train. Under the second was a shooting victim. Under the third was the woman in the suitcases, except the body parts had been removed and assembled in some kind of order.

Once again the sight of the lifeless bodies, even the particularly gory ones, had little effect on him. Yes, it was eerie and scary, but it was exciting too, like jumping into a body of dark water. Under the fourth sheet, though, was something that made him turn away in horror. A young man, no more than a teenager, looked as if he had suffered the most gruesome death—shot in the head and burnt— and his face seemed to be frozen in a terrifying scream.

The ninth gurney was number 5233. After wheeling the woman out into the hall, Frank took some photographs of her face. He didn't really know what he was doing, but he kept thinking about what Tony Greenwood, his sculpting teacher, had said: "If you can't see the form, then *look*. Go up and look at the model. Look and look, and then look again."

Her face had sunk in some more, and so had her eyes, and the nose seemed thinner. Under the matted and bloodied hair were the gunshot wounds. The artist in Frank was fascinated by the way the blood in her body had settled in the lower part, creating hues of red, purple, and brown that were almost vibrant.

At first he touched her wearing rubber gloves, but he took them off when he was taking measurements. The sensation of her closed eyes and her mouth against his fingers took him by surprise— cold, plastic, unreal. Once he was finished doing sketches and taking photographs and measurements, this time in millimeters, he put her back in the storage room, said goodbye to Fillinger, and went home.

‖‖‖‖‖‖‖‖‖‖‖‖‖‖‖‖‖‖‖‖‖‖‖‖‖‖‖‖‖‖‖‖‖‖‖‖‖‖‖‖‖‖‖

In a hoagie shop across Arch Street from the studio a few days later, Frank saw a woman whose nose and forehead made him think of case number 5233. The woman told him she was Polish, which made him think that perhaps the murder victim was of Eastern European ancestry. He already knew he was going to sculpt someone who was neat and precise, and now he had a nose and a forehead.

Frank had never sculpted a full bust before. In Greenwood's class, they had gone only as far as they could get in an evening, at which point they threw the clay from their half-completed work back in the barrel. This would be his first.

Less than a week after seeing the murdered woman for the first time, he began to sculpt her. He worked at night, after he had finished with his photographic clients. Not knowing how they would react to his new sideline, he said nothing about it.

He layered the clay onto an armature, a twisted framework of aluminum, in the same way they did in class. Greenwood came by several times to look at Frank's progress and to offer advice. He had suggested using oily clay, since the water-based kind had to be kept covered or it would dry out and crack. "If you want it softer," he added, "just add some Vaseline." To make the reconstruction even more lifelike, Greenwood also recommended that once the clay bust was complete, Frank should make a plaster mold of it and paint it.

Several other artist friends who were sharing space with Frank in the fourth-floor loft on Arch Street regularly popped in to see how he was progressing on number 5233. When it was time to paint the plaster mold, Tom Ewing and Marguerite Ferrari, who were dating, both had suggestions.

"Here's how you do it," Ewing said.

"No, Tom," Ferrari said. "I'm already showing him how."

Frank waited until they were gone before he started painting the skin and the eyeballs. He had left the head bare so he could fit it with a wig later on. If he was having any doubts about what he was doing, he called Greenwood.

The medical examiner's office had, in the meantime, informed the police about the bust, and a policeman wearing a trench coat and a fedora arrived at the studio one afternoon. His name was Larry Grace.

"No one's ever done this kind of art for us before," the detective said.

Most law-enforcement units relied on composite sketches done by an artist who took down information from the victim of a crime or a witness and then drew a likeness.

"The artists we use aren't that good," Grace confessed. "We seldom get an ID from what they've drawn."

That was why he was similarly skeptical about what Frank was doing, but he nevertheless came by the studio almost daily to see how it was going. On one of his visits, he told Frank that the chief of homicide wanted to meet him. "He also says he's never heard of such a thing as sculpting a victim. But he says we have nothing to lose."

The police wanted to get a story about the bust in *The Philadelphia Inquirer* and asked if someone could come by to take a photograph.

"It will still only be clay," Frank warned Grace.

"That's okay. We just want to see if we get any reaction."

Knowing what the woman's hair length and color were, Frank

went to a secondhand store with Grace and bought a wig that he thought would also fit her face. He didn't tell Jan that it cost him thirty dollars. He was so caught up in helping get an ID for the woman that he didn't mind paying.

A story on number 5233 ran in the paper, as planned, and although the police didn't get a reaction, Frank did. A day later, a man called to say that he was very concerned about the dead woman and wanted to give the authorities money so she could have a proper burial. Then he asked if he could come by the studio and see the bust. Someone else wanted to bring his daughter over because she was doing a school report on sculpture. All the callers came from northern New Jersey and had Italian names.

"Why do you think they'd be interested in a corpse found outside the Philadelphia airport?" Frank asked Grace.

The police thought there might be some connection to the Mob.

Once Frank had cast the clay in plaster and painted it, flyers of the bust were sent to police stations and post offices all along the East Coast. Five months later, a New Jersey policeman working the night shift was going through bulletins of missing people when he noticed a similarity between the woman on the flyer and a mother from Arizona who had been reported missing by her family. Her name was Anna Duval.

Duval had lived on the East Coast until recently moving to Glendale. She had allegedly invested in a real estate deal that had gone bad, and she'd come to Philadelphia to get her money back. Then she disappeared. The resemblance between the bust and one of the last photographs taken of her was uncanny.

Fillinger was one of the first people to call Frank and congratulate him. "Now I've got someone else down here you might want to put a face on," he said. "And this time I'll pay you for it."

"I'll be right down," Frank said.

"You might remember him," Fillinger said before hanging up.

It was the boy who had been shot and burnt to death, his face frozen in a scream.

## A BRONZE DEATH MASK

Since Frank had last seen him, the Burnt Boy had been moved to the decomposition room. His skin was now dark, pinched, and hard to the touch, although the scream on his face was as terrifying as the first time Frank had seen it.

Fillinger explained what they knew about him. A slender white male in his late teens with brown hair, he had been tied up with an electric cord, beaten, burnt, and shot in the head with a .22. They had also found drugs in his system. His body had been dumped not far from the railroad tracks near the Walt Whitman Bridge.

The detective responsible for the case was Ellis Verb, who immediately took to Frank. That wasn't unusual; most people took to him. He had an easy, likable way, always curious and asking questions, a guy's guy as much as a lady's man.

But there was something else, too. Frank's work on Anna Duval had put him on a new footing with some members of local law enforcement. He was no longer just a civilian but someone who had helped them break a case. Verb even asked him to consult a psychic, saying that policemen weren't allowed to do it themselves. Verb and Fillinger knew of a woman in New Jersey who had a good reputation, and once Frank had agreed, an appointment was made.

At the same time Frank started having nightmares about the Burnt Boy. In one of them, the youth met a black man in his thirties who was wearing a light, large-brimmed straw hat and a plain sport coat. As the two of them stood on an unfinished portion of the I-95 near the Philadelphia airport, the man gave drugs to the youth. In another dream, Frank became the boy and was running through a warehouse. In a third dream, he saw the boy killed in front of a row house.

Two days before Frank's meeting with the psychic, she phoned him and described his nightmares, even though she knew nothing about the case. When they finally met, she told him that she would require something metallic from the person being sought—a bracelet or a ring, perhaps—but it turned out that there had been nothing on the body that she could use. Frank immediately thought of how he could help. He asked if a bronze death mask of the youth would work. She said it would be fine.

Frank had never made a death mask, but he figured that the procedure couldn't be that much different from sculpting. Instead of making a plaster cast of a clay bust, he needed to make one of the Burnt Boy's leftover face.

First of all, he had to find some kind of material with which to make an impression of the Burnt Boy. He couldn't pour plaster over the face, because that would destroy evidence. Fillinger said that Haskell Askin might have an idea.

A forensic dentist who also practiced as a dentist in Brick Township, New Jersey, Askin had looked at the Burnt Boy earlier on in the case. At the time he'd discovered that the victim had a short lingual fraenum, or tongue tie, which meant that he probably spoke with difficulty. Askin told the police they should perhaps be looking for a missing person with a speech impediment.

Askin suggested that Frank try making an impression of the face with dental alginate, a material used for creating teeth impressions. It was soft and could be easily removed once the cast was made and wouldn't harm the face, although it had to be applied quickly and be kept moist; once it dried, it cracked and fell apart.

Late one night, when the medical examiner's office was less busy, Frank went down and entered the decomposition room armed with his container of alginate powder and an empty bucket. Mixed with water, the alginate turned into a gooey, molasses-like substance that he poured over the youth's face and into his mouth.

Within minutes the alginate had set to a consistency like Jell-O, over which Frank poured plaster. When that shell was dry, he pulled it off, placed it upside down on the table, peeled off the limp half-inch-thick alginate, and carefully laid it inside the plaster shell so that it kept its shape. He wrapped the two molds in damp towels and headed home.

The next step was to create a version of the alginate in plaster, so it could be given to a foundry to make the bronze death mask. A second mold of the youth's face, or a plaster positive, was created by pouring plaster into the alginate, which was held in shape by the original plaster shell. Once the plaster positive was hard, Frank coated that imprint with several layers of latex, on top of which he poured more plaster to create the final mold, the so-called mother mold. That was the version he took to a foundry outside the city.

The foundry went through its own labor-intensive procedure of making a wax casting inside the mother mold (the third imprint of the Burnt Boy's face), which, when hardened, was covered in ceramic. When the ceramic was baked, the wax became liquid and flowed out through a hole. The hollow was then filled with hot liquid bronze.

On learning that the bronze wasn't a commercial job but was being used to try and ID the Burnt Boy and find his killer, the foundry manager charged Frank only for the materials, which was a fraction of the cost of the entire job.

But it was all in vain. Once the psychic had the death mask in her hands, it told her nothing.

## HOMICIDE HAL

"If I never do another forensic case in my life," Frank told Fillinger, "I will feel good for having helped identify Anna Duval."

The pathologist smiled. He could see that Frank was basking in the glow of his first ID.

"Once you're bitten by the police dog, you won't want to turn back," Fillinger said. "You'll want to keep working in the field—just like I did."

They pulled into the parking lot at Temple University, Philadelphia, where Fillinger lectured in criminology. As he set up his slide show, students kept streaming into Bright Hall. It was a popular class, and even students who weren't studying criminology came to listen to him. Not only did he know what he was talking about, but he knew how to tell a good story. Tonight it was about the Circus Killer.

Several years earlier, the bodies of half a dozen young boys had been discovered in the basement of a house in a run-down area of Philadelphia, their partially decomposed remains covered in chemicals. The investigation by the police and the medical examiner's office eventually led to a Russian immigrant who liked to stalk his prey on circus fairgrounds. The chemicals that were meant to destroy the bodies did the opposite—they preserved them.

At the end of the class, Fillinger turned to Frank expectantly. "Well?"

"That girl with the glasses in the back and that one to the side dressed in pink," Frank said.

It was a game they played every time Frank came to Temple with Fillinger. As the pathologist was talking, Frank had to pick two students who didn't like Fillinger, and at the end of class, the two men would compare notes. Frank wasn't sure how Fillinger had found time during his lecture to single out a few people in several hundred, but he always did.

"I think you're right," Fillinger replied.

The Who Doesn't Like Me game was one of various ways in which Fillinger tested Frank and made sure he was serious about forensics. He also asked Frank to lecture himself. Barely a week after Anna Duval was identified, Frank was addressing the International Association for Identification, one of the oldest forensic organizations in the world.

"Don't you think I should build up a track record first?" Frank asked. He felt totally inadequate to talk about forensic sculpting, a subject he had only just been introduced to.

"Nonsense," Fillinger replied. "Come have dinner with me, and then we'll go to the meeting."

Frank accepted the offer for two reasons. First, he was still a bit mystified by his own success with the bust of Anna Duval, and he wanted to learn more about forensics. Second, the person he wanted to learn more from was Fillinger.

||||||||||||||||||||||||||||||||||||||||||||||||||||||||||||||||

Most people called Fillinger Doc or Homicide Hal.

He wasn't as well known as Thomas Noguchi in Los Angeles, who autopsied Marilyn Monroe, Robert Kennedy, and Sharon Tate, or New York's Michael Baden, who would later autopsy John Belushi and give evidence at the trial of Claus von Bülow. Fillinger's most famous case—at least where a famous person was involved—was Holly Maddux, the woman whom Philadelphia counterculture personality Ira Einhorn killed in the late 1970s and stored in a trunk in his apartment for eighteen months before she was found.

But most of Fillinger's autopsies—by the 1970s he had done more than ten thousand—were of people who weren't famous at all. He also testified in numerous trials and got the police involved in cases that they might have overlooked otherwise.

Though only an assistant medical examiner in Philadelphia, Fillinger was regarded with enormous respect. In many ways, he wasn't unlike the character Jack Klugman played on *Quincy, M.E.* In fact, Klugman, who was also a Philadelphian, often came by to have dinner with Fillinger. So did Peter Falk, the actor playing the TV detective Columbo.

Fillinger, who was in his early fifties, conducted autopsies around the country and at all hours of the day and night, as many as forty a week. When he wasn't working at the Philadelphia medical examiner's office, he was doing freelance jobs. The license plate on his Thunderbird was HOM-HAL, for Homicide Hal. At the medical examiner's office, he preferred the late-night hours, when the place was quieter. For Frank, that was also when it was easier to come and watch him dissect a body. Fillinger told him to see a dead body as "the shell of a soul."

Pathologists often got a reputation for specializing in a particular field. No one knew stab wounds like Robert Catherman. Another colleague was an ace at discerning blunt trauma. With Fillinger, it was gunshot wounds.

In the autopsy room one night, the team was having a problem with the body of a black male who had been shot to death only a day earlier.

"Doc," one of them finally called out to Fillinger, who was working on another body, "I can't find the bullet. I can see the bullet entrance, but it doesn't have an exit, and I can't find it inside him. It's got to be in there somewhere."

Fillinger came over and took a quick look at the body and the place where the bullet had entered the chest. "Let me show you something," he said. He placed his left hand over his eyes and then put his right hand into the opened chest cavity. Unlike his colleagues, Fillinger worked without gloves, even after contracting hepatitis C several times. "I can feel the tissue better with my bare hands," he once told Frank. "The resilience and surface tension and texture tell me a lot about a body."

With his arm deep inside the body, he felt around and then came out with the bullet in his bare hand. "Here it is."

||||||||||||||||||||||||||||||||||||||||||||||||||||

Fillinger had an ulterior motive in cultivating Frank's knowledge of forensics. He needed someone who could assist him with his freelance autopsy jobs. He was already using a detective from Pennsylvania's Montgomery County named John Durante, and they sometimes went out at seven at night, came back at six the next morning, had a few hours of sleep, then went back to work.

But Frank wasn't interested. His photographic work was full of deadlines that often changed at the last minute. He couldn't give that up to help cut up bodies. "I've got a career already," he said. "And I'm not looking for a new one."

But he kept going down to see Fillinger work whenever he could. And he joined Fillinger and Durante when they drove up to Lancaster, Pennsylvania, to see the legendary Wilton Krogman.

## TISSUE THICKNESS

Wilton Krogman was one of the most famous people in forensics at a time when few people knew what the word meant. Sometimes called "the bone detective," he had worked with Eliot Ness, had taught many of the country's leading figures in the field, and had been an expert witness in countless murder trials. Long before Fillinger was keeping classrooms and courtrooms on the edge of their seats, Krogman was.

In 1939 he wrote the FBI's "Guide to the Identification of Human Skeletal Material," a brief work that was one of the first important works in forensic anthropology in the United States. His book *The Human Skeleton in Forensic Medicine*, published in 1962, became a bible for crime-scene investigators and remained so for decades. At that time there were perhaps only a dozen people in the country who focused on what was more commonly known as "Skeletal ID." Besides practicing forensic anthropology, Krogman was also an expert in dentition, osteology, racial studies, genetics, and paleoanthropology, a combination of interests making it almost inevitable that he would eventually look into the possibility of putting a face on a skull.

Not that Krogman was the first American to do so—in 1914 J. Howard McGregor of Columbia University had attempted a facial reconstruction of a prehistoric man—but he gave impetus to the art. The skull, Krogman wrote, told not only the age, sex, and race of a person but was also "the matrix of the living head; it is the bony core of the fleshy head and face in life."

Using the skull to build upon, a reasonable facsimile of the face could be created. But science was able to go only so far, and an artist's touch was needed from a certain point forward. Krogman himself had worked with various artists—creating sketches, mostly, but also some busts—since 1946.

By the late 1970s, his procedure was fairly well known. First you cut a series of wooden dowels and attached them to the skull to show the depth of the flesh at various points. Next, clay was put on the skull until it was the right depth, and the facial features were shaped. After hair was added, photographs of the bust were taken. Unofficially, this procedure became known as "Krogman's rules."

||||||||||||||||||||||||||||||||||||||||||||||||||||||||

Krogman came out of the building to meet Fillinger and his two passengers. Now seventy-five and semiretired, he was director of research at the H. K. Cooper cleft palate facility in Lancaster.

A lanky man, he was dressed in a powder-blue shirt and a tie, his thinning gray hair neatly combed. He had large ears and a long head, which somehow made him more imposing. Despite being almost blind (he had lost the sight in his right eye in 1941), he was full of energy and enthusiasm. He went up to the visitors and greeted them.

Fillinger had brought a head and some bones that he wanted Krogman to look at. The four men walked into Krogman's office, a badly lit, old-worldly place of crammed dark bookcases and hutches that went up to the ceiling. In one corner was a table where Krogman could study skeletons.

"I want to be with my work," he said, putting out the bones that Fillinger had brought. He had to hold the skull until it was almost pressing against his black-rimmed glasses before he could see it properly.

Frank had a million questions he wanted to ask. When the two doctors had finished talking, he got his chance. He told Krogman that he was about to start sculpting the Burnt Boy. He explained how he had reconstructed Anna Duval, even though he hadn't really known what he was doing, first sculpting her in clay and then making a plaster mold. Was that the proper way to do a facial reconstruction? Were there any other people in the country doing this kind of work?

"What did you use for tissue thicknesses?" Krogman asked.

Frank didn't understand.

Krogman explained that the depth of flesh and muscle covering each person's skull, male or female, well fed or undernourished, was different. Once you had determined these thicknesses, depending on age, sex, and race, you marked them on the skull. The measurements could be found in several charts, the most famous of which dated back to two Swiss colleagues, Kollmann and Büchly, in the nineteenth century. But they weren't the first people to study the subject—Hermann Welcker was.

A German anatomist who specialized in skulls, Welcker knew them so well he maintained that he could tell which of two skulls belonged to the painter Raphael by comparing them to his self-portrait. In the same way, a German cardiologist and internist named Wilhelm His identified a skull, exhumed in Leipzig, as that of Johann Sebastian Bach, and helped create a bust of him that still stood outside the city's Thomaskirche.

In 1883 Welcker studied the bodies of thirteen middle-aged white males to find out how much soft tissue there was over the skull. In 1895 Wilhelm His did a second study and put together a chart of the measurements. Whereas Welcker had used a double-edged knife to test the tissue depth, His opted for a needle with a rubber stopper attached to the end that was displaced upward until the needle reached the bone. He chose fifteen points, from the hairline to the chin to the center of the eyebrow to a point on the lower jaw. Because the skin from the hairline over the back of the head remained relatively thin and even, and was often covered in hair and didn't usually figure in the recognition of a person, it was thought unnecessary to give any points there. His, meanwhile, tested over sixty bodies, all suicide victims, and listed them according to the categories All, Males 17 to 40, Males 50 to 72, and Females 18 to 52.

Three years later, in 1898, Julius Kollmann, a Swiss anatomist, and his countryman W. Büchly, a sculptor, expanded on His's findings. They used a soot-covered needle on twenty-three points on the corpse, from the upper forehead to the cheekbones, from the mid-eyebrow to the height of the upper lip. They also described bodies' nutritional condition: Thin, Very Thin, Well Nourished, or Very Well Nourished.

Despite slight adaptations over the years—usually to add other races and to allow for diets divergent from those of the original specimens, most of whom came from Central Europe—Kollmann and Büchly's results remained the foundation on which future charts were based.

"The various charts are listed in my book," Krogman said. "I will give you a copy." As he walked over to his bookcase and pulled out a copy of *The Human Skeleton,* he continued. "You needn't take measurements of the skull the way you did. You can sculpt directly onto it. The skull is strong enough to take it, and you won't have errors in measurement."

Krogman knew a woman in Oklahoma named Betty Pat Gatliff who was doing reconstructions, and she was thought to be quite good at them. However, she never made a plaster cast—she ended her process with the clay bust, which she took pictures of. The clay was then removed from the skull.

"But that means there is no bust later on," Frank said. "There are only photographs." To Frank, it made more sense to have the head in plaster and painted, a permanent three-dimensional figure.

Krogman sat down at his desk and opened his book to the title page. "You should carry on doing it the way you think best," he said.

"Just make sure to use the tissue-thickness markers and get as much information about the skull as you can. After that, it's up to you."

Before they left, Krogman inscribed his book for Frank: "To a fellow-seeker in the vineyard of the forensic sciences."

||||||||||||||||||||||||||||||||||||||||||||||||||||||||||||||

Upon Krogman's suggestion that Frank put the clay directly onto the skull, Fillinger had the head of the Burnt Boy removed from the body and cleaned of any remaining flesh. The procurement officer at the medical examiner's office had to put through a request for payment.

"We've never done anything like this before," he told Frank. "We can't really offer you much more than two hundred dollars."

"Two hundred's fine," Frank said.

When the head was cleaned and ready to be picked up, Frank rode his Harley down to University Avenue and put the head in a cardboard box, which he tied to the sissy bars with a bungee cord. Gerry White was watching him.

"See," Frank called out, "it fits perfectly."

It was twilight by the time he got back to Arch Street, and several prostitutes had gathered at their usual place, sitting on the parking lot wall next to the St. Charles Hotel. One of them had modeled for Frank several times, and he always made sure to greet her.

"Hey," called out a woman seated next to her, who was wearing a big Afro. "What's in the box? Something for me?"

"It's a head, honey. You want to look?"

She smiled back uncertainly. "You're sick, man."

Around the back of the building, there was an industrial elevator that Frank used to take his motorcycle to the fourth floor. Once he had parked in an unused part of the loft, he went across to his workbench, untied the box, and took out the head.

No longer covered in leathery skin, which meant the horrific scream was hard to see anymore, the skull was clean and smooth, the bones almost white. Frank ran his hands over the cranium. The fine cut going across the top of the head, where the medical examiner had run the saw in order to take the brain out, came to a two-inch V shape at the forehead. The cap was loose, so Frank stuck it in place with Elmer's glue. He also glued on the lower jaw.

The phone in the studio rang. One of the advertising agencies he worked for needed some shots delivered within the next twenty-four hours, so Frank put aside the Burnt Boy. No matter how much he wanted to start working on the bust and help solve a crime, it was paying only two hundred dollars. An advertising job took a fraction of the time and paid up to ten thousand.

Sculpting the Burnt Boy several nights later, Frank found himself working a lot quicker than with Anna Duval. He thought that was probably because he didn't have to take measurements, putting the clay right on the skull. He also used the tissue-thickness charts in Krogman's book, even sculpting the boy's hair instead of buying a wig.

But the bust wasn't nearly as good as that of Anna Duval, or as human-looking. The boy appeared almost comical, his ears protruding, his upper jaw pronounced, two front teeth overlapping his lower lip, as if he had a severe overbite. Flyers of the bust were distributed, but several months passed without any ID, and the case went cold.

Frank was disappointed, although Fillinger told him not toworry. They were driving to Temple University for his weekly lecture.

"Not every head is going to be identified as fast as Anna Duval," Fillinger said. "It might never be identified. It depends on who sees it. There are lots of factors to take into consideration—especially luck."

## IN RUSSIA

The same year that Wilton Krogman was born, 1903, so was Mikhail Gerasimov. Even though they quite likely didn't know about each other, the two men followed very similar paths. From childhood, they developed a fascination with fossils and ancient artifacts, then later became physical anthropologists who split their time between academia and helping to solve murders.

A doctor's son who had grown up outside of Irkutsk in Siberia, an area rich in prehistoric remains, the young Gerasimov dug for bones in summer and assembled them in winter. His playroom shelves were filled with his discoveries: the bones of a woolly rhinoceros and a mammoth's tusk, horse skulls, elk antlers, and flints from Stone Age man. By the age of ten, he knew about the Swiss anatomists Kollmann and Büchly, and he had even read about the ongoing argument over whether a skull in Weimar belonged to the Austrian playwright Friedrich Schiller (a case he himself would be called in to help resolve forty years later).

By his late teens, Gerasimov had befriended zoologists, archaeologists, and physicians at Irkutsk University, and had started reconstructing skulls, a technique he further developed at the Irkutsk Museum and then in Leningrad. Being one of the few scientists who was also an artist, he didn't need someone to help him the way Krogman did.

In 1937 Gerasimov addressed an esteemed group of scientists at Moscow University, explaining his methods and displaying several busts he had made. Alongside each one was a photograph of what the person had looked like when he was alive, although he assured them that he never looked at the photograph until he had completed a bust.

His audience was skeptical, so he suggested they test him. They could choose any skull they wanted, and he would put a face on it. Confronted with their eventual choice, however, Gerasimov knew he was in trouble. It clearly wasn't a Caucasian or a Mongoloid, so he assumed it was a Negroid, a race he'd never worked on. With several scientists watching over him at all times, and without using the tissue-thickness charts of Kollmann and Büchly, he finished the bust in less than two hours.

The scientists didn't have a photograph of the person the skull had come from, but they had a death mask. It was a Papuan. Even though Gerasimov had chosen the wrong hair and the mask was full of ornament—there was mother-of-pearl around the forehead, a boar's tusk through the nose, and pendants in the ears—the likeness was unmistakable.

His audience remained unconvinced. It was just a coincidence, they said, adding that in any case, Papuans all looked alike.

At the outbreak of World War II, Gerasimov got his first forensic case. Bones were found in a Leningrad forest, clearly from a human, but the age, sex, and manner of death were unclear. The presiding magistrate was about to give up on the case when a detective approached Gerasimov for help.

From the teeth and the open sutures of the skull, Gerasimov determined that the victim was about thirteen. The sex was harder to figure out, although the large mastoid process—the bony protuberance behind the ear—as well as the relatively large lower jaw and the prominent supraorbital region led him to believe it was a boy. Hatchet marks on the right side of the head, just above the mastoid process, led Gerasimov to believe he had definitely been murdered.

Gerasimov told the detective to look in the missing persons' reports for a boy of about thirteen, short but thickly set, with a head that stuck out in the back and was covered in light reddish hair that was cut short. Then he set out to make the bust.

Kollmann and Büchly's charts did not cover children, so Gerasimov made up his own measurements. Using numerous sets of X-rays of boys aged nine to thirteen, he estimated tissue thicknesses. He gave the victim a snub nose and chubby cheeks, a high forehead, a thick upper lip, and slightly projecting ears.

In the meantime, the police had come up with the name of a boy who had been missing for several months, though his parents said that he often ran away. Without a similar case to serve as a precedent, the police didn't know what their next step should be. The magistrate and the detective feared showing the bust to the parents, who still didn't know that their son might be dead. The shock could prevent them from making a proper ID. The detective suggested putting a photograph of the very lifelike bust with several others.

In Gerasimov's presence, the parents identified the photograph of the bust as their son. So real did it look that the father even commented on the quality of the coat the boy was wearing and said that he must be doing well for himself.

Gerasimov never learned the outcome of the case. It dragged on for another two years, by which time he was deeply involved in the mystery of Valentina Kosova.

Married and eight months pregnant, Kosova had suddenly gone missing. Several months later, skeletal remains were found in a forest near her home and were presumed to be hers. Kosova's husband was interrogated but let go. At that point the anthropologist was called in.

As was his custom, Gerasimov received the head through the mail, and he let one of his assistants open the box for him. At the bottom, in an envelope, was a photograph of Kosova that he left unopened and put in a safe.

On studying the skull, he determined that it belonged to a woman in her mid-twenties. Because the lower jaw was missing, Gerasimov went to look for a similar head. After going through more than three hundred specimens in the anthropological collection of the Russian Academy of Sciences, he found one "with due regard to the general breadth of the trochlea, the shape of the dentition, the mass and form of the lower jaw." It wasn't perfect, but it was the best he could do.

When he was finished with the reconstruction, he retrieved the photograph from the safe. It had been taken when Kosova was about sixteen, but the bust was clearly a match. Two pieces of evidence seemed to corroborate this: the age of the bones and the fact that several of her friends said she had a gold crown on her second incisor, which the skull also had.

With this information, the police once again brought in Kosova's husband for questioning, and he finally confessed to killing her.

||||||||||||||||||||||||||||||||||||||||||||||||||||||||||||

By the end of his career, Gerasimov had undertaken more than a hundred forensic cases in which he gave faces to the unknown. But he spent almost as much time reconstructing the very well known.

Early on, he was approached by a colleague who wanted to prove that a skull in his possession was that of Fyodor Dostoyevsky's mother, Maria. Which he did. Before long, the authorities had seized on Gerasimov's talent to put faces on famous deceased Russians. One of his first jobs for them was to reconstruct Tamerlane, the great and merciless fifteenth-century warrior who was a descendant of Genghis Khan and founder of the Timurid Empire.

In 1941 the tomb containing Tamerlane and several of his sons and grandsons was opened, and Gerasimov was put in charge of the removal of gravestones, the recovery of textiles and bone fragments, and their preservation. Most important, he had to make documentary portraits of the famous warriors' skulls.

In preparation, Gerasimov read whatever he could about Tamerlane, not only for pieces of information, such as old wounds, to confirm whether the skeleton was his but also for any reference about what he might have looked like (which he would then test his final bust against).

The legend of the Central Asian conqueror was known far and

wide, and while many of the records spoke of his riches and how famous he was from China to Europe, they referred only briefly to his appearance—and even those texts often contradicted one another. The bust, once it was finished, depicted a man who looked like everything one would have imagined—mean, his full beard flaming, his face terrifying.

Twelve years later, Gerasimov had to put a face on a Russian leader with an even more villainous name, Ivan the Terrible, who lay buried in the Kremlin's Archangel Cathedral.

Gerasimov had read in various accounts that Ivan was a complex character, "outstanding and remarkable" yet bloody and cruel, but he didn't want to let the many literary and artistic portraits of the tsar get in the way of a realistic reconstruction. For that reason, as with many of his busts, he first sculpted only one side of the face and let the other half of the skull show how he had reached his outcome.

The bust of Ivan, as with Tamerlane, seemed to confirm the legend, and only Gerasimov knew how vital a role artistic license had played. His own words, in his book *The Face Finder,* seem to suggest he was as much scientist as artist. "The face was hard, commanding, undoubtedly clever but cruel and unpleasing with pendulous nose and clumsy chin," he wrote. "The lower lip was indicated by the occlusion of the teeth and the face was set off by a powerful neck and a massive, well-filled torso."

In the 1950s Gerasimov was made the chief of the newly created Laboratory for Plastic Reconstruction at Russia's Ethnographical Institute in Moscow. His students repeatedly asked him two questions over the years: Could a skull be re-created from a face? Never, he said, for the skull provided much more information than the face.

And second: Was it possible to look at a skull and imagine its face? Yes, he said, but that came with experience.

"Usually, it is thought that all skulls are more or less alike," he told them. "But this is not so. Absolutely similar skulls do not exist and cannot exist."

## A WALL OF SKULLS

1980

Anna Duval was enough to get Frank noticed. Police departments in a number of states started calling to find out if he could help them, although that was easier said than done. Or rather, it was easier said than getting the heads to him.

Few police departments had the facilities to separate a head from a body and to deflesh it before mailing the skull to Frank. Fillinger said the Philadelphia medical examiner's office could deflesh the occasional head for him, but someone still had to detach it. Confronted with those obstacles, most police departments gave up.

John Durante, the detective from Montgomery County who'd accompanied Frank and Fillinger to see Krogman, sent Frank the head of a man whose decayed body had been found hanging from a tree in Whitemarsh Township, Pennsylvania. From the police in Belle Glade, Florida, Frank got the skull of a man who'd been murdered and dumped on the bank of a canal.

Fillinger remained Frank's biggest supporter, sending him his third job, the first since the Burnt Boy. A man found floating in the Delaware River was suspected of having drowned when a Russian ship, the *Corinthus,* had caught fire and sunk. The medical examiner's office got little cooperation from the Russian authorities, so they didn't know whether any sailors were missing or, if so, what their racial background was. The suspected Russian was possibly Mongoloid or Asian. Never having worked on anything but Caucasians, Frank went down to the Mütter Museum to get some ideas.

The Mütter was a small museum located in the College of Physicians of Philadelphia. In the nineteenth century, the city was a well-known center of medicine, with hospitals, medical schools, and pathological and anatomical collections called cabinets, one of which belonged to Thomas Dent Mütter. On retiring as a professor of surgery in 1856, Mütter donated his array of medical objects to the college.

Most people came to the museum to see the oddities, the human monstrosities and malformations, the famous Siamese twins Chang and Eng, the fetuses in bottles, the stomach the size of a car engine, and the Soap Lady, a woman who died in 1792 but whose body, instead of decomposing, had been preserved by adipocere, the hydrolysis of fat in wet ground that gave her a coating like soap. But Frank came to see the skulls.

He walked through the marble foyer of the Beaux Arts building and headed past the grand staircase and the paneled library to the back, where the museum was. Ignoring the displays of murder victims and obstetric tools—forceps, specula, and pessaries—he made his way to the eastern wall on the mezzanine floor. Almost half of it was covered in an assortment of skulls, 139 of them.

Collected by a Viennese anatomist named Joseph Hyrtl from

across Central and Eastern Europe, the skulls had come from prostitutes, soldiers, children, Calvinists, Slovaks, thieves. The description
of each person was brief. From Moravia, a seventeen-year-old shoe-
maker's assistant. From Parma, a fourteen-year-old who died after
a botched amputation. From Naples, a fisherman. From Dalmatia,
an idiot.

For those who understood anatomical terminology, there was
occasionally more information—*Frontal groove from a laterally positioned right supraorbital foramen. Defects in tooth enamel. Moderate
overjet. Small cranium, short face*—but to most people inspecting
them, the skulls were merely a dozen rows of ghouls, all of whom
had taken their faces to the grave.

Frank came down to the Mütter Museum as often as he could—
whether it was for fifteen minutes or an hour—to compare what he
had in his studio with what was on the wall. He tried to find similarities. How did the elongated skull compare to the round? Were
there characteristics common to either? Where were you most likely
to find large orbits? Or heavy jawbones? Did the size of the nasal
opening bear any relation to the cheekbones or the jaws? In the
midst of comparing and studying, he found bits of a face emerging
on a skull.

He tried to use the terms he'd learned in the medical examiner's
office—the nasal aperture (the pear-shaped opening in the face where
the bones and cartilage of the nose would have been), the nasal bone
(the little bone at the top of the nose and the only indication of the
nose's shape absent the cartilage), the zygomatic bone (the upper
cheekbones).

Today he focused on the nasal area. A "brigand" who had died
in prison in Naples had a square head and a nose whose nasal bone

suggested it had been long and straight. A mason from Lombard had a nose that curved to the side. A Venetian sailor's head was rounder, but the nasal bone spiked out and down, which meant his nose was probably more hawkish.

In the middle of the third row, Frank noticed a skull that bore a slight resemblance to the Sailor from the *Corinthus*. A soldier from Dalmatia, he had a prognathism on his lower jaw, or an underbite. The nasal bone was upturned and came out at a sharp angle, suggesting a small nose. His skull was marginally wider than those nearby, and the supraorbital ridges, where the eyebrows would have been, stuck out more prominently.

A group of schoolchildren started flocking into the museum and headed straight for the Soap Lady, which was located to the left of the skulls.

"You're going to look like that one day," a girl said to her friend, giggling.

Frank laughed too.

With a clearer image in his head of what the sailor might look like, he headed out of the museum and back to his studio.

## TUG McGRAW

Frank began to lead a double life. By day he was a photographer, shooting ads for agencies like Spiro and Aitken Kynett. By night he worked on the heads.

In the two years since he had reconstructed Anna Duval, the fourth floor of the building on Arch Street where he had his studio had become an art commune. He'd been given the loft for free when he was a photographer for Faraghan Studios, located two floors down.

Since the building wasn't in a particularly safe part of town, the owner, Hercules Membrino, liked the idea of someone being there at odd hours. When Frank left Faraghan to freelance full-time, he started paying rent. There was so much space in the place that a few artist friends from the academy asked if they could move in too. Membrino didn't like the idea. "No more artists," he said. "Artists have parties and take drugs."

But soon he relented, and a number of people moved in: Tom Ewing and Marguerite Ferrari, who helped with painting case number 5233, as well as Paula Lisak, Bruce Samuelson, Raquel Higgins, Russ Veeder. They all worked at different hours, and the amount of room they got depended on what kind of work they did— sculpting, macramé, oil painting. Anyone with a big canvas usually constructed his or her own workspace out of wire mesh in the large central area.

Frank had one of the few rooms, a large airy space at the front of the building looking across at the St. Charles Hotel. The other artists knew about his foray into forensics, and they sometimes looked in to see what he was working on. When he couldn't get to a skull immediately, Frank occasionally left it in the fridge in the communal kitchen. More than once Ferrari had grabbed the wrong brown paper bag, thinking it was her lunch, only to open it and find a head. "Frank!" she'd scream.

He came running from his studio, but when he saw the horror

on Ferrari's face, he burst out laughing. "I warned you that I put heads in there," he said. "Besides, it is my fridge."

Frank could get away with it because, macabre as it was, everyone knew he was doing it for a good cause. He also liked the idea of being seen as a forensic artist, often playing up the role by looking through his eyebrows and trying to appear mysterious.

But he was also the first to admit that he had very limited experience. He had done only five heads and had gotten the ID of Anna Duval. For the man found hanging in the tree in Whitemarsh, Frank's bust had just confirmed a tentative ID given by the family. Moreover, several months had passed since he'd finished the Sailor from the *Corinthus,* but no one had contacted him with another skull.

In the meantime, he had a big photographic job to keep him busy. Philadelphia had recently won the World Series, and in honor of the Phillies pitcher Tug McGraw, a World War II diesel-powered tug had been named after him. Frank had been commissioned by Blue Cross to fly over the Delaware River and shoot the boat, which had been specially painted in blue-and-white trim for the occasion.

The day he gave in his final photographs, Frank got a call from Gerry White, the investigator at the medical examiner's office, who told him to come down to University Avenue. They had an unknown white female who had probably been murdered and had been found in the basement of a house in North Philadelphia.

Normally, Frank didn't inquire about the details of a case before he got down to the medical examiner's office, but this time something made him ask. As soon as he heard that the body had been found at 2526 North Leithgow Street, he froze. It was three houses down from where he'd grown up.

## ▍TALKING HEADS

Frank was born at 2520 North Leithgow Street in 1941, when the area was more commonly known as West Kensington. The blue-collar neighborhood was so close to the factory district where many of the residents worked that the streets were often filled with the smells of jams and grape jellies, leather, candle wax, and spices.

Until Frank was almost five, his father, Frank Sr., was away at war, serving as a Seabee and fighting in Okinawa and Iwo Jima. Frank Sr. wrote to the family almost every week, always making sure to draw a train at the bottom of each letter.

Frank developed a fascination with trains and, when his father came home, guns. Frank Sr. took his son fishing and told him stories about how he'd carried a heavy Browning automatic rifle up the beaches of Iwo Jima, which made Frank want to learn how to shoot. He already possessed a .22 rifle that he'd found in the basement after his grandfather had told him and his cousin that he'd misplaced it. "Whoever finds it can keep it," he said.

The .22 became the first gun in Frank's collection. Lots of soldiers had brought weapons home from the war as mementoes, although their wives didn't like their keeping guns around the house. Frank's mother, Sarah, didn't mind if Frank took them, so long as he was careful.

Frank was barely six when Sarah and Frank Sr. started taking him to the Fleisher Art Memorial on Saturday for art classes. At first they waited outside in the courtyard for him, but by the following year he was catching the trolley downtown on his own. He sketched and painted, developing an early fascination with the relationship between form and function, and with the way something very efficient could also be wonderful to behold. Guns and trains being his passions, they were where he noticed it first. The Colt .45, the German Luger, the Hudson locomotives designed by Henry Dreyfuss for the Twentieth Century Limited, and the trains of Raymond Loewy.

When he was a sophomore at Edison High School, several of his paintings were considered good enough to be shown at a student exhibition held annually by Gimbels department store. He received a gold seal for a watercolor of a maritime scene, which Walter Stuempfig, an artist who taught at the academy, bought for five dollars. Frank never got the money, although Stuempfig offered him a scholarship to study art at the academy while doing his academic work at the University of Pennsylvania.

After Frank's paintings were taken down from Gimbels, some of them were exhibited by his high school, but they were never given back to him. The incident had an almost inexplicably profound impact on him and annoyed him so much he decided that he didn't want to be an artist anymore—at least not one who had exhibits. It was a decision he would stick by for many years. If he was to become an artist at all, his art would have to serve a different purpose, although he wasn't sure what that was.

When his friend Franny Gerbelni, who was second in line for the scholarship, told him that he really wanted to go to the academy, Frank said he could take the prize. Sarah was furious. "You're not going to make anything out of your life without a college education," she said.

"We'll see," Frank replied.

||||||||||||||||||||||||||||||||||||||||||||||||||||

Frank Sr. got him a job at the Curtis Publishing Company, where he was employed. Curtis produced *The Saturday Evening Post* and *Ladies' Home Journal.*

Working as a messenger for the photographic department, Frank picked up tips from the photographers and the guys in the developing room. He visited the studio on the twelfth floor, where they did portraits and photographed Norman Rockwell's paintings for the covers. He met Rockwell.

In his spare time, he sneaked into the studios and the darkroom to do his own photographs. He asked young women he chatted up in the hallways if they wanted to model for him, and he eventually put up one of his shots anonymously for an in-house competition. His boss liked it, but when he found out it was Frank's, he told him that, as a messenger, he was out of the running.

With the military draft still on, Frank followed the family tradition of joining the navy. He was given the chance to serve in a photographic unit but turned it down to become a mechanic. He was posted to the U.S.S. *Calcaterra,* a destroyer escort ship that patrolled off Greenland and Nova Scotia, looking for Russian trawlers that had come within the three-mile limit.

In 1962 Frank left the navy and went back to Curtis, but the company was in financial trouble and he soon lost his job. With a portfolio of his sketches and the girls he'd photographed at Curtis, he went to studios around the city looking for work. One of them was Faraghan on Arch Street.

"If you can draw like this," George Faraghan said, "I'll hire you."

‖‖‖‖‖‖‖‖‖‖‖‖‖‖‖‖‖‖‖‖‖‖‖‖‖‖‖‖‖‖‖‖‖‖‖‖‖‖‖‖‖

The moment Frank met a girl named Jan Proctor a few years later, he was hooked.

She had been living in Philadelphia's Center City for a year. Three days before her eighteenth birthday, she had run away from home in West Kensington with five dollars she'd stolen from her father's wallet. It wasn't the first time she had run away, but it was the last. She left her one-year-old daughter, Lisa, with her parents.

After renting an apartment in the city, she found work dancing at a club, and she sometimes modeled. With her ash-blond hair, wide-set eyes, and long lashes, she looked not unlike Jean Shrimpton. Joe Petrellis, a photographer friend, introduced them.

Jan posed in the nude for Frank and got him work at her go-go club. The club needed a new batch of slides—colors, shapes, anything psychedelic—to project during the girls' performances. Frank was eager to help out, less because he needed the work than because he was intrigued by Jan.

She was wild. She took acid, smoked pot, partied, and even experimented with girls. But she wasn't interested in him, even after he moved into her apartment on Spruce Street. They each had a room—Frank the kitchen, Jan the living room—and they were separated by the bathroom.

They started hanging out together, going to Kensington nightclubs like the Randolph Social Club, run by Tommy the Boot, and the Saint Giorgio on Fifth Street. Frank took Jan with him on some of his photographic jobs, even one in New York, and she rode on the back of his Harley 1200. When they got back to Spruce Street, they drank Ripple and smoked marijuana that Jan had stashed in the back of the television. Frank began showing her how his camera worked, and before she knew it, they were in bed together.

"You got me with the old camera trick," she joked with him afterward.

When Frank brought up the subject of marriage, Jan said she wasn't interested. Her own parents had a bad marriage, and she didn't want to repeat their mistake. But she soon started caving in. Frank cut a very sexy figure—blue eyes, tattooed boxer's arms that he showed off in muscle shirts as he sat astride his Harley, a rock-hard stomach that she loved clutching as she sat behind him—and he was a great lover. She felt flattered that of all the girls he could have, he had picked her.

On Halloween 1969 Jan took Frank to a party at a friend's house.

"I've never seen you getting on so well with a guy," her friend said. "Are you two an item?"

Jan looked at Frank across the room. "I guess we are."

She told Frank about the conversation.

"So," he asked nonchalantly, "you want to get married or something?"

"Sure."

They got married the following Halloween. Jan made cupcakes to hand out to any trick-or-treaters who came by during the ceremony. Quite unintentionally, there were thirteen guests. Frank's mother thought the whole thing was not only macabre but unlucky.

"Isn't it sacrilegious to get married on Halloween?" she asked.

"I hope not," Jan said, still unsure she was doing the right thing. "We're going to need every blessing we can get."

The couple's first house was a compact three-bedroom on Bingham Street in Lawndale, right next door to Frank's parents. Jan thought it would be good for her to live in the suburbs, away from her wild life of parties and drugs. Within a year, Vanessa was born. Lisa, Jan's first daughter, came to live with them when she was seven, and Frank adopted her. She always called him Frank, not Dad, but in no time she adored him. After being raised by her grandparents for most of her childhood, and rarely seeing Jan, she saw Frank as the person who had brought the family together. He joked with her and made life fun. Before taking the girls to church on Sunday he'd stop at a bakery and buy them all something to eat on the church steps.

The day in October 1977 when Frank went down to see his first autopsy with Bart Zandel, Jan didn't think anything unusual about it. She had read *Dracula* countless times as a teenager, and she was so fascinated by human anatomy that it wasn't long before Frank took her to meet Fillinger and to watch an autopsy.

After Anna Duval was ID'd, Jan wrote the word "forensics" and its dictionary explanation on a piece of paper that she stuck to the fridge in their kitchen. She was convinced it was a word that was going to be important in their lives, and she believed Frank had an extraordinary talent.

From about the time when Frank worked on the man found hanging in Whitemarsh, he started bringing the skulls home. He didn't want to spend his nights in the studio and not see the girls. He transported the skulls home in anything that was the right size—cardboard boxes, wood boxes, Igloo coolers, beer coolers—which the family made jokes about.

"Wouldn't it be funny if he were on the train and the head fell out?" Lisa said.

"And it rolled around," Vanessa added.

They all laughed. Frank, in turn, wasn't beyond using the skulls to play the occasional joke on his family. One night some friends of Lisa's were at the house for a sleepover. They all knew what Frank did with the skulls, which they thought was cool, and they called him the Head Man or the Skull Guy. On their way to bed, the girls came out of the kitchen to find a skull on the bookshelf. Unlike other skulls they had seen in the house, this one was glowing. They thought something was wrong, and were about to call Frank when he jumped out from the doorway where he'd been hiding.

"Gotcha!" he cried out, then burst out laughing.

The skulls lying around the house didn't bother Jan, but one day Frank went too far in the way he co-opted household items for his forensics work. He had brought home the Sailor from the *Corinthus,* although the skull was still too wet for him to layer clay on. He and Jan had an old Hotpoint stove whose door was so loose that they jammed bits of foil into the sides. Frank thought thirty minutes in the oven might dry out the skull. When Jan went into the kitchen, she found bugs crawling out of the Hotpoint.

"Frank!" she screamed. "Come take this fucking head out of here and go visit your mother!"

He took the skull next door and finished drying it while he had a cup of coffee with his parents.

When Frank and Jan bought their first house, it was only a few blocks away, on Palmetto Street, but it had enough space for the girls to live alone upstairs. They each had a room on either side of a bathroom and a small kitchenette, which, seeing as it wasn't being used for anything else, Frank turned into a workroom.

The kitchenette didn't have a door, so whenever Lisa went to the bathroom, she could see what he was working on. She found it especially hard at nighttime. She tried not to look in, or to see the skulls, but she couldn't help herself. She also noticed strange things that she couldn't explain. One day the arm of a skeleton was lying on the table, the upper and lower arms straight, and the fingers too. But the next day the index and middle fingers were crossed. Was Frank playing a practical joke on her?

Knowing that Frank sometimes kept a head in the kitchenette's small fridge, Lisa also started having nightmares about the fridge door opening. Inside, there would be several heads having a conversation. Finally, she asked Frank to do something about it, so he put up a curtain in the doorway.

## FROM SUPRAGLABELLA TO MANDIBLE

Gerry White and Frank pulled up outside 2526 North Leithgow Street.

The skeleton that had been found by a homeless man in the basement belonged to a white girl. Going by her wisdom teeth, or third molars, which weren't fully out yet, she was probably under eighteen.

Even before they reached the address, Frank could see how much the neighborhood had changed. The trolley no longer ran down Germantown Avenue; the Admiral Theater where he and his friend Leon Small had watched the *Rocketman* serial had become a church; and many old buildings were windowless. Low-income housing had replaced several factories, including the one where his grandfather had mended looms. Franklin Square, where they used to have stone fights as kids, was now full of weeds and trash.

"Kids shoot up there," White added.

Frank's own home, at 2520 North Leithgow, had been knocked down. The Union Hall across the road where he had played handball against the wall was still there, but it was abandoned. Hookers hung out on some of the corners.

White parked in front of 2526 North Leithgow Street, which was derelict, and led the way in. As Frank followed him down the broken stairs to the dank basement, he remembered playing there as a child.

"What was a white girl doing in a neighborhood like this?" he asked, not expecting an answer.

|||||||||||||||||||||||||||||||||||||||||||||||||||||

The girl's skull was ready for Frank to take back to his studio a few days later. He put it in a cooler that he strapped to the sissy bars and rode across the Schuylkill.

He had developed a routine by now. He put the skull on a table in the corner of the studio or the kitchenette for a while, looked at it, turned it over in his hands, left it for several hours or an entire day, and looked at it some more in between his photographic work.

On the third day he began adding the tissue-thickness markers. By 1980 Frank was using a very recent chart, which had been produced by Stanley Rhine of the University of New Mexico and his colleague Homer R. Campbell, who combined Kollmann and Büchly's landmarks with new data that they had collected under a very limited set of conditions. Their most important contribution was to measure the faces bilaterally to ascertain whether there were differences in thicknesses from side to side, something that other investigators had not done.

The Rhine & Campbell chart distinguished between Black, European, and Japanese, which were then subdivided into male and female, and then into Emaciated, Normal, and Obese. They identified twenty-one points on the skull—ten down the center and eleven on each side—although when both left and right sides were taken into account, they added up to thirty-two points. Number 1 was the supraglabella, or upper middle forehead, and Number 21 was the Sub $M_2$, indicating the area below the second molar on the lower jaw.

Frank had already removed the clay that was on the Sailor from the *Corinthus* by peeling it off with a wooden spatula. The shoulders he usually kept the same from one bust to the next, although some of his other methods he had already started adapting. For tissue-thickness markers, he no longer used wooden dowels but pieces of eraser he cut from a seven-inch eraser stick.

After checking a figure on the chart—for example, the upper lip margin, or Number 6, on a European woman was just over eight millimeters deep—he measured it off on the eraser with his caliper, cut it, and stuck it to the skull with model glue at a point that corresponded to a diagram at the top of Rhine & Campbell's chart. When all thirty-two markers were in place, the skull, with it acne-like markers, looked vaguely human.

After finishing a photography job for Bell Atlantic the next day, Frank had time to work on the skull again and began layering the clay in between the markers. By the time he rode home, the clay was flush with the markers, and by the end of the week, he had refined the face enough that he was almost ready to make the plaster mold. He took the bust home to show Jan and the girls.

Jan was walking back from the store with Vanessa when he pulled up in the alleyway behind the house. They waved as he climbed off his motorcycle and unstrapped the Igloo cooler.

"Another head?" Jan asked.

Vanessa giggled.

"The Girl from North Leithgow Street," he said.

Frank had a nightmare that night. He and his childhood friend Leon Small were in a basement full of roulette wheels, looking for his grandfather's .22, when they saw some bones. As he reached for them, they turned into sand. He woke up, convinced that the dream was about the Girl from North Leithgow Street and that he had made her face too thin for someone her age.

"I think I'm going to remake her," he told Jan that morning. The bust was on the table between them.

Jan looked at it. "You sure?" she asked.

"I had this nightmare."

Jan seldom offered her opinion. She had complete faith in what Frank did with the skulls. But this time she said something: "What does your gut tell you?"

He took the bust back to the studio on Arch Street and put it in a corner, where he looked at it throughout the day. During lunchtime he went down to the Mütter Museum to study the wall of skulls.

Maybe something he saw there would reassure him that the Girl from North Leithgow Street's face wasn't too thin.

By nightfall he was happier with the bust. He started painting latex onto the clay, the first step toward creating the plaster mold.

## BEHIND THE CURTAIN

By early 1981 Frank had done six heads, less than two a year. At two hundred dollars apiece, that hardly added up to pocket money, let alone a salary that could support him, Jan, and the girls.

But whenever he had a spare moment, he went down to the Philadelphia medical examiner's office to chat with Fillinger, White, and Suplee. Fillinger also made sure to get him to address various law-enforcement groups, and he passed Frank's name to people who could use him. In February Bob Gerken from the Pennsylvania State Police called.

Several months earlier, a skeleton had been found by a hunter on a hilltop near Slatington, Pennsylvania, a small town just north of Allentown. The coroner believed that it belonged to a white woman between the ages of eighteen and twenty-five, and that she'd been dead between nine and twenty months.

"The pelvic bones, the mastoid bone beneath the ear, the lack of a bony ridge above the eyes—all say this was a female," the coroner told the local paper, *The Morning Call.* "The skull of a Caucasian has a more gradual slant than that of a black or Oriental. The shape of the eye sockets and the facial slant all say this was a white girl."

The cause of death was uncertain, and an investigation of missing persons' reports from the surrounding counties turned up nothing. Around the skeleton they had found the following items: a few articles of clothing, charred sneaker soles, a blue star-sapphire ring, and a single photogray eyeglass lens.

The skull of the Girl from Slatington sat on Frank's workbench for a few days before he got to the tissue-thickness markers. Almost immediately, he noticed something about the girl's mouth—it seemed a bit misaligned. It was nothing pronounced, but he needed a second opinion. He had learned by this stage that a coroner could tell him only so much about a skeleton, and often too little. He took the skull to Krogman, who immediately knew what was wrong—the girl had not only a cleft palate but a severe overbite. "She will be a mouth breather," he said.

To show Frank how the defect changed the thickness of the tissue in the upper and lower jaw areas, Krogman gave him cephalometric X-rays of four people, two with normal palates and two with cleft palates. As Frank headed home from Lancaster, he already had a better idea of the girl he was going to sculpt. Besides a prominence in the upper jaw, her mouth would be slightly open, with one or two of her upper incisors showing.

It was nighttime, so he drove the skull home, put it in the kitchenette, and pulled the curtain across the doorway before going back downstairs. After dinner, he took out the eraser sticks and his blade. Referring to the Rhine & Campbell chart, he looked under the table EUROPEAN FEMALE and began at Number 1, the supraglabella, or upper middle forehead. Next came the glabella, the prominent point between the supraorbital ridges just above the nose. Third was the nasion, or indent where the bridge of the nose meets the forehead. The tip of the nasal bone was fourth.

The remaining midline locations, Number 5 through Number 10 (the mid-philtrim, or nose-lip furrow that lies over the top row of teeth; the upper and lower lip margins; the chin-lip fold; the mental eminence, or the most projecting part of the chin), were in the area affected by the overbite. Although he gave the girl the tissue thicknesses specified by the chart, he knew that he would probably make changes as he added the clay.

Sticking on the markers could be a laborious process, because whenever he turned the skull on the cork base that held it in position, several erasers fell off onto the floor or into the skull itself. They also fell off if the skull hadn't been properly degreased. Once he'd retrieved the erasers, he had to add more glue and sometimes hold them in place. He didn't affix the markers numerically, from Numbers 1 to 21, but at random, as the inclination took him.

The following eleven points were the bilateral ones. They were positioned on either side of a line running down the center of the face, from the forehead to the supraorbital and the suborbital, which were above and below the bony socket of the eye, and outward to the cheekbone area. These included the inferior malar, which was Number 14; the supraglenoid, Number 17; and the occlusal line, Number 20, although Frank seldom used the scientific terms. Even when he did, he often mispronounced them, calling an aperture an "aptature" and a diastema, which was a gap tooth, a "diasmus." He was more concerned with dimensions and appearance than with words.

Once the glue had dried, Frank placed the skull on the clay

shoulders that had last held the Girl from North Leithgow Street. Out of a small plastic box he took a pair of plaster eyeballs from a dozen he'd made, each twenty-four millimeters in diameter. In the back of each orbit he pushed a piece of clay, into which he embedded the eyeball, then put more clay around it, making sure to keep it centered and in line with the canthus marks at the corner of each eye.

At first it appeared that the girl's left eye was slightly higher than the right, but after studying the skull again, Frank decided they were fairly even. Unlike tissue thicknesses, there were no charts specifying how far the eyeball should protrude. Krogman suggested following an average: The cornea should come out no farther than a line drawn from the superior to the inferior orbital margins. Once the eyes were in place, and he was happy with what he had done that night, Frank pulled the curtain across the kitchenette's doorway and went to bed.

He wanted to take the bust with him to Arch Street the next day, in case he got a chance to work on it, but it was too fragile to move with the tissue markers attached. He left it at the house, where it stayed untouched for four days, as he completed an urgent job shooting the satellite dishes on the city's rooftops.

By then he knew where he would start layering the clay first—at the girl's mouth. Where he began on a skull wasn't crucial, and he never really knew why he chose a particular point, but the mere act of choosing a starting point made him feel more comfortable. On the Girl from North Leithgow Street, it had been her cheeks; on the Sailor from the *Corinthus*, the back of his cranium.

He used the same clay skull after skull, and it grew darker with each job as it gathered bits of grit and bone from a previous job. Frank took a handful of clay from the barrel and put it on the workbench, then pinched out a small piece, maybe a square inch at a time, and pressed it onto the skull.

First he went to the upper jaw and worked outward from there. He had to be careful when he worked anywhere near the tissue-thickness markers, especially if they were close together, like at the top of the nose or around the mouth. It didn't take him long to cover most of the bony surface, its ivory color transformed to a shade of brown. On either side of the skull was a small hole left for the ears.

The yellow erasers faded into the clay to become minor blemishes, and the oily sheen added a touch of life. She was almost human. Though most of the initial process—gluing the markers, putting the clay between them—was random, the next part was not. The ears, mouth, and nose Frank worked on at the same time. In his mind they were connected, and one feature looked the way it did because of the others.

First of all, he fashioned a nose. With the cartilage gone, the end of the nasal bone was a major clue to how it might have looked. Did it tip up, stick out, curve to one side? The length was standard. For women the nose was three times the length of the nasal bone; for men, three and a half times.

The photographs of the skull he had taken from various angles were spread around the workbench, and he kept referring back to them as he added clay. He needed to remind himself of the bare bones that he had started with.

After molding a crude strip for the upper lip, he attached it, pressed at it, and then took it off again. He did that twice more before leaving it in place. Counting three teeth to either side of center, he inserted a toothpick where the edge of the inner lip would be, then cut the lip division with the pointed end of a stick.

Whenever he came across a bit of bone from a previous head, he picked it out.

There was no clue as to what the ears looked like, so he took his lead from the nose and the mouth. He constantly thought back to advice Krogman had given to him on one of his trips to Lancaster, and which he'd written about in his book: "So much of what we key in to in recognizing a face are features like the eyes, nose, and mouth, the very things that the skull does not directly tell us very much about. The flare of the nostrils, the bulge of the nasal tip, the thickness and eversion of the lips, the details of the eyelids that are so telling for ID are left up to the carefully controlled discretion of the facial reproducer, not to go overboard with nifty-looking warts, dueling scars."

Frank's hands fluttered around the sculpture like a pair of butterflies, adding clay more than refining. That came later. With all its blobs and chunks, the Girl from Slatington resembled something that might have come from the mind of the sixteenth-century artist Giuseppe Arcimboldo, who painted faces as composites of other things, often fruit and vegetables and plants.

Frank smoothed the line from the nose down to the bottom of the cheek, then pressed up the back of the nose with the flat part of a sculpting stick. The tip of the nose altered imperceptibly over the hours, its shape becoming less bulbous and more feminine. That— like the lips, the shape of the eyes, and the eyelids—was a part of the face he was less certain of, and it was always determined by what he did around it.

With short strips of clay, he created eyebrow ridges, which he worked with a flat piece of wood. He pushed them with his left thumb as the right hand held the skull from behind, the way a doctor might hold a patient, his grip strong but mindful of the skull's fragility. Tiny bits of clay pushed into the chin disappeared like makeup.

In between, he kept returning to the mouth as if it was bothering him. He didn't hear Jan call him from downstairs when she went to bed, and he didn't hear Lisa or Vanessa say good night when they passed by on the other side of the curtain. It was two A.M. by the time he finished working.

In the middle of the night, he woke with a start. He had an idea about the chin—it needed to be more pointed. Not wanting to forget, he went back upstairs, took a small bit of clay, and stuck it to the chin to remind him when he returned to her. Then he crept back into bed.

## COPYING LISA'S EARS

On her way to school later that same morning, Lisa stopped outside the drawn curtain to the kitchenette. Out of curiosity, she peeked in to see how the Girl from Slatington was coming along. Even though she'd asked Frank to cover his work, she was fascinated by it. Sometimes it felt like watching a puzzle come together.

The last time she'd seen the girl, there had been only a skull. Now she had a face, her upper jaw protruding and the corners of her mouth turning up a bit, almost in a smile. As Lisa approached it a bit closer, the head started moving.

"Frank!" Lisa called out. "You better get up here!"

Frank was downstairs making coffee. When he got to the kitchenette, he saw Lisa standing frozen in the doorway. She pointed to the Girl from Slatington, whose chin had started sinking toward the table.

"It's the clay," he said. "It's too heavy."

Propping a wooden block under the bust's chin, he made sure nothing was damaged. "You okay?" he asked Lisa.

She nodded, taking a better look at the bust. "It looks like she's squinting."

"I did that on purpose," Frank said. "The glass lens found with the body was for an extremely nearsighted person."

"What happened to her?" Lisa asked.

"They're not sure," he said.

Lisa knew that was the end of the conversation, because Frank never liked to disclose details about his cases.

Later that morning he took the bust to Arch Street in his van, careful to keep the block lodged under the chin and to wedge the sculpture in place so it didn't fall over. Unable to get to her for the next few days, he took her home to finish on the weekend.

Once the bust was set up on his workbench in the kitchenette again, he saw the small bit of clay he'd stuck to the chin as a reminder. Immediately recalling what he wanted to do, he narrowed the chin and then went back to her mouth. The lips were full and, since she was a mouth breather, they were parted, the upper row of teeth barely visible.

The face was almost complete, but there were still several things marring the picture. The toothpicks stuck out of her mouth, he'd left slits in her temples, and the ears bothered him. He took them off, loosely shaped some clay in his hands, and held the new ear against the skull. He reshaped it several times, but it wasn't working. He called Lisa, who was doing her homework.

"What is it, Frank?" she asked.

When she came in, she noticed that something about the girl's mouth had changed. The girl also looked as if she were craning her neck, trying to see something in the distance. The eyeballs were the only white thing in the midst of the brown clay, but the bust was closer than ever to being a person.

Lisa watched Frank cut into the eyelid, then smooth the skin around it. He dug into the nostrils and put a bit of clay on the tip of a stick and applied it to the lower lip like rouge.

"She looks sweet," Lisa said.

"I need you to help me with the ears." Frank had never used anyone in the family for a sculpture before. "She's your age," he said, "and I'm having trouble with the ears."

Lisa didn't like the idea of her ears being on a dead person, but she would do anything for Frank. Her relationship with Jan was often turbulent, while Frank, even though he was strict, made her laugh and got her to help him with his wood carvings. For her he was the glue that kept the four of them together.

As Lisa sat down on the stool, she found it hard to believe that the lifeless skull had until not long ago been a girl.

Frank held up a limp piece of clay next to her ear. "There are no rules for ears," he said. "All you have to work with are two small holes. That's why lots of artists put hair over the ears and try to hide them, because they usually stick out or look like little vegetables."

Lisa laughed.

He took the ear away from the skull, shaped it some more, and then put it back on the skull.

"The ear holes are so low down," Lisa said. "I'd never noticed that."

"That's because there's no hair," he said. "You'll see, it looks normal when there's hair." Frank held up another piece of clay to her left ear, then attached that one to the bust.

"They look like ears, but they also don't," Lisa said.

Frank never heard her, because he had his ears and he could carry on now. She left the room without him noticing. A week later, the mold of the Girl from Slatington was completed and painted. Now all he needed was a wig and glasses.

"What color hair are you going to give her?" Lisa asked.

There had been no hair with the skeleton, so he had to guess. Should it be straight? Long? Curly? Dark? He didn't have even a strand to go on. The colors of the hair and the eyes were always so critical, and yet they were pure guesswork.

"I'm not sure yet," he said, but he had some ideas. "I'll see where the face takes me."

Lisa groaned. She could always count on Frank to be evasive. The only thing she knew was that the Girl from Slatington was her age.

Frank decided to go with reddish hair and green eyes. There was nothing to suggest either, but he had to make a decision. It was like so many things about a face that could determine the way someone looked—scars, tattoos, piercings, skin color—but couldn't be predicted from the skull. When he looked at the bust in front of him, the form, the overbite, he saw red hair. Even if it was wrong, he knew that it wasn't enough to destroy what he had created. As Krogman had told him, people looking at a reconstruction recognized the tiny details and subtle nuances, some of which they didn't even consciously register. There was just something about the bust that made them say, "That's her."

Frank went to an optometrist with Bob Gerken. It didn't take long to find what he was looking for: a large pair of eyeglasses with thick tinted teardrop-shaped lenses, something that matched the photogray lens found on the hillside.

The police came to pick up the bust. Unlike Verb and Grace, Detective Gerken had hardly visited the studio during the sculpting process. He had dropped off a skull and was getting it back as a full face.

"That's what she looked like?" he asked when he came by the Arch Street studio.

"Let's see," Frank said.

||||||||||||||||||||||||||||||||||||||||||||||||||||||||||||||||

On February 27, 1981, *The Morning Call* ran a story on the Girl from Slatington and a photograph of the bust. A man who lived in Salisbury, about 250 miles away, thought it looked like his daughter, Linda Keyes. He hadn't seen her in two years. A second daughter was struck by the detail in the story about the blue star-sapphire ring. Another relative thought Frank's likeness was all wrong. The police checked the dental records of Linda Keyes, and they matched the skull.

The newspaper tracked down a farmer who owned land near where the skeleton had been found. He said that in April 1979 he had seen and spoken to a woman who was wandering across his property before she disappeared up a nearby hill. A fire started shortly afterward, although he thought she must have left by then. The fire brigade was called in to put out the blaze, but they didn't find anything suspicious.

Before Linda Keyes was positively identified, the police showed the farmer a number of photographs, one of which was of the bust. He immediately picked out the Girl from Slatington as the girl he'd spoken to.

Frank was overjoyed. It was his second ID, and it proved that Anna Duval hadn't been just a lucky break.

# MEXICO

# TEN THIRTY-GALLON BARRELS

October 2003

It was Frank's third day in Mexico, and he was agitated.

He sat in his room at the Hotel Lucerna in Juárez. From his balcony on the sixth floor, he had a view of the neat, palm-lined figure-eight swimming pool, the bar area next to it, and a small fountain. To the right, behind a wall, was a starker scene: the hotel's parking lot, always half empty, and beyond it, a dirt road used by trucks coming from across the border.

He had asked the Mexicans to put him in the Lucerna. No, he'd demanded it. That had been a condition he made during the first visit, when Esparza showed him a small, lightless room in the former police academy outside of town, where his bed would be a mattress on a concrete slab.

"I don't want to be stuck in the middle of nowhere," Frank said. His workspace was his only condition. "The atmosphere has to be right when I sculpt. If I want a sandwich at two A.M. when I'm working, I want to be able to get it."

Organizing a room for him at the four-star Lucerna wasn't a problem, seeing as it was partly owned by Governor Martínez. Frank was nevertheless instructed to keep his expenses to a minimum. He wasn't allowed to make phone calls to America unless they were crucial, which, since he phoned Jan every day, was a penance.

His room was comfortable, although now it felt a bit too comfortable. He had been in the city for seventy-two hours, and there were still no heads for him. Whenever Esparza came by, Frank complained about the delay. "Manuel," he said, "you told me the heads would be ready when I got here."

"Dr. Sánchez is still working on them."

"Can't you get me just one to start with?"

"I'll see what I can do."

Frank tried to keep himself busy by going for a swim every morning and then having a long breakfast. He was advised not to leave the hotel alone, other than to go across the road to Sanborns, a local chain drugstore that doubled as a restaurant. Each trip to Sanborns, he made sure to spend as much time there as possible. The store sold none of the music he normally listened to—no Tom Petty or Rolling Stones—so he bought jazz, show tunes, Tommy Dorsey, Maurice Chevalier.

He reorganized his room not once but several times. On arriving, he'd first put out his little hat-shaped Vietnamese coffeemaker, his good-luck charm, and a chicory blend that he'd gotten from the Café du Monde in New Orleans.

From Philadelphia he had sent ten thirty-gallon plastic barrels of equipment. Inside them he'd packed clothes, facial charts, reading material, reading glasses, toiletries, paintbrushes, caliper, eraser sticks, pencils, sketching paper, vernier scale, X-Acto knives and blades, eyeballs attached to cutoff golf tees, drop cloths, a cutting board, dozens of black trash bags, measuring tape and rulers in centimeters and inches, toothpicks, lollipop sticks, Krazy Glue and Zip Kicker, several pairs of hemostat clamps, a palette for mixing glues and paints, clothespins to hold things, a nail brush to clean off the head at the end after the clay had been peeled off, a Pentax digital camera, his rock and classical music, and a Walkman with small speakers. In two separate barrels, there was also a tripod lighting system and a video camera from a producer at a company called BrainBox, who wanted Frank to shoot himself making the heads.

The rubber that Frank ordered in Philadelphia had arrived, but three hundred pounds of gypsum cement to make the plaster casts hadn't. On the second day Esparza drove Frank to El Paso to buy some from a distributor.

The way Frank had planned it, he wanted to pack the items in the order they would be needed. The things that he required last—the plaster, the rubber, and the paint—went in the barrels on the bottom. Everything else went on top, where it was easy to get to.

As he listened to Tommy Dorsey playing "I'm Getting Sentimental over You" and "The Lady Is a Tramp," Frank checked the barrels in the corner once again to see if everything was ready. Then he did it again. And then he waited.

Esparza drove a metallic-blue Beetle. He took Frank out on Barranca Azul, past the prison, to the Juárez headquarters of the investigative team.

There was more time now to study the office. It was located in a one-story section of the former police academy, and it was drab and sparsely furnished. The walls were painted maroon in some places, hospital green in others, and were hung with a few pictures of Mexican tourist spots or the president, Vicente Fox. Straight ahead as you entered the building, there were several women sitting at computers behind a window. No one seemed bothered by the stray dogs wandering in and out. To the back of the office was a bleak courtyard with an untended garden and a broken walkway. The building that faced onto the courtyard from behind went up three stories and, Frank was told, was sometimes used to house prisoners. Esparza's office, which looked out over the courtyard, was next to the American Slater's and across the hall from that of the assistant prosecutor, Angie.

Esparza's cell phone rang. It was Attorney General Solís, who told Esparza he was needed in Chihuahua immediately, so Gus took Frank back to the hotel. As they turned onto the road, Gus said that at least eleven bodies of murdered women had been found not far from the former police academy.

Back in his room, Frank put on some Tommy Dorsey and then waited. At sunset, he went onto the balcony and took a series of photographs of a hill overlooking the town called Cerro Bola. One of the very first bodies had been found on Cerro Bola, and ten years later, she remained one of the women who were still unknown. In the interim, several more bodies had been found on the mountain.

Through his telephoto lens, Frank could see that someone had painted words on the hillside. When he went down to El Acueducto bar that night for some wine, the bartender Jackie told him what the words meant.

THE BIBLE IS THE TRUTH. READ IT.

||||||||||||||||||||||||||||||||||||||||||||||||||||

## Day 4

Esparza came by and said he had good news. He had been able to get a head for Frank. "This is a very special head," he added. "It is a girl from Chihuahua."

Frank wasn't sure whether it was the same girl from Chihuahua about whom Esparza had called him so frantically in Philadelphia.

"This head has to be kept very secret," Esparza continued. "No one is to know about her. Not even Dr. Sánchez."

"Why?" Frank asked. "Is she someone famous? Is she the daughter of someone important?"

With so many of the victims being poor, someone with money instantly stood out. Was the killer changing his pattern? One of the times the media had made a bigger story than usual about the murders was when Viviana Rayas, the sixteen-year-old daughter of a union leader, had been kidnapped and killed. The police later tried to pin the murder on a Mexican artist, Ulises de Perzábal, and his American wife, Cynthia Kiecker, who sold T-shirts on the road between Juárez and El Paso. Could the girl from Chihuahua be someone like Rayas?

"I haven't been told," Esparza said. "But no one is to know about it. If anyone who is unauthorized comes up to your room, hide the head."

Frank thought that the cover-up might also have to do with the location of the body. Until now most of the victims had been found in Juárez, although a recent report in a U.S. newspaper, *The Arizona*

*Republic,* noted that thirteen murders in Chihuahua City seemed to have very similar patterns. What if the killings were spreading to other parts of the state, like some kind of disease?

## FRAGILE. DON'T TOUCH

### Day 5

Frank prepared the room. He moved the dining table in front of the balcony doors so that he had a view when he worked, and then he covered the table and the floor around it with black trash bags.

He kept thinking of the job ahead of him. He had twenty-five days left to do five heads. He had never worked that fast, and only once before had he done multiple heads at the same time.

Ten years earlier, riding the wave of fame after John List, he had been commissioned by a New York gallery to do the busts of ten children who had died in the Holocaust, in Khmer Rouge execution camps in Cambodia, and in the Alabama fire bombings of 1963, to show what they would look like if they had grown up. Sculpting them from photographs, he'd had a lot more time to complete them—numerous months, in fact—and they had been for an exhibition and not to help catch a possible serial killer.

His plan even before he got to Juárez was to do all five heads at the same time. He would line them up on the table, put on the tissue-thickness markers, give them each a face of clay, create five molds, and then paint them. In unison. But already things were going wrong. Time was running out, he still hadn't received a single skull, and there was only the possibility of doing one. Who knew if he'd even be able to do more than one at a time?

Later that morning Esparza arrived carrying a plastic box with a lid. A label on the side read FRAGIL—NO TOCAR. Fragile—Don't Touch.

"Here it is," he said, "the girl from Chihuahua. And remember, no one is to know about her."

"What kind of information do you have on her?" Frank asked.

Esparza shrugged. "She was eighteen years old," he said, then pointed at the box. "They just gave it to me like that."

"Can you ask them if they have anything more?"

"I'll try," Esparza said before leaving.

After photographing the box and the label, Frank lifted the lid. Inside was only the cleaned skull, wrapped in a layer of soft cardboard. He picked it up and noticed that the molars were gone, which meant she was at least older than a teenager. He used some Elmer's glue to fix the two jaws together.

Setting the skull on the table, he photographed it from every side. With the case being kept a secret, he took more photographs than normal, just to be safe. Once he had taken four rolls of film, he went across the road to Sanborns to have them developed. They said he could pick them up the next day.

Back in the room, he turned on Beethoven's *Emperor's March* and then, with the music filling the room and going out the open balcony doors, positioned the skull on the table between two large pieces of clay. He started cutting pieces of eraser and sticking them in place.

While the glue was drying, he walked to the corner of the room where the barrels were stacked. He had opened one of the barrels of clay the previous night, hoping that it would soften some more. He pressed it with his finger; it felt pliable enough. At least he wouldn't need to ask for a microwave.

# THE ENEMY

### Day 6

Six people from the United Nations who were in Juárez to investigate the murders were also staying at the Lucerna. It was arranged by the federal government to take them to the various sites where bodies had been found. Esparza told Frank he was welcome to come along.

He had worked through the night on the Girl from Chihuahua and had already covered the skull in a layer of clay. Needing a break, he thought a tour of the murder scenes might somehow help by giving him some more insight. He didn't know what he'd learn exactly, but he had so little information he was sure that anything would help.

In the hotel foyer, Esparza introduced him to the members of the UN team, which included five Europeans and an American, a retired FBI agent from Virginia.

The UN members stood to one side, clearly wanting to keep to themselves. Everyone had been told that there wasn't going to be any publicity, but as soon as they walked out of the hotel, where four cars were waiting for them, they were met by a group of journalists.

"We didn't want this," one of the UN representatives told Esparza. "Who told them about us being here?"

Frank, who was walking with the group, didn't see any harm in the publicity. In his experience, the more exposure you gave a crime, the better chance you had of solving it. His busts would have been largely ineffective in the past without publicity. Newspaper stories, TV shows like *America's Most Wanted*, police flyers—they had all been part of the identification process. If an effort was being made to solve the Juárez murders, everyone should know about it.

Standing near Frank was a smartly dressed man with a neatly trimmed goatee. At the very moment he put out his hand to greet Frank, someone took their photograph.

"What do you think of what is going on down here?" a female journalist asked Frank.

"I can't comment," he said.

The motorcade left, surrounded not by the state police and Esparza's colleagues but by federal police, who were there to protect the UN members. The *federales,* riding motorbikes and armed with machine guns and AR-15s, stopped traffic and kept their sirens blaring as they sped around.

They drove through downtown, where many of the women were last seen. Next, they drove out Rivereño, the Juárez equivalent of the I-10 along the other side of the Rio Grande, which petered out into a pitted track entering Anapra and its puzzle of shanties and shops called *abarrotes.* But their main stop was really the cotton field where eight bodies had been found two years earlier.

This time Frank had a chance to get out of the car and walk around. He noticed how close the murder site was to the vehicles driving along Ejército Nacional Boulevard and Paseo de la Victoria. It was hard to imagine bodies lying here unfound or unreported for so long that they could decompose into skeletons. When Frank said something about this, Esparza told him that people they'd interviewed had confessed that they'd smelled something, but it was a section of the cotton field that they didn't go to because it was sometimes used to dispose of dead dogs and animals.

Frank walked close to the pink crosses, one of which had been knocked over. They were about six feet tall and had names on them: Laura, Berenice, Veronica, Esmeralda, Lucita, and *Desconocida*—or Unknown. He wanted to take some photographs, but Esparza told him it would be better to move away from them.

"That is amnesty," he said, pointing at the crosses. After a moment Frank realized he must mean Amnesty International. "They are the enemy."

The words stuck in Frank's head. The motorcade drove for an hour into the desert before pulling off the road and stopping at a place where more bodies had been found. One of the policemen remarked that it was strange to think of the bodies being found here. "As teenagers, we used to bring our girlfriends here to make out."

||||||||||||||||||||||||||||||||||||||||||||||||||||||||

Frank went to have a glass of wine at the hotel bar, El Acueducto, and to talk to Jackie the barmaid.

"Calafia, *por favor*," he said. He liked the regional wine she had introduced him to.

"You're famous," she said, putting his drink in front of him.

"What do you mean?"

She pulled out that afternoon's edition of the local daily, *El Diario*. It had a photograph of the UN team outside the hotel. Frank was standing next to the well-dressed man with the goatee.

"What does it say?" he asked her.

She translated. "It says you are Frank Bender and that you have done these busts of many"—she paused as she thought of the English word—"*fugitivos.*"

"Fugitives," Frank said.

"*Sí*, fugitives. A man named John List and another from Puerto Rico."

Frank asked her if he could see the paper. He couldn't understand what was written, but the names caught his eye—John List and Hans Vorhauer and Robert Nauss. The story even mentioned the Puerto Rican he had forgotten from a long time ago, a murderer who had fled the United States and had cut off his fingertips to avoid being identified, but whom Frank had picked out of a crowded courtroom.

But nowhere in the article did it mention Anna Duval or Linda Keyes or Rosella Atkinson, the cases that were much closer to the work that he was being employed to do in Mexico.

Frank was looking absentmindedly at the newspaper, wondering why they would write about fugitives he'd helped track down instead of murder victims he'd helped identify. "Who is this man?" he asked, indicating the man with the goatee.

"He is very famous too," Jackie said. "He has many enemies. He is the man prosecuting the drug cartel."

## FIFTY-FIFTY

### Day 7

With a dozen five-by-seven photographs of the Girl from Chihuahua spread around the bust, Frank continued to work the clay. In the last two days, he had gotten so far that he had even shaped the important trio—ears, nose, and mouth.

There was a sharp knock at his door, and he quickly covered the head. But it was only Esparza. When he saw that Frank was dressed in jeans and a T-shirt spattered with bits of clay, he told him he needed to get cleaned up. "We have a press conference to go to," Esparza said.

Frank didn't understand. "I thought you didn't want publicity."

"The heads are ready. We want to make an announcement and to introduce you."

"That's great," Frank replied, putting down his sculpting stick and going to the bathroom to wash up.

After he had changed, they drove to the main police station in the center of town. A table had been set up in a conference room, and four skulls on it faced the audience. Frank and Esparza joined two other people behind the table, the tall woman Angie and the assistant attorney general, a man named Oscar Valadez Reyes.

Valadez and Esparza briefly addressed the audience in Spanish, little of which Frank understood, although he saw them repeatedly pointing to the skulls and to himself. When it was Frank's turn to talk, he said he hoped that once he had finished the busts, images could be spread far and wide, and hopefully someone would come forward to identify one or more of the women.

⁣⁣⁣⁣⁣⁣⁣⁣⁣⁣⁣⁣⁣⁣⁣⁣⁣⁣⁣⁣⁣⁣⁣⁣⁣⁣⁣⁣⁣⁣⁣⁣⁣⁣⁣⁣⁣⁣⁣⁣⁣⁣⁣⁣⁣⁣⁣

At the same time that Friday, September 26, a very different kind of gathering was taking place to publicize the *feminicidios*. A group of Mexican and American activists placed flowers at the Paso del Norte Bridge that crossed the river to El Paso.

One of those people was Esther Chávez Cano, head of the Casa Amiga rape crisis center, which had kept a list of the murders since 1993. Chávez told reporters that she didn't believe the authorities were doing anything to help the situation.

"We don't trust the people in charge of the investigation," she said.

⁣⁣⁣⁣⁣⁣⁣⁣⁣⁣⁣⁣⁣⁣⁣⁣⁣⁣⁣⁣⁣⁣⁣⁣⁣⁣⁣⁣⁣⁣⁣⁣⁣⁣⁣⁣⁣⁣⁣⁣⁣⁣⁣⁣⁣⁣⁣

Several hours later, four state policemen came by the Lucerna to drop off four cardboard boxes. Before Frank let them in, he hid the Girl from Chihuahua.

Once the policemen were gone and Frank was on his own again, he opened the boxes. Two of them included, besides a skull, a Ziploc bag with some hair in it. The last skull was also missing its lower jaw, something he had already noticed during the press conference at the police station.

He took the lids off of four barrels in the corner and arranged them alongside one another on the table like a set of dinner plates.

On each lid he wrote any information that came with the skull, no matter how brief it was—*Admixture, 16–17, flat upper (for the teeth). Normal upper 2 gold teeth. 22–23. Pointed upper 13/2/2002. 23902. Upper normal, Caucasian? Admixture, flat upper.*

Afterward he dug into one of the barrels for four miniature tires—his latest discovery for resting a skull on, instead of cork—and inflated them with a small pump. He arranged each skull on the lid that bore its information. At the end of the table, the Girl from Chihuahua stood alone, temporarily set apart from the others.

He photographed the skulls from every angle, the sides, the top, underneath, always making sure to get bits of the information he had written on the lid in the frame of the picture. He didn't want any confusion about which skull he was doing once they were covered in clay.

While his film was being developed at Sanborns, he took some time to consider the skulls, individually and together. Putting the tissue-thickness charts out of his mind for the moment—that was the technical part—he wanted to find any peculiarities, things that stood out, the width of the nasal openings, the cheekbones, the chins. As he had seen so many times at the Mütter Museum, each skull was different. You just had to look closely, look, and look again. What made each one of these girls special?

He glued the jaws together on the first three. The last skull, besides having no mandible, was also very white, as if it had been bleached too much or had been lying in the sun for a long time. He put the hair from the second and third girls alongside the skulls.

Picking up the remaining skull, the first one he'd taken out, he held it up to the light. It wasn't until now that he noticed the asymmetry. The nasal aperture, which was shaped like an upside-down heart, was slightly misshapen. The right side of the face was almost indiscernibly compressed.

Frank put the skull down. At that moment his task seemed enormous. He had twenty-four days to create four—no, five—different people out of very little information. The fact that one of them was missing a lower jaw didn't bother him as much because he'd already had a case like that.

Two years earlier, he had received the skull of a man whose head had been hidden in a block of concrete; he too had been missing a lower jaw. The Girl from Manlius, New York, had been missing even more of her face. Frank had done reconstructions of both of them and had gotten one ID, which had also helped track down a murderer.

If those results were anything to go by, his chances of success in Juárez were fifty-fifty.

## PRAYING

When Maurice Chevalier finished singing "Le Chapeau de Zozo," the album started playing all over again. "Louise" was followed by "Mimi," and Frank absentmindedly hummed along.

Sometimes he thought that what he did with the skulls was like someone composing music. He wasn't a musician, but he imagined someone's fingers running across a keyboard the way his did on a cheek or along an eyebrow, refining it, seeing something that was wrong and didn't fit with the rest of the piece, adjusting it, refining again, until the composition was perfect.

> *My left shoe's on my right foot,*
> *My right shoe's on my left.*
> *Oh, listen to me, Mimi.*

With the tissue-thickness markers now firmly attached to the four skulls, he began to press clay between them. At first he concentrated on the fourth skull, the Girl Without a Lower Jaw, making an approximation of a mandible before he did anything else. Then he moved between the skulls, starting each one at a different point, noticing things as he worked.

The second girl had one orbit smaller than the other one. The third girl's nasal bone suggested a nose that would be flatter than the others. These weren't traits that you would immediately notice on the sculpted face, but a friend or a relative would see them and register them somewhere deep inside. That's what had happened with the Boy in the Bag.

The skull he had taken out first was the one whose face he had already started to visualize, even before he had gotten far with the clay. The asymmetry—along the mouth, the cheek area, the nose—made it look as if the right side of her skull had fallen just a bit, nothing that would make her look unusual or ugly. For him, it was a face full of character.

He took a step back from the table, appraised what he'd done so far, and then returned to the Girl from Chihuahua and smoothed her out some more. When he couldn't go any further on her, he went back to the other four.

He moved around the table, working on one bust until it had progressed more than the others, turning to another that caught his attention for some reason—an ear that was too long, a shallow cheek, a narrow lip—and then going from the jaw of one to the nose of another. When he was tired or didn't know where to go next, he stretched out on his bed and slept for a few minutes. Or maybe an hour.

But then, from his reclining position, he saw something that made him get up—an eyelid, the end of a nose that needed changing—and that was the very point where he started again.

He seldom left the room and didn't answer the door if someone knocked, unless he knew it was Esparza. In any case, the housecleaning service had been told to leave his room alone. He developed a routine of washing his T-shirts and underwear in the bathroom.

In Philadelphia, if he got stuck, he made a point of leaving his studio, going out to a café or to visit friends. But his only escape outside the hotel was Sanborns, where he would go to have coffee or a sandwich. Esparza visited him once or twice a day, always briefly. As a precaution, Frank covered the Girl from Chihuahua or put her in the bathroom, in case someone else was with Esparza. It became habit.

On two occasions the Mexican brought people especially to see the busts. The first time it was Assistant Attorney General Valadez and Angie. The second time Esparza came with two members from the UN team, after which the four of them went to eat at a taco place on Hermanos Escobar.

On their way out of the restaurant, a small, plainly dressed middle-aged woman came up to Frank and threw her arms around him. She said something in Spanish that he didn't understand. Once they had left the restaurant, he asked Esparza what she'd said.

"She is praying for you at church. They pray for you and hope that you can help them with the murdered women."

## A WARNING

Day 10

When Jan called that afternoon, Frank knew something was wrong. She usually called from home at night, but she was still at work.

"You sound upset," he said.

"I was going through your e-mails, and there was one that I think you should know about."

Jan did all Frank's correspondence because he didn't use a computer. Any e-mails to him had to be clearly marked. Since his correspondence came from addresses that she didn't always recognize—the FBI, Interpol, police departments, fans, museums, plastic surgeons, people around the world who wanted to start sculpting heads, spam—she opened only the ones that looked safe and had something in the heading to identify them.

He asked what the e-mail was about.

"I'm going to read it to you," she said. "It says, 'Look out your window.' And it comes from Mexico." Jan paused.

"That's all?" Frank said. "There was nothing else?"

"No, that was it."

Instinctively, Frank looked at the large doors that opened onto his balcony. He had been out there countless times—in between sculpting the women, to watch the city, to take photographs of life on the streets below—and he worked in front of the open doors every day and night. Was someone watching him?

"You think it's a threat?" Jan asked, reading Frank's mind.

"No, I'm sure it's nothing," he said.

He didn't want to worry her unnecessarily, but he immediately thought of the story in *El Diario*. Not only had it focused almost entirely on his work with fugitives, but it had pictured him alongside the man with the goatee, the prosecutor of the drug cartel. Maybe the threat, if it was a real threat, had something to do with drugs and not with the murdered women. Could someone think he was in Mexico doing busts of people in the drug trade?

"Frank," Jan said. "I'm worried about you."

He reassured her that he was fine. He would speak to Esparza and see what he thought. "I'll call you back once I know what's going on," he said, then hung up.

In the hotel lobby, he saw two representatives from the United Nations and told them about the e-mail. They were visibly concerned and said he should ask not just the state police for protection but also the *federales*.

Frank thought they were overreacting, but they had already gone to the lobby phone and put through a call to the *federales*. Several policemen and Esparza came to the hotel. They asked for a copy of the e-mail, which Jan faxed through. After the police looked at it, they decided there was reason for concern. They asked Frank if anyone suspicious had approached him in the last twenty-four hours. The only stranger he'd talked to was a man at El Acueducto, whom they ruled out after Frank drew a quick sketch of him.

"We're going to give you a full-time bodyguard and change your room," Esparza said. "And the *federales* will put two agents outside your room and two outside the hotel."

"Is that really necessary?" Frank asked.

"Yes, it is necessary."

It was late at night, but they began moving Frank's room from the sixth floor at the back of the hotel to the fourth floor at the front, facing Sanborns. Frank packed up his materials in the ten barrels and carefully wrapped up the five heads in cloth; he took them downstairs with Esparza and the state policeman Gus.

Frank was no longer allowed to open his curtains, and Esparza said that Gus would have to stay with him in his room at all times. Having a stranger in the room would disturb his work, but Frank didn't tell Esparza that yet. He would try having Gus with him for a night.

When the two policemen left to go downstairs, Frank started spreading trash bags on the floor of his new room and across the furniture, unwrapping the heads, and laying them on their little tires on the table. An hour later, Gus returned.

Frank felt crowded by the policeman, so he went down to El Acueducto. Gus followed him but sat a few tables away. As Frank drank his glass of wine, the former FBI agent from the UN team came up and sat with him.

"I heard about your e-mail," he said. "If I were you, I'd get out of Dodge. Right now."

# The Murders

# REESE'S PIECES

## 1982

During the Linda Keyes case, Frank saw a dilapidated building on South Street—an old meat market—that was for sale. His photographic business was going so well that he decided he could afford his own premises.

In early 1982, he had barely moved his equipment from Arch Street to the new location when he received a call from Detective Ellis Verb. It was about the Girl in the Steamer Trunk, who had been found under the Platt Memorial Bridge. The body was examined by Fillinger's colleague Robert Catherman, who said she probably had been beaten regularly.

Since she was the first child Frank had sculpted—and since there were no tissue-thickness charts for children—he wanted to gather as much information about her as he could, anything that might give him a clue to her features. But there wasn't much. The forensic dentist Haskell Askin, who had already examined her teeth, gave Frank what little he had. On Krogman's suggestion, Frank also took the skull down to Lawrence Angel, a physical anthropologist at the Smithsonian in Washington, D.C.

Back at his freezing studio, he chose to sculpt the girl in the old meat freezer in the back not only because it was small and easy to heat but also because he wanted to keep the skull away from his photographic clients. Not many of them knew about his other profession, and he wasn't sure he would tell most of them. Nor was he eager to show his clients the South Street space—at least not before he could fix it up—although he knew that someone was bound to come by unannounced. He was lucky it turned out to be someone as easygoing as George Beecham.

Beecham had just commissioned Frank to shoot an ad about Reese's Pieces, a candy that was to feature in an upcoming movie called *E.T.: The Extra-Terrestrial*. To save money, Frank created a fake theater in the meat market, renting thirty movie seats and bringing in models to act as an audience. Everything worked out fine, although the models had to close their mouths whenever he photographed them so their breath wasn't visible in the freezing air.

When Beecham asked to come see the studio, Frank tried to put him off, but Beecham insisted. On seeing the makeshift theater with holes in the floor and the roof, he burst out laughing. He was one of the few ad people who knew about the forensic work, so Frank also took him back to see the Girl in the Steamer Trunk.

A huge consignment of Reese's Pieces was delivered to the meat market during the shoot, and Frank left them at the front door. Whenever Ellis Verb came by to see how the Girl in the Steamer Trunk was coming along, he grabbed a few packets.

Before Verb took the completed bust from Frank, he consulted a psychic about the case. Unlike the case of the Burnt Boy, when he'd asked Frank to go on his behalf, he went on his own. He never told Frank what the psychic said, but it didn't matter. Nothing she told him helped give the girl a name.

〰〰〰〰〰〰〰〰〰〰〰〰〰〰〰〰〰〰〰〰〰〰〰〰〰

Two artists who had also been on Arch Street asked if they could rent space at the meat market. They didn't care how broken down it was. Bob Barfield set himself up in the pit, and Paula Lisak took the basement. She wasn't bothered by the low ceiling, the mushrooms growing out of the beams, or the fact that it smelled like a freshly dug grave.

## LETTERS TO THE FBI

Jan took a job as a fragrance sprayer at Strawbridge's department store in Center City. Before that, she had been a waitress at Milly's Luv Inn Diner on Rising Sun Avenue; a house cleaner; and a model at the Pennsylvania Academy of the Fine Arts, even though Frank didn't like her taking off her clothes in front of the other students.

"I did it for you," she reminded him, "and that was for free. Why can't I make some money off of it?" Frank knew she was right.

On her lunch hour at Strawbridge's, Jan sometimes walked down to the main branch of the Free Library, near Logan Square. There she hunted for anything she could find on facial reconstruction.

To anyone who didn't know Jan, this behavior might have seemed odd, because she didn't pay much attention to Frank's forensic work.

She loved the fact that he was doing it, helping to find people's IDs and to solve murders, but the minutiae of it all bored her. Admittedly, this was partly Frank's fault. He seldom talked about the skulls—inexplicably, he treated every case as if it were top-secret—so Jan and the girls saw skulls arriving at the house and then completed busts leaving, but they knew little about their histories. If Frank spoke about a case, it was after the fact, when it wasn't exciting anymore. One of the few exceptions was the Man in the Cornfield, which became one of Jan's favorites. Most of the skulls, however, were indistinguishable and started morphing into one. Much of the time she hardly noticed Frank even working on them.

But Jan was also Frank's biggest fan. She believed he had a rare talent, and she did everything she could to promote him. After Linda Keyes was ID'd, she sat down at the kitchen table with her friend Sally Bischoff and started composing a résumé of Frank's forensic work. She sent it off to police departments around the country, the FBI, Interpol, the CIA, and any law-enforcement agency she and Sally could think of.

At the library, meanwhile, she looked for articles about other people who sculpted the dead or did forensic art, not only to get whatever information she could for Frank—who was still making up many of his own rules as he went along—but also to prove to herself that what he was doing wasn't crazy.

One day she came across an article from the British *Daily Express* about a facial reconstruction of a famous Nazi who was thought to have fled to South America after the war. When Berlin police suspected that a skull found by workers digging near the Lehrter station might be that of Hitler's deputy Martin Bormann, a reconstruction was done by a West German police inspector named Moritz Furtmayr. In 1977 Furtmayr had used a system of mapping out the skull to determine whether Anna Anderson, a woman who claimed to be the last surviving daughter of Tsar Nicholas, was indeed the grand duchess Anastasia. He concluded that she was.

The *Daily Express* article said that the Berlin reconstruction proved Bormann hadn't escaped to South America, as many believed, but had died in 1945. To Jan it proved something else: There were people in Europe doing work just like Frank.

In a copy of *Science Digest,* she found a short article by Skip Rozen about facial reconstruction in the United States. He mentioned Betty Pat Gatliff, Wilton Krogman's friend, who, it said, had worked on the busts of nine unidentified bodies found in the crawl space under the home of the serial killer John Wayne Gacy. After writing to Rozen, Jan got Gatliff's address in Norman, Oklahoma, then wrote to her on Frank's behalf.

Rozen's article also referred to *The Face Finder,* the book about the Russian Mikhail Gerasimov. The library had to order a copy for Jan, and when it finally arrived, she immediately sat down and started paging through the black-and-white photographs of his busts. She was so entranced that she was late getting back to work.

At Strawbridge's, she found herself sneaking off from customers buying perfume so she could read bits of the book, which she hid behind the Estée Lauder counter. She was fascinated by the photographs of several of Gerasimov's busts—the playwright Friedrich Schiller, the murder victim Valentina Kosova, as well as Jan's favorite, Ivan the Terrible. They looked so lifelike and full of character. And she couldn't get over how much they reminded her of Frank's work.

## SHATTERED

For his tenth skull, which arrived in August 1982, Frank's payment went up to three hundred and fifty dollars.

The police knew who the killer was but not the victim. A year earlier they had arrested a man named Michael Taylor, who admitted to killing three women over a four-week period. He was tried and convicted and received three life sentences, although only two of the victims were identified.

The third woman was found shot to death in a field in Upper Darby, Pennsylvania. Taylor claimed to have picked her up on the road from Philadelphia and taken her to a bar, where they got drunk. She told him she wanted to own a gun, and he offered to sell her one. They took a shotgun out to a field near his apartment, where they attempted to have sex, after which he shot her. He told the police he didn't know who she was, and fingerprint searches turned up nothing. All they knew was that she was black, in her twenties, about five feet four, and weighed 120 pounds. She had a vaccination scar on her upper left arm and a chipped left front tooth.

Detective Raymond Grazel warned Frank that the skull was severely damaged, since the right side of her face had been virtually destroyed by a blast from the shotgun.

When Frank got home one night later that week, Jan said that UPS had delivered a box for him. After dinner, while Jan and the girls were in the kitchen washing up, he opened the box on the dining table. Besides a large portion of skull, there was a plastic bag containing dozens of smaller pieces that ranged in size from a fingernail to a dime. As he took them out one by one, Frank had no idea how he would put them together. He paged through a copy of *The Face Finder* that Jan had brought home, to see if Gerasimov had ever tackled a similar case, but found nothing. Once again he made up the procedure as he went along. Even if there was someone out there who could do the job, the police didn't have the money to pay for it. If Frank didn't put the skull together himself, the bust wouldn't get made.

"Yech," Vanessa said as she came into the room. She was almost eleven.

"It's just a head," Frank replied.

She helped him count all the pieces, which came to about three hundred. Frank started trying to match them by color and shape.

"How did that happen?" Lisa asked.

"A gun," he said. "Four-ten-gauge shotgun."

"That must be big," she said, looking at all the fragments.

"Not as big as a twelve-gauge, but a good hunting rifle for kids," he said, holding up a piece of bone and trying to fit it into the cheek area. "Big enough to do damage."

Frank knew all about guns from collecting them. On weekends he also sometimes went to the shooting range with Tony Greenwood and one of his photographic clients.

Lisa kept looking at the pieces on the table. "Who was it?" she asked.

She always asked Frank about his cases, no matter how secretive he was. For once he said more than usual, maybe because he was distracted by putting the skull together.

"A girl in her twenties," he said. "They think she was a prostitute."

"What happened?"

"Once they've got an ID, maybe we'll find out more. Right now she's just known as the Girl with the Shattered Head."

Lisa thought for a moment. "You said she's in her twenties. The same age as the Girl from Slatington?"

"Yeah."

"And the same age as the Girl in the Sewer?"

He didn't know where she was going with her questions.

"So why do you always say 'the Girl' and not 'the Woman'?" she asked.

Frank looked up. Lisa was seventeen now, finishing high school and getting ready to leave home for business school. For her, twenty was womanhood.

"Maybe it's because they were all so young when they died," he said. "They hadn't had a chance to grow up yet. Maybe that's why."

After Frank gave the bust of the Girl with the Shattered Head to Grazel, the detective compared it to hundreds of photos that the killer had taken of women he'd come into contact with. One face in particular looked just like the bust's.

"It just about jumped out," Grazel told a reporter. "It looked about identical."

But there was no name on the photograph for him to follow up on.

## ◼ DR. ANGEL

In the summer of 1983, Frank and Jan went to see *Gorky Park*. Martin Cruz Smith's novel, which the movie was based on, was said to have been inspired by Gerasimov, a fact the movie clearly hinted at.

In one scene, the fictional anthropologist, who was named Andreev, showed the main character, Detective Arkady Renko, a bust he'd made, and it was none other than Tamerlane. It didn't at all resemble the one created by Gerasimov, but the reference was obvious. In another scene, probably put there for some extra shock value, Andreev stood next to a glass case containing a head covered in a writhing mass of insects feeding on the flesh.

"Demmestoid beetles," Frank whispered to Jan, but she elbowed him to keep quiet.

Frank knew about dermestid beetles—he pronounced it "demmestoid"—because the assistants at the medical examiner's office often talked about them, although he had never seen them used. More commonly, they were found in carrion or roadkill, where they laid eggs that took several days to hatch.

"The beetles are good on small things, like birds," one of the assistants told him. "On skeletons, they'd take a long time to do the job."

The assistants preferred to soak the flesh off a head with a strong solution of bleach, which worked much faster and wasn't as awful to look at as bugs. Which was why Frank was surprised when, a few weeks later, Lawrence Angel sent him a report recommending using dermestid beetles to clean off a head he'd evaluated. The victim, a woman, had been shot in the head, which was also badly burnt.

Angel, the head of the anthropology department at the Smithsonian's Museum of Natural History since 1962, was a brilliant, diminutive man who often wore bow ties and had an explosive amount of energy. He had been doing important forensic work for the FBI for many years and lectured at George Washington University. Frank had gone to see him for the first time in 1978, when he was working on the man found in Belle Glade, Florida. Over the past year or two he had been turning to Angel more and more for advice on the possible sex, age, race, and individual characteristics of victims, especially since Krogman was getting older and unable to take on as much work.

The burnt skull was the first Frank had taken to Washington since the Girl in the Steamer Trunk, although the case had more in common with the Girl with the Shattered Head. The victim was probably a prostitute, and a man had been arrested and accused of killing her. He told the police that he didn't know her name. After they had sex in his apartment, he went to the toilet, and after he came out he found his wallet gone. Suspecting her, he shot her. It wasn't clear if she had died immediately, but he had taken her into the house next door and set her on fire.

The skull was missing a good portion of the right side, part of the right orbit and cheek area, although most of the teeth were still there, except two at the upper front. Angel's report, as usual, gave Frank lots of details to work with. He could almost picture her in his head.

The girl, Angel wrote, had "an extreme prognathism with quite big teeth, a large gap between the upper central incisors, a rather small, broad but not low-bridged nose with uptilted tip, square orbits, rather small and horizontal, suggesting wide open eyes without eye-folds, forehead rather high with sagittal bony ridge perhaps perceptible, average and not extreme muscularity. The face is not wide and the upper part is not high compared to the teeth and chin." In spite of Angel's report, the assistants at the Philadelphia medical examiner's office chose to use bleach and detergent, not beetles, to remove the flesh.

When Frank was almost finished with the bust, he decided to do one version with sculpted, shortly cropped hair, and another with a wig that was large and the hair loose and curly. He took black-and-white as well as color photographs of both versions and gave them to Ellis Verb, who was handling this case.

The detective looked at the images for a while before saying anything. "It could be two totally different people," he said, as if he had only just realized how drastically a face could change simply by altering the hairstyle.

Verb showed the photographs to people in different bars around North Philadelphia. One of his informants pulled out one of the photos and said it resembled a girl named Wanda Jacobs. Wanting to get a more positive ID, Verb asked who she was friendly with. He got the name of a woman who lived in the projects in South Philadelphia.

Gerry White at the medical examiner's office took up the case from there. On a cold gray day, the trees bare and the swirling current on the Delaware River almost the only sign of life as they drove alongside it, White and Frank went to meet the woman in South Philadelphia. It was a bad neighborhood, and White warned Frank that people sometimes took potshots at you from the windows in the projects.

When they located Wanda Jacobs's friend, the three of them went to sit on a bench out in the open. Frank kept looking around expectantly, waiting for someone to shoot at them. White took out the photographs and asked the woman if they bore a resemblance to anyone she knew. One of the black-and-white pictures in which the girl had short hair drew her attention.

"Oh, you know my friend Wanda," she said. White told her it

was a plaster bust. She turned to Frank, who had said nothing until now. "Did you do that sculpture of her?"

Frank said he had. The woman didn't understand why her friend would have a sculpture of herself made. She didn't know that Wanda was dead.

"Where'd you do that?" she asked.

In his studio, Frank replied.

The woman still didn't get what was going on, so they finally showed her a photograph of the burnt skull.

"Oh my God," she cried out. "Wanda's dead."

## A BODY ON THE NEXT SEAT

### 1984

Frank took the day off from his photographic work to visit Washington, D.C. A group of students from the Fleischer Art Memorial were going to see a Rodin exhibit at the National Gallery, and he used the opportunity to catch a ride with them. Once in the capital, he wanted to see a friend of his at the Pentagon.

Through Doc Fillinger, Frank had met numerous people in law enforcement—Texas Rangers, polygraph experts, anthropologists, even officers in the military—and whenever they said he should come by and visit them, he made sure to take them up on the offer.

For him it always meant possible forensic work. No one would know about what he did if he didn't tell them.

Once they arrived at the National Gallery, he peeled off from the group and walked down Constitution Avenue past the National Archives. As he was right next door to the Museum of Natural History, he decided to pop in and see Stephanie Damadio.

Damadio was a young anthropologist who worked with Lawrence Angel and acted as a liaison between him and law-enforcement members seeking his help. More and more police departments were learning that, as government agencies, they could make use of the Smithsonian's services for free. Need a skeleton evaluated? Send it to the Museum of Natural History.

The trouble was getting an appointment with Angel, who, besides having a hectic schedule, was in demand across the country. Even when his health began failing, he kept working almost till the day he died. If he took in a skeleton—and it was always stipulated that no flesh could remain on any skeleton submitted—it was unlikely that he would get to it for a while. Skeletons sometimes lay around Angel's laboratory for weeks and started to smell.

The fact that Frank knew Angel meant he could help the police fast-track a case. The last time he had done that, several months earlier, it had been for two detectives from New York. The case concerned a woman who had been shot and left in Harriman State Park, New York. She was between thirty-five and forty-five, white, had a medium build, and was wearing some inexpensive jewelry. Frank had to do a bust of her, but the detectives also hoped Angel could give them some more information.

The three of them drove down to Washington from New York

with the skeleton in the back of the policemen's station wagon. Angel took a quick look at the body, and Frank scribbled some notes from his initial remarks: *Well nourished. Teeth well cared for. Age 40. Canine muscle strong. Remarkably long face. Strong chin. Low forehead. Small person. Slight features. High bridge nose slight tip. Non-prominent cheekbones. Big nasal bone. Fairly wide orbits. Pink tooth time of death. Molars extracted. Big long teeth. Weak jaw set back.*

The skeleton was left with Angel, who later mailed the skull to Frank for his bust. What Frank didn't know was that the detectives had never returned to collect the rest of the bones, which had been left lying in Angel's laboratory all that time awaiting pickup. When he arrived at Damadio's door, she didn't realize that he'd come for a social call and not for the skeleton.

"You've got to take these bones away," she insisted.

She had to remind Frank which body she was talking about.

"You mean the police never came back to fetch it?" he asked. She shook her head. "But it's been here for several months."

"Right. And we need it out of here now. We've got nowhere to keep these bones. They aren't part of our collection."

Frank told her he couldn't possibly take the skeleton. He was visiting by bus with a group of art students.

"I'm going to get in a lot of trouble if the bones stay here," she said. "I did you a favor by helping those cops and getting them in to see the boss. Now you've got to get this body out."

"How am I going to take it on the bus?" Frank asked.

"I'll put it in some boxes and then cover them with a trash bag and duct tape, and you can throw it over your shoulder. Just get the bones out of here today."

He had no choice. If he wanted to stay in good favor at the Smithsonian, he would have to take the skeleton.

Once Damadio had wrapped everything up, Frank threw the loose package over his shoulder like a sack and left. Encumbered with the skeleton, he could no longer go see his friend at the Pentagon, so he headed back down Constitution Avenue to the bus. With several hours to spare, he decided to go see the Rodin exhibit after all.

It being winter, he was sure the attendants at the coat-check room would think nothing of the package he was carrying. Other people had heavy coats and big bags. When he handed the trash-bag-covered boxes over the counter, one of the attendants almost dropped it.

"Man," he said, "this is heavy. What have you got in here?"

Frank said it was clothes.

"Well, you come put them on the shelf yourself, then," the attendant said.

After going through the exhibit, Frank picked up his coat and the bag. It was dark by then, and the weather had turned bitterly cold. He asked the bus driver if he could put the bag in the luggage compartment under the vehicle.

"I don't have the key," the driver said. "This was only meant to be a day trip. Just put it inside."

The bus was crowded, but Frank was able to use the seat next to him for the bag. Soon after they set off, the driver turned up the heat. Frank knew that the warmer the bus became, the quicker the skeleton would start to smell. To avoid having people suspect the odor was coming from the black package, he immediately said something himself: "Where is that stench coming from?" he asked, loud enough for the people around him to hear. It did the trick. Even when the smell got worse, no one said anything about it.

The bus dropped everyone at Eighth and Catherine streets, and with the bag over his shoulder, Frank walked the twenty blocks to the meat market, where he left it on the floor of the studio. It had been a long day, and he wanted to get home.

Early the next morning, he got a call from Bob Barfield, one of the artists renting space from him. He had found the bag on the floor as he came in. "Is that what I think it is?" he asked.

Frank said it was.

"Jesus, Frank. You can't just leave bodies lying around. What are you going to do with it?"

"I've got no choice. I'm going to have to leave it at the studio until the police come from New York to pick it up."

Barfield sighed. "You mean I'm going to have to look at this thing every day?"

"Well, I can put it in the basement, I guess."

When Paula Lisak heard about Frank's plan, she told him the basement was her space and she didn't want a skeleton down there.

"Okay," he said, "I'll put it in the meat freezer in the back."

What Frank didn't tell Lisak was that there was already a body in the basement. While still on Arch Street, he had received a case from Montgomery County, Pennsylvania. They hadn't detached the skull but had sent him the whole skeleton instead. When he finished the bust, the police never picked up the body, so Frank put it in a metal case and eventually forgot about it. During his move to South Street, he found it again and, not knowing what else to do with it, took it with him. It was still in a corner of the basement, barely a few feet away from where Lisak worked.

## AXION AND BIZ

In 1985 Barfield and Lisak had to move out of the meat market because Jan was ready to move in. She hated the suburbs. She had given them a try after her wild early days, but she decided that she preferred living closer to the city.

Frank liked the idea of having his home and studio in the same place. It meant he would no longer have to drive the busts and heads between the two locations. And now that Lisa had moved out, only three of them would be living together.

The meat market, by this stage, was almost habitable. The roof was repaired, and the holes in the floor had been closed up. There were enough rooms to live in, except there was still no proper bathroom, and getting one installed was proving impossible.

The plumbers took more than a month to put in a sink, and when they finally installed the toilet, it was too close to the wall and it leaked. They said they would come back to fix it, but they never did. Frank kept phoning them, explaining that he had sold his house in Lawndale and the place needed to be ready for his family. "Until I get the bathroom fixed, they can't move in."

When the police in Luzerne County, Pennsylvania, contacted Frank to say they had a job for him, he told them not to mail the skull. Needing a break from the construction work at the studio, he offered to pick it up himself. His contact was a coroner named George Hudock.

It took Frank two buses and several hours to get to the town of Wilkes-Barre, where Hudock had arranged to meet him and take him to his office. When they met, the doctor was apologetic because things hadn't worked out as smoothly as he'd hoped.

"The head is still on the body," he said, "and it hasn't been cleaned yet."

Hudock was performing the autopsy for another county that didn't have its own facilities, so he'd been obliged to rent space from the Wilkes-Barre hospital. The first available time he could get was later that same morning.

"The good news is that I have a homicide detective coming to help me," he said.

Hudock suggested that Frank return the following week to pick up the head. Not wanting to make the trip all over again, Frank said that he would wait for them to finish the job.

They drove to the hospital and went downstairs to a small autopsy room in the basement. The body, which lay on a stainless-steel table, was decomposed, although Frank already knew it was a white female in her twenties.

"We don't know how she died," said Hudock. "The hyoid bone isn't broken, so it's unlikely she was strangled. It could have been drugs, but I haven't gotten the toxicology report back yet."

When the detective arrived, Frank asked if he could watch. As soon as Hudock started cutting into the neck area, the detective got sick and said he couldn't continue. Hudock looked over at Frank, who was clearly at ease in the autopsy room. "You ever done this before?" Hudock asked.

"I've watched the attendants in Philly deflesh a head," Frank said. "But I've never seen a head being taken off."

"Good, that's a start."

After the detective left, Frank put on rubber gloves. Hudock used a scalpel and a small curved knife to get between the vertebrae in the neck and then pry them apart to cut the muscle. He asked Frank to pass him a pair of stainless-steel pliers.

"There's lots of muscle," Hudock said. "I could cut right through it with a saw, but I don't want to damage any evidence."

As Hudock continued cutting, Frank held the head at different angles for him. When it was removed at last, they began slicing at the dried skin and tissue, which was rigid because nothing had been done to soften it. Again Frank held the head tight, and if Hudock's hands got tired, Frank took over.

An hour later, most of the flesh had been cleaned off. Frank told Hudock that he could finish the job back in Philadelphia. It was for this exact reason that he'd had an industrial sink installed in the studio; there was already a drain in the floor from when the building served as a meat market. With the head in a plastic bucket, the two men set off for the bus station. It was late by the time Frank got to Philadelphia, so he went straight back to Lawndale.

The next morning he left home early with the bucket strapped to his Harley. "I wouldn't come down to the meat market today," he warned Jan, just in case she wanted to transport more things from the house. "I'll be boiling up a head."

The kitchen at the meat market was still very simple, although Frank did have a single gas burner for cooking. He put the head in a large pot, to which he added enough water to cover it and a quarter cup of bleach. The attendants at the medical examiner's office used a lot more than that, but it made the skull too white and often burnt off important markers, such as the nasal bone and the canthus marks on orbital bones. Finally Frank put in equal measures of Axion and Biz, two detergents that Wilton Krogman had suggested because they contained phosphates that helped break down the flesh.

He left the pot on a low simmer and then carried on with a photographic job that had just come in. The agency had given him two days to go out by helicopter and find an exact replica of a quarry written about in the text of an ad they were working on. Frank knew there had to be an easier, quicker, and cheaper way of doing it: a sculpture. If he could make a face out of clay and plaster, he could make a quarry.

At lunchtime he headed out to Brown's market to get a sandwich. When he got back, the plumber and his assistant were standing outside. "We've come to take a look at that toilet again."

Frank said he hoped they could finish the job today, but the plumber didn't seem to hear him. The two men had to pass through the kitchen to get to the bathroom. The smell of the head boiling in the pot permeated the place.

"Hey," the plumber said, "what's cooking?"

"A head."

The man laughed.

"Take a look for yourself," Frank said, without thinking twice about the reaction the plumber might have upon seeing the head. The prankster in Frank also wanted to play a joke on him for delaying the construction work.

The plumber put down his tools, went to the burner, and lifted the pot's lid. The skin had floated to the surface, the water had turned a murky brown, and the skull was facing upward with its vacant eyes. The plumber dropped the lid as soon as he saw it.

The toilet was installed by the end of the day, and the job was done so well the plumbers made sure they never had to come back again.

# MURDER À LA CARTE

Once a month they met at Day by Day, a diner on Sansom Street where Frank's friend Wendy was a waitress, or at Seafood Unlimited, between Spruce and Locust. Usually it was just Frank and Bill Fleischer, although sometimes an FBI agent named Kevin O'Brian also joined them.

Frank had met Fleischer several years earlier, when he went with Fillinger to address a meeting of Philadelphia's Jewish policemen. A jovial teddy bear of a man with a beard and a lustrous crop of black hair that he combed back, Fleischer was no longer a cop (he had also worked for the FBI) but a U.S. Customs agent.

On this particular weekday in 1986, the two men met at Day by Day. Within minutes they were talking about their latest cases. Frank's concerned a young woman whose skeletonized body had been found by two hunters in the woods of an industrial zone in Croydon. About twenty miles northeast of Philadelphia, Croydon was only a short distance from the bridge to Burlington, New Jersey, which led police to think that she might have been murdered in one state and the body dumped in the other.

Fillinger had done as much of an autopsy as he could, given the state of the body, and determined that she had been dead for about two months and died from two bullet wounds in the chest. On further inspection, a forensic anthropologist concluded that she was between twenty-three and thirty and about five feet five. She had shoulder-length brown hair, some of which had been found with the body.

Frank seldom got hair with a subject. In this instance, it had been cleaned off the head and was delivered to him, along with the skull, in a separate plastic bag.

"I've got your order," Wendy said, interrupting the two men's conversation to put their sandwiches and soup on the table.

Frank ignored his food and carried on telling Fleischer about a discovery he had made on the victim. Sometimes he called her the Girl from Croydon, sometimes the Girl from Bensalem, a town near Croydon, and sometimes the Girl in the Woods. For once a particular name didn't stick.

When trying to neaten the hair, he told Fleischer, he had found some twigs and a little eighteen-karat gold medallion that the X-ray machine in the medical examiner's office had failed to detect. There was a picture of Jesus on one side, a heart and anchor on the other, and the words *Dio ti protegga*.

"It means 'God protect you,'" he added.

Insubstantial though the clue was—and Frank never tried to figure out how the puzzle of a face worked itself out in his head, or which clues played more of a role in his artistic decisions than others—it was only after the discovery that he decided to sculpt the girl's hair and not to use a wig.

Other than for Wanda Jacobs, Frank hadn't used a wig in several years. The last time he had felt the impulse, it was for the Girl in the Sewer, whose body had been found at Twenty-first and Bellevue streets. Her head had been crushed and her body covered in lye, some of which was still sticking to the head.

It wasn't that he disliked wigs. If he saw a wig that he thought would work with a bust, he bought it.

"But wigs cost money," he told Fleischer as he bit into his sandwich, "and the police don't want to pay the extra thirty or forty dollars—so I have to. If I buy a cheap wig, the bust suffers. And I don't want the bust to be at the mercy of a cheap wig."

Nor was there any guarantee with a wig that the hairstyle would stay the way he'd created it. Even before a case went cold, he'd seen busts end up in a detective's drawer, where they would roll around and the wig would get destroyed. By sculpting the hair, he could choose the exact style, and afterward it stayed that way.

Frank pulled out a photograph of his bust of the Girl from Croydon/Bensalem. Her hair came down to her shoulders, and Frank had styled it so that it covered one ear but was tucked behind the other.

Wendy came over to take their plates and saw the photograph. She always asked him about his technique. "Why'd you do it that way?" she asked.

Frank took a serious tone, as if giving a lecture. "I looked at her face and the pieces of hair that I was given, and I had to make a choice," he said. Hair was an illusion, not a solid form, and it had to work with the other elements of the face. "There is a harmony of form, and I apply it to all the face."

Frank gave his completed bust to Al Eastlack and Thomas Mills, the two detectives handling the Croydon case. Using the three-year-old computer list compiled by the FBI's National Crime Information Center, they came up with more than three hundred missing persons who resembled the bust. But one girl in particular stood out. She was twenty-three-year-old Yvonne Davi, from Bethpage, Long Island. Dental records confirmed that it was her.

|||||||||||||||||||||||||||||||||||||||||||||||||||||||||||||

In November 1987 Wilton Krogman died at the age of eighty-four, and the Girl in the Steamer Trunk was identified as Aliyah Davis, five years after Frank had sculpted her.

The girl's father, Robert Davis, had been trying to find out about his daughter, whom he hadn't seen in five years. Two of his other children, who lived with his ex-wife, told him that their stepfather had beaten Aliyah to death. Davis took the children down to the police station, where a detective showed them some photographs, one of which was the bust of the Girl in the Steamer Trunk. They all recognized her as Aliyah.

The girl's mother, Maria Davis Fox, was already on probation for the death of another child in 1973. She and Aliyah's stepfather were charged with her murder.

Frank and Ellis Verb went to the trial, where they met Robert Davis. He said the bust even had Aliyah's skin tone and hair correct. Frank recalled the night in 1982 when he'd been woken by a nightmare that had caused him to change her pigtails to braids.

During a break in the trial, he and Verb were introduced to Aliyah's grandmother in a hallway outside the courtroom.

"You did such a good job on Aliyah," she said. "I recognized her from five and a half years ago, when she was first shown on television."

Frank and Verb were surprised by her remark. She had recognized her granddaughter at the time but had said nothing.

"Why didn't you tell us about it back then?" Verb asked.

The woman was embarrassed. "The family told me not to get involved."

## THE SHIP 'N SHORE BLOUSE

### December 1987

The skeleton was found by a group of children in a thicket at the edge of a high school football field in North Philadelphia. At first they thought it was an animal, but then they saw a few articles of clothing lying nearby.

By the time Gerry White called Frank, the medical examiner's office had already explored various ways of identifying the girl. She was African-American, between the ages of fifteen and twenty-five, and had been dead for about a year. Besides a bit of decomposed pierced ear, there was no flesh on the bone. Apparently, she had been raped, but it wasn't certain if she had been murdered. Even if a bullet were found at the scene, White said, there needed to be a mark on the skeleton to prove it had caused her death.

Little about the skull stood out for Frank—a slight underbite but nothing else—although he did notice that her teeth were in very good condition. She didn't have a single cavity. White showed him the belongings found with the body, among which was one item in particular that Frank remembered: a Ship 'n Shore blouse.

Back at the studio, he put on some Rolling Stones and started cutting the tissue markers. The process went more quickly nowadays, ever since he had started using Krazy Glue, which dried quicker than model airplane glue. He'd also discovered hemostat surgical clamps, which he used to retrieve erasers that fell into the skull.

To the side of his workbench was a tool kit where he kept a growing array of sculpting knickknacks. It had begun as a storage place for his tools, paints, and the Plasticine eyeballs, but it now included ice-cream sticks, toothpicks, pieces of wire, sprays, baubles, and anything that might come in handy while he was sculpting.

He took out an eyeball and was about to fix it to the anterior part of the eye socket with clay. Until now he had been following the rule Krogman had suggested—to let the front of the cornea come out as far as an invisible line drawn between the lower and upper orbital ridges. In the past few years, however, he had done several skulls on which the eye sockets were shallower—the Girl in the Sewer, Wanda Jacobs, and Valerie Jamison, who'd been murdered by the serial killer Marty Graham—and the victims all had one thing in common: They were African-American. If he followed the rule about eyeballs, it meant that either there was less tissue, muscle, and fat behind their eyes or their eyes were pressing down into it, which would have caused them excruciating pain.

Frank called the Wills Eye Hospital on Walnut Street. He explained to the receptionist that he sculpted dead people's faces for the police and needed to speak to someone about eyes. All the doctors were busy, she said, but she would try and get someone to contact him. A few days later, Frank received a call from a doctor in the oculoplastics department.

The doctor said that Krogman's suggestion was perhaps a good average for artists to follow, but eyes could differ from case to case. An obvious example was someone who suffered from Graves' disease, or hyperthyroidism, which caused the eyes to protrude.

Frank said he was having particular trouble on the skull of a young African-American woman. The doctor said that in many cases the eye sockets on African-Americans were indeed shallower, as Frank had suspected, which could cause their eyeballs to project a bit more than those of other racial groups, perhaps by two millimeters or so.

The doctor added something else: No matter what race the person was, the amount of muscle, nerves, blood vessels, and fat behind the eye was the same. The distance from the back of the globe to the back of the orbit was less than the width of the eye. Even though the optic nerve leading between the two was between twenty-four and thirty millimeters, it was in an S-shape. A good distance to keep behind the eye was about eighteen millimeters.

For Frank, these were two very important indicators. From now on he would have to start placing eyeballs according to the back of the eye socket and not the front.

That night he sat in front of the skull, wondering how he could make sure the depth behind the eye was always the same. Looking around the studio for something, he wasn't sure what, he finally dug into his tool kit. There he found some golf tees. He took one, measured off eighteen millimeters and cut it, glued the cup part to the back of his premade Plasticine eyeball, and let the other end rest at the back of the skull. To keep the eyeballs centered, he packed small pieces of clay around the golf tees.

With the tissue markers and the eyeballs in place, he put the skull on top of the clay shoulders that had last held his bust of Valerie

Jamison. As he started fixing clay to the skull, he focused on the girl's mouth and its set of teeth without any cavities. He looked at the shape of the teeth, the configuration of the upper and lower jaws, the slight prognathism. In between, he kept looking back at the photographs of the skull on his workbench.

Once he had shaped a nose, he returned to the girl's lips. He made them full and then less full. He switched his attention from the mouth to the ears to the nose—the crucial three—but his movements were erratic. He knew he sometimes had to go with averages, especially when there was any doubt, but something about the head kept bothering him.

He was refining the clay several days later when his friend Joan came around. Joan Crescenz was the same age as Jan, blond and pretty, and she had modeled for Frank in the 1970s, when Frank worked at Faraghan's. Now married with two children, she visited the studio once or twice a month to do Frank's books. Ever since Lisa had moved away, Joan had also become the person Frank relied on most for opinions about his busts.

Joan knew something was bothering Frank about the latest skull. In her presence, he once again ran through all the facts he knew about the case—the football field, the depth of the eyes, the underbite, the clothes found near the body—because talking about a case often led to some new insight.

That was when he realized what didn't fit in the picture—the Ship 'n Shore blouse. The feminine, frilly shirt wasn't the kind of clothing an African-American girl her age in that part of North Philadelphia would have worn.

Joan agreed. "I used to wear that brand," she said. "If she bought Ship 'n Shore, she was going somewhere."

Frank thought for a moment. "So she was quite possibly a girl who was looking for something better in life."

"I think so."

Frank knew that he would dress the final sculpture in the blouse. If there was clothing with the victim, he always used it. But that night he decided to do something else too. He tilted the girl's head upward slightly. In the morning he found Vanessa staring at the bust.

"Who is she?" she asked.

"I think she is a girl with hope," Frank said.

"A dead girl who had hope?"

He nodded.

"What are you going to do with her hair?" she asked.

Frank hadn't decided until that moment. "I'm going to give her a pompadour."

"But why?"

"It goes with her face."

When Frank delivered the bust to the medical examiner's office, Gerry White was surprised. He was used to Frank putting expressions on his busts, parted lips, showing their teeth, but the girl with the blouse had something more.

"You've never done one like this before," he said. "She's looking up."

"Yeah," Frank said, "with hope."

Frank headed back to the meat market. His job was over. He knew that the girl might never be identified. Even if she was, the police didn't always bother to tell him. Until he heard otherwise, she would remain the Girl with Hope.

# HARMONY

## January 1990

Gretchen Worden wanted to use five of Frank's heads for an exhibit. "I think it would draw us a better crowd," she said.

Worden was the director of the Mütter Museum and a well-known personality in Philadelphia society. Under her guidance, the museum had gone from a little-known and little-visited collection of eccentricities to a world-class museum. It even produced a sought-after calendar shot by photographers such as Joel-Peter Witkin and Arne Svenson. In addition to showing the heads, Worden wanted Frank to give a talk at the opening of the exhibit.

Frank was overjoyed. He had gone to the Mütter Museum on every case since Anna Duval, to look at the Hyrtl collection of skulls. Now his busts would be there on display. The young boy from Edison High who had wanted his art to mean something was getting his wish.

Worden specified the five busts that she wanted: the Girl from Slatington, Linda Keyes; the Girl in the Steamer Trunk, Aliyah Davis; Wanda Jacobs; the Girl in the Well; and the Girl with Hope.

Frank had some of the heads in his possession, if he'd made copies of them, but the others he needed to get from various police departments. Worden wanted him to drop them off by the end of the month.

A group of about thirty people gathered in the foyer of the Mütter Museum the day Frank gave his speech. The five heads had been arranged in a glass case nearby, and it was the first display you saw on entering the building.

There were mostly women, housewives probably, and they were quite unlike his usual audience of Texas Rangers, forensic specialists, and policemen. He told them that there were three important things for him in his sculpting work: getting the skull; getting as much information as possible about the victim; and then, hopefully, getting an ID.

As an example, he took the Girl in the Well, who was white and in her twenties and had been found with the skeleton of an unborn six-month-old child, lying on some plywood above the pipes in a concrete well on the grounds of an abandoned whiskey distillery in Bensalem, Pennsylvania. Scattered around the body were magazines, candy wrappers, and clothing of different sizes and styles.

Besides the other things he looked at—Was there any hair? If so, was it dyed? What condition were the teeth? Did the face have any asymmetry?—Frank noticed that she had an overbite as well as a narrow mandible and maxilla. When he created the bust, he made sure to give her a pinched mouth and to show some of her teeth and her chipped incisors.

Other information also provided him with important clues. Was there jewelry? Clothing? Because the Bensalem girl was living in an old well and had clothes that looked like they'd come from the Salvation Army, he gave her the ratty hairstyle of a homeless person.

"The skull is a road map to the face," he told the women, "and when I look at the skull, I can see the details. It's nothing psychic. There are charts too, for tissue thickness, but each person is an individual. And where character changes, you have to change the facial tissue thickness, a bit here and there.

"When you look at a nose, a mouth, you can see a repetitive form happening. There's a harmony. That's why you can't go entirely by what the forensics people or the physical anthropologists tell you. Some white people have black features and vice versa. They might not even know it themselves."

Frank had several slides of the case, and when he showed the skeleton of the Girl in the Well, several women near the front shifted uncomfortably. He focused on one middle-aged woman in particular, dressed in a coat with a fur collar. It was a trick Fillinger had taught him at Temple University.

"You can't change one part of a face without taking the other parts of it into account. If you go wrong, you can tell. It's like a bad plastic surgery job—you can instantly spot this tiny nose on a face with a lot of character. You cannot only see it, you can feel it."

A woman in the back asked how close his reconstructions came to the individual when they were actually identified.

"Close," he said. "Close enough for the person to be ID'd in a lineup."

The same day that Frank gave his talk at the Mütter Museum, a brief article appeared in *The Philadelphia Inquirer,* announcing the exhibit. Alongside it was a photograph of the five busts in the glass case.

Lois Brown, a cleaner at an office block in the city, saw the picture in a newspaper that someone had thrown away. Something about one of the heads in the photograph caught her attention, and she decided to go to the exhibit to have a closer look.

Several weeks passed before Brown made it to the museum. She got off the bus on Walnut Street and then headed around the corner and into the museum. She hadn't been there before and expected to find a crowd, but there were only a few other people in the foyer.

Sitting behind the front desk was Paul Reilly, a heavyset, soft-spoken man who normally worked as the mail clerk but was filling in over lunch hour. Brown paid her admission and immediately saw the glass case. She had barely taken a look at the heads inside when she let out a scream: "It's her! I know that girl!"

Reilly got up and quickly went over to the woman, who was shaking. He had never seen anyone react this way in the museum before. Brown's voice drew the attention of other people, who came from the gift shop and from the back to see what the commotion was about.

"Please calm down," Reilly said.

She turned to him. "I know that girl."

"Which girl?"

"The girl in the case."

She was pointing to a sign under one of the busts that said UNKNOWN. It was the African-American girl whose head was tilted up slightly, the one Frank called the Girl with Hope. Brown suddenly started walking out of the museum. "I'll be back," she called.

An hour later, she returned with an older woman and a young girl of about four. They all walked straight past Reilly without paying and went up to the glass case. Both women started talking loudly. Again Reilly went up to see what the commotion was about.

"It's her," the first woman said, while the second woman kept peering into the case.

Reilly went back to the reception desk and called Worden. "Doctor," he said, "I think we have a problem here. You better come down right now."

Before Worden reached the foyer, she could hear the loud talking. She went up to the women, introduced herself, and asked if she could help.

"She's a relative of mine," Brown said, pointing to the Girl with Hope. "I'm her aunt, and this is her mother and her daughter." She paused. "Rosella went out food shopping two years ago and never came back."

Worden thought for a moment. "Are you sure that's her?" she asked.

"That's Rosella. I'm positive. Even the hair is right. That's her."

Worden turned to Reilly. "You better notify the police."

Reilly didn't know whom to call. How did you report an ID from a sculpture? He dialed 911. "We have a dead woman who has been identified," he told the woman who answered. "Can you send someone over here?"

Before the police arrived, Worden called Frank, who was sitting in the room at the back of the meat market that he now used as an office. Worden told him that they might have gotten an ID for the Girl with Hope. Frank was skeptical and asked to speak to the mother. Brown got on the phone and told him she was the girl's aunt. Frank explained that he was the sculptor of the bust.

"I'm sure that's her," Brown said. "Even the hair's the same."

She told him that the girl's name was Rosella Atkinson. She had been eighteen years old when she disappeared, leaving behind a two-year-old child. They never knew what had happened to her. It was information that could fit many a young woman, but then Brown added something that caught Frank's attention: "Rosella was a healthy girl. She didn't even have a single cavity."

"No cavities?" he asked. The skull had no cavities, either.

"Not one."

Frank said he would be right down. By the time he got to the museum, a police car was there, and the women were being taken away to give a statement. Frank called Gerry White at the medical examiner's office.

"Gerry," he said, "I'm at the Mütter Museum, and I think we have an ID on the girl who was found at the high school."

White knew that Frank liked to play detective, meeting with Fleischer to talk about cases over lunch, and that he sometimes took his sleuthing too far. "You have a *possible* ID, Frank," White corrected him. "We're following up some pretty good leads of our own."

Frank couldn't wait to tell him the news. "Her aunt said she didn't have any dental work. No cavities."

There was a pause.

"I'll be right over."

Even though Atkinson didn't have any cavities, which meant there might not be any dental X-rays to check, the medical examiner's office found some records. And they matched the skull. *The Philadelphia Inquirer* ran a story on April 25, 1990, VIGIL FOR DAUGHTER ENDS IN MUSEUM.

Frank was on a roll. The story made newspapers and television stations around the country. This was his most public ID of a murder victim since Anna Duval. The attention almost made him forget that another one of his busts was causing even more of a sensation around the country. It was of the fugitive murderer John Emil List.

# MEXICO

# THE SECRET

The policeman Gus lasted only one night sharing Frank's new room on the sixth floor.

After talking with Esparza about it the next morning, the Mexican agreed that Frank could be there alone, but it wasn't safe for him to go anywhere outside the hotel without a bodyguard. As a result, Frank stayed indoors most of the time.

"The less visibility, the better," Esparza told him.

Even though he wasn't scared after the warning e-mail to Jan, Frank suddenly became overly cautious. When he answered the door, he made sure to stand to one side, so that if someone shot through it or pushed it, he wouldn't be hurt.

By late afternoon, he had sneaked off to Sanborns on his own, telling the bodyguard that he was going to the swimming pool.

||||||||||||||||||||||||||||||||||||||||||||||||||||

Anyone who looked at the busts probably would have thought Frank was almost finished with them, whereas the truth was that the longest part of the reconstruction process lay ahead—the refining.

The changes would be so slight as to escape the untrained eye, but from here on he instilled the character and traits that someone who knew the victim would hopefully see and register.

Working on five skulls at once also gave him the chance to do something he had never done before—let the victims interact.

He moved the heads around the table, put one in the place of another, turned them around so he could see them from different angles, noticed how they looked near one another, in couples and in trios, or how they changed in shadows and brightness as he pointed his tripod light at the table or bounced it off the walls.

What he was doing with the heads—letting them "converse," if you will—reminded him of what would happen when he watched living people, whether in a bar, at a party, in a church pew, on a beach, or on a bus. When one person left the company, whoever was left behind looked different. It wasn't as if the lighting had changed, but something was different. Their appearances altered once again if someone else joined them.

The sound of a knock at the door startled Frank. He had been warned that the coroner, Maria Sánchez, might come by to see how the busts were getting on. Before answering the door, he did as he'd been instructed and hid the Girl from Chihuahua, putting her in the cupboard. The four remaining heads were in a row on the table, their chins resting on wooden blocks, as if with an air of expectation. The Girl Without a Lower Jaw was more finished than the others, her face round, her nose small, her mouth turned down slightly at the edges.

Sánchez came in, looked at the heads, and asked Frank about the fifth bust. Surprised that she knew about it, he acted as if he didn't know what she was talking about and said there were only four.

She turned to him abruptly. "I know there are five heads," she said in halting English. "I know about the Girl from Chihuahua."

She was angry at him for lying to her. Frank couldn't understand why he had been told to keep the Girl from Chihuahua a secret from her.

## MAKING A MOLD IN THE NIGHT

Frank looked at the heads in the darkness. They were the last things he saw at night, their silhouettes framed by his lighted balcony window, and the first things he saw every morning. Never before had he been with a bust so utterly, and now he had five as his companions all day long.

He was trying to find something in each of them, a smile, some sadness, a brooding quality, a touch of playfulness. The Girl from Chihuahua was at the front of the table, more refined than the others, her eyes almond-shaped and her nose-lip furrow, or philtrim, fairly obvious. He had already done her hair, which he parted in the middle and let fall to her shoulders.

The second girl, the one with the different orbits, was happier, her teeth partly visible through her opened lips, and she was looking up—another girl with hope. The third girl had a broader nose, and her head was tilted almost imperceptibly to the right. She seemed serious, the most serious of them all, a student perhaps.

The Girl Without a Lower Jaw was thoughtful, and Frank already knew that when he painted her, he was going to show her looking to one side, as if averting someone's stare. Each time he looked at her, or any one of them, it was hard to imagine a man's hands around her neck, the young woman beaten, raped, and struggling for her life.

Behind them all, almost in the shadows, was the bust Frank was coming to think of as the Girl with the Crooked Nose. The downward shift on the right side of her face was not immediately obvious. It was something her mother or her sister might notice, a characteristic she would have probably tried to hide with her hairstyle or her manner, lifting her hand up to cover it when she was talking to a boy she fancied. Frank couldn't tell whether it was the abnormalities, but he knew that if he'd met her, he would have liked her.

Together the girls could have been five young friends at a party or on their way to a dance, they looked so carefree and unharmed by the world. All of them had an air of hope, which wasn't the only thing they had in common with Rosella Atkinson. But Rosella had been identified, while each one of these girls remained nameless.

It was four A.M., but Frank couldn't sleep. He had been thinking about Rosella Atkinson's hairstyle. It had seemed so obvious at the time that he would give the Girl with Hope a pompadour. But what would he do with the girls of Juárez?

Ever since arriving in Mexico, he had watched the women around him—whether they were walking on the roads through town, standing at the pink crosses, sweeping the floor in Sanborns, working behind the counter at El Acueducto, or waiting at the bus stops—knowing that what he took in were clues he would eventually put into the busts. Few of the women he had seen wore their hair short; instead they seemed to keep it long, parting it in the center or to the side or pulling it back in a bun.

As for makeup, they didn't wear much more than some eyeliner. The girls who had better jobs might wear something more, some lipstick and nail polish, and look more American, with shorter skirts and hairstyles they had spent money on. But it didn't seem like they were the ones the killer was going for.

Frank got out of bed and started adding dollops of clay to the scalp of the second girl, the one with the slightly open mouth, and then layered it down her neck. At first it looked like clods of earth. He hit the mass softly, twisting on more curls as if screwing them into the skull, straightening them slowly as he progressed. He didn't normally cover ears with hair, but that was the way girls here seemed to like it. Then again, he could change that if it didn't work with a face.

Frank smoothed down the clay with his thumbs, intermittently going back to the features, pushing the nose in from both sides with his thumb and forefinger, distracted by the smaller details—the eyebrows, the lips, the mouth, inside the eyes, toward the canthus points, around the ears, into them.

Then he was back at the hair. With a large wire-ended sculpting tool, the kind he preferred when working with hair, he made big movements. As excess pieces of clay fell to the table with little thuds, his movements became more constricted.

He hadn't been thinking about it, but before the night had turned to morning, he had decided what he was going to do with each girl's hair. He would give long hair to three of them—the Girl Looking Up, the Serious Girl, and the Girl with the Crooked Nose. The Girl Without a Lower Jaw, he was going to give a bun.

The traffic outside his window began before six A.M., but he didn't notice it. Two hours later, he heard a knock on his door. He got ready to move the Girl from Chihuahua to a corner and cover her with a sheet.

"It's Hector," a voice called out.

Hector was a big, solid state policeman who sometimes accompanied Esparza. Frank liked him because he seemed like a straight shooter, and he always said what was on his mind. As soon as Hector came into the room, he stopped.

The four heads had taken shape quickly and were almost as far along as the Girl from Chihuahua. To Frank, the four still needed more refining, but to an amateur, there was no difference. The way the busts were arranged on the table, the Girl from Chihuahua was to the right, at the rear.

"It's the Girl from Chihuahua," Hector exclaimed, pointing at her. "It's the Girl from Chihuahua."

"Are you sure?" Frank asked.

"Yes, it's her," he said.

Frank thought that maybe Hector had made a lucky guess. But when Esparza came by later that morning, the same thing happened. At first he stood behind Frank, saying nothing. His presence made Frank self-conscious.

"Keep working," Esparza said.

Frank turned. "I can't work with you there. What's on your mind?"

"That girl," Esparza replied.

"Which one?"

"That one," he said, pointing. "That's the Girl from Chihuahua."

Even though Esparza had come into the room many times in the past ten days, Frank had always covered the bust. So the Mexican hadn't seen her properly until she was with the others. There was no way he could have known it was her.

"How can you be sure?" Frank asked.

"I've seen pictures of her."

Besides Frank, only seven people at most had seen the busts. The fact that two of those people had identified the Girl from Chihuahua was, to his mind, as close to an ID as you could get without a DNA test.

"Who is she?" he asked. "What do you know about her?"

Esparza held back for a moment. "I'm not allowed to say."

His caginess was less mysterious than annoying. Frank was used to secrecy—when he'd done the bust of the mobster Alphonse Persico, he couldn't even say the man's name out loud—but here he didn't see the point. Whom would he tell, anyway? He didn't know anyone and was virtually locked in his room all the time.

"You know, Frank," Esparza said, changing the subject, "you're doing such a great job here, it's a pity we aren't publicizing it."

Frank thought Esparza was going to suggest they get in touch with *El Diario* and *El Norte* to come and photograph the Girl from Chihuahua. But the Mexican actually meant newspapers outside Juárez, in America.

"That'd be great," Frank said.

Esparza hesitated. "But I don't know how to contact them," he said. "Could you maybe help us do that?"

Frank didn't hesitate before answering. "Of course I can." He knew lots of people he could call. And publicity of the busts was the key to getting them identified. "But is that okay? Am I allowed to do that?"

"The attorney general has personally asked me to ask you."

"Sure, then. I'll make some calls."

By the time Esparza left, Frank had decided that the Girl from Chihuahua was ready.

||||||||||||||||||||||||||||||||||||||||||||||||||||||

The sounds of the city at night—a siren, a truck lowering its gears, blaring music from a cantina, someone whistling, a scream—traveled through the hot air of Juárez and up through Frank's open balcony doors. He hadn't put on any music tonight because he also liked to listen to what was going on outside.

He coated the bust of the Girl from Chihuahua with releasing agent, shellac, and finally, synthetic rubber. As it was drying, he prepared the bathroom by lining the tub with trash bags.

All the while he thought about Esparza's request for help. It was strange, yes. Frank was, after all, an outsider, practically a stranger to Mexico, an American who spoke hardly a word of Spanish, someone not even in law enforcement. But he tried not to dwell on that or, for that matter, on several other things bothering him. For instance, why keep the Girl from Chihuahua a secret but publicize the other four girls? Why wasn't he allowed to tell the coroner, Sánchez, about the Girl from Chihuahua when she already seemed to know about her?

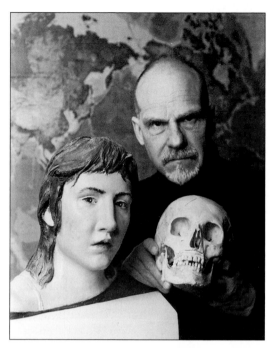

Frank with the Girl in the Well, who had been found alongside the skeleton of a six-month-old fetus on the property of an old whiskey distillery.
© *Janice Bender*

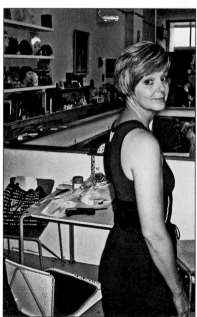

Jan Bender in the meat market, Philadelphia. © *Frank Bender*

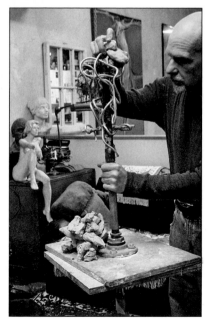

Frank applies clay to an armature.
© *Janice Bender*

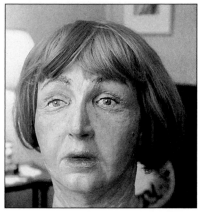
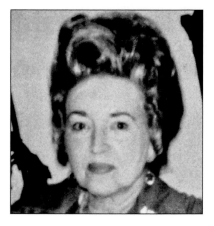

LEFT:

One of the last photographs taken of Anna Duval before she was murdered.
*Photo courtesy of the family of Anna Duval.*

RIGHT:

The bust of Duval was identified by a policeman who matched the bust with a missing person's photograph. © *Frank Bender*

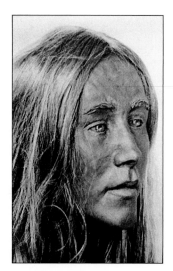
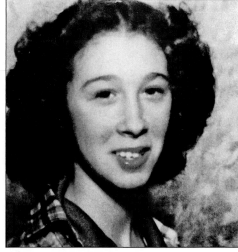

LEFT: The Girl from North Leithgow Street, whose skeleton was found in a basement. She was sculpted in 1981 and identified . . . © *Frank Bender*

RIGHT: . . . as Jacqueline Gough, thirteen years later.
*Photo courtesy of the family of Jacqueline Gough.*

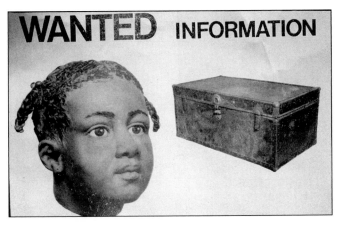

A poster publicizing the five-year-old Girl in the Steamer Trunk, cast away below a bridge in Philadelphia. *Poster courtesy of the Philadelphia Police Department.*

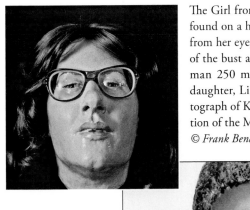

The Girl from Slatington, whose bones were found on a hilltop in Pennsylvania. One lens from her eyeglasses lay nearby. Within weeks of the bust appearing in a local newspaper, a man 250 miles away claimed it to be his daughter, Linda Keyes. The bust and a photograph of Keyes are in the permanent collection of the Mütter Museum in Philadelphia. *© Frank Bender*

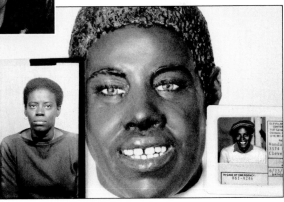

Wanda Jacobs was shot and then burnt, which severely damaged her skull. The bust was identified soon after police began showing images of it around Philadelphia. *Mug shot courtesy of the Philadelphia Police Department. Photo of bust © Frank Bender.*

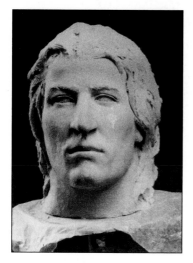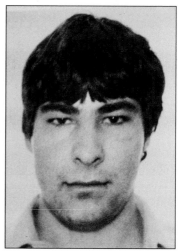

A half hour after seeing the unpainted bust of the Man in the Cornfield, who was murdered and buried on a farm, Detective Paul Schneider happened to see a photograph of Edward Myers.
*Photo of bust © Frank Bender. Mug shot courtesy of the Delaware County Police Department.*

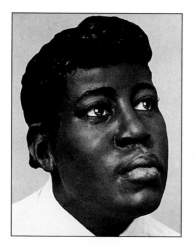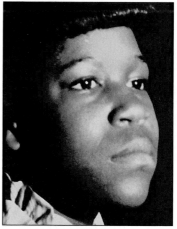

The sculpture of the Girl with Hope, whose skeleton lay undiscovered on the edge of a high school football field for a year, and Rosella Atkinson. Of all Frank's work, this bust struck many people as the most uncannily like the victim.
*Photo of bust © Frank Bender. Portrait courtesy of the family of Rosella Atkinson.*

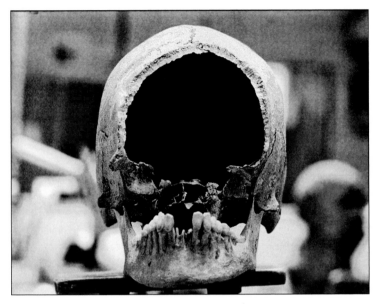

The faceless skull of the Girl from Manlius, who was killed in 1986, although her body was only found ten years later. © *Frank Bender*

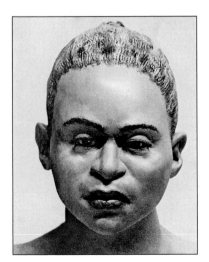 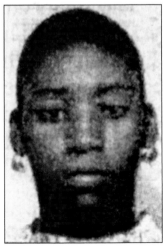

LEFT: The Girl from Manlius, as Frank imagined her in 2001. © *Frank Bender*

RIGHT: Lorean Quincy Weaver. *Mug shot courtesy of the Manlius Police Department.*

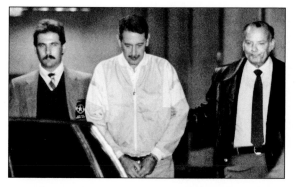
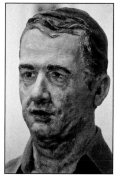

One of the most secretive manhunts undertaken by the U.S. Marshals was for Alphonse "Allie Boy" Persico, an underboss of the Colombo crime family. To make an age-progression bust of him in 1987, all Frank had to go on were several photographs taken twelve years earlier. *Persico photo © Brad Clift. Bust photo © Frank Bender.*

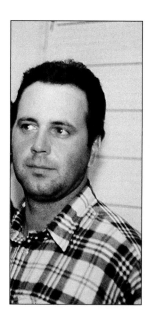
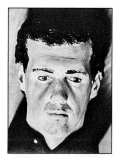
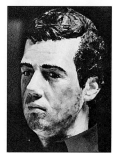
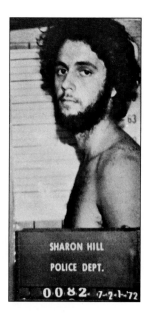

Biker and murderer Robert Nauss was captured in 1990, three years after Frank created his bust. In the last photos of Nauss, taken in prison in 1977 before he escaped, he had a thinner face, a beard, and long scraggly hair.

*The 1990 mug shot courtesy of the United States Marshals Service.*

*Photos of bust © Frank Bender.*

*The 1977 mug shot courtesy of the Sharon Hill Police Department.*

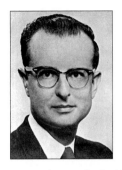 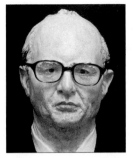 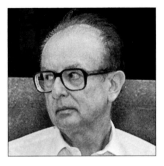

How John List looked before he disappeared in 1971; how Frank imagined him to look in 1989; and how he looked when he was captured eleven days after his bust was broadcast on the TV show *America's Most Wanted*.
*Courtesy of the New Jersey State Police; © Frank Bender; © AP Images*

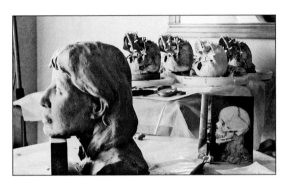

Frank did the Girl from Chihuahua in clay before even starting on the four other skulls.
*© Frank Bender*

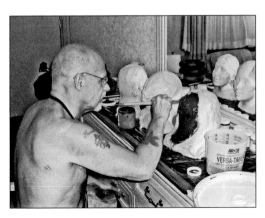 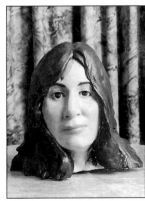

LEFT: Painting the three busts. *© Frank Bender*

RIGHT: The Girl with the Crooked Nose. *© Frank Bender*

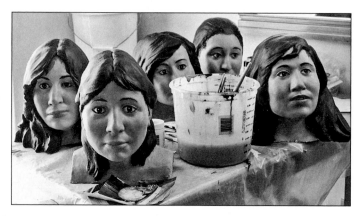

The five heads, painted. Two of them were identified after Frank left Mexico.
© *Frank Bender*

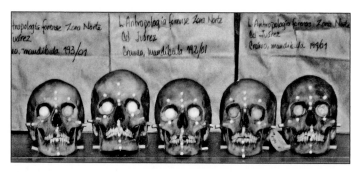

The second set of five skulls, lined up on a chest in Frank's hotel room. Two would eventually be removed because of a lack of money and confusion over which skeletons they came from. © *Frank Bender*

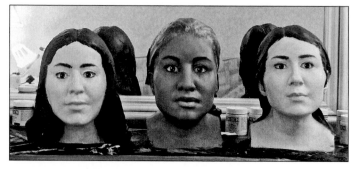

One of the busts, which Frank finished in twelve days, would be identified within several months. © *Frank Bender*

No. He had to focus on the main issue. He was helping the Mexicans get publicity, and all publicity was good. If it weren't for newspapers and television showing his busts to the world, Anna Duval and Linda Keyes and Rosella Atkinson would be in a potter's field, and Robert Nauss and John List probably wouldn't be behind bars. Yes, publicity was good.

Once the rubber coating had dried, he took the bust of the Girl from Chihuahua to the tub and slathered plaster on it with his hands. Waiting for the plaster to dry, which would create a mother mold, he made several calls to America. He tried *20/20, 48 Hours, America's Most Wanted,* and CNN, all of which had made shows about him in the past. He knew they were always interested in a new case because they regularly phoned to find out if he had another Rosella Atkinson or anyone else who'd make a good story.

Frank briefly explained what he was doing in Juárez, but each producer gave him the same answer: Juárez had been done, and they didn't need an update.

Finally, Frank tried Ed Barnes, a journalist at Fox International in New York. They had known each other for many years, and although Barnes had wanted to do a story on Frank in the past, it had never worked out.

"Let me run this by my people," Barnes said. "I'll call you back."

Barnes liked the idea. Not only was Juárez one of the biggest unsolved murder cases in the Western Hemisphere, but Frank could get him access to the police and the government. Barnes had worked in enough third-world countries and had dealt with enough corrupt policemen to know what that meant. Having Frank on his side would be invaluable.

Before Frank went to bed that night, the mother mold was ready.

He pulled it apart, lined it with the rubber sheeting, tied the two sides together, poured plaster through the neck opening and into the inverted mold, and left it to dry overnight. By morning the Girl from Chihuahua would be ready for painting.

Day 13

Shortly after Frank called Esparza to tell him that the Girl from Chihuahua was finished, three policemen arrived at his room to take her away.

## NO GUNS ALLOWED

Ed Barnes arrived in Juárez the following day.

A wiry man in his fifties with gray hair, a trimmed beard, and an infectious smile, Barnes had been a newspaper reporter for many years. He had covered organized crime in the 1980s before becoming a war correspondent for *Time* and *Life*. His most recent assignment had been in Iraq, where he had been stationed since the overthrow of Saddam Hussein.

Barnes and Frank met that night at El Acueducto, where they ordered drinks.

"I've got three days," Barnes said. "Then I have to get back to

New York and head off to Russia. Think I can do a story in three days?"

"Sure," Frank said. He was excited that Barnes had come down so soon. "They [the Mexicans] told me you can go anywhere you want—the police station, the laboratory, to meet the coroner, Dr. Sánchez. You can talk to Manuel Esparza. He's a great guy."

Barnes liked the idea of open doors, but he was immediately suspicious. "There's no such thing as a free ride," he told Frank. Most of the stories about Juárez that he'd read before coming down had dealt with the drug traffickers and the killings relating to the drug cartel. "I read that at least five journalists have been killed because of the cartel. Other people too. There are still people being shot in the street."

"Yes," Frank said. He got daily updates from Jan, who faxed him articles about Mexico that she found on the Internet. "But the police really want to solve the murders of the women. They've had Bob Ressler down here, now me. And Manuel's really helpful."

Barnes thought that Frank was overplaying his role and sounded like a publicity machine for the state of Chihuahua. He told him so. "Whose side are you on, anyway?" he asked.

They laughed and then ordered another round of margaritas.

"You'll see," Frank said.

The next morning Frank introduced Barnes to Esparza, and they sat by the hotel pool. Barnes asked questions about the *feminicidios,* but Esparza said he should put them to the attorney general. Esparza would organize an interview.

The three of them went off to meet the coroner and to visit the former police academy. When Barnes asked to see any evidence that had been found with the murdered women, he was shocked. The evidence room was not only poorly maintained—it was hard to tell what article of clothing went with which body—but the lock on the door was so flimsy it could be kicked open. He had enough years covering the crime beat to know something was wrong.

"It looks like a piece of shit," he whispered to Frank. "Are they even interested in finding a killer?"

|||||||||||||||||||||||||||||||||||||||||||||||||||||||||||

An interview with Attorney General Solís later that afternoon was canceled. As an alternative, Esparza offered to take Barnes on a tour of Juárez, and Frank joined them. They drove through the old section of town and then headed to some of the industrial parks, where groups of women were coming off of the early-morning shift.

"You know," Barnes said, looking out the window at the bad roads, "except for the traffic flow and the lights, Juárez reminds me of Kinshasa."

The comment wasn't a good sign. Barnes was growing irritated with driving around and not meeting anyone in government. When they reached the last factory of the day, the sun was already setting. The previous time Frank had been there was during the day. The place seemed even eerier in the dark, somewhere he wouldn't want to walk alone.

"They should put in some lights," Frank said, and immediately felt stupid for saying it. He had to keep reminding himself that this wasn't his country.

"Maybe the women go into the cars of their own accord," Esparza said. "Maybe they aren't kidnapped. At least not to start with."

They drove down Lerdo, one of the main streets near the Rio Grande, and famous for all its *quinceañeros,* shops selling party dresses. They passed several bars on seedier streets like Mariscal and Juárez, and then stopped at one called Lucy's. Frank and Barnes hesitated before going in. What would have been an everyday act for them back home was suddenly clouded in suspicion. This was the very kind of place where the girls were said to be taken before being killed. A large sign outside announced that guns weren't allowed: NO SE PERMITE PISTOLAS.

The men were frisked before entering the bar, which was large and poorly lit, with dark walls, colored lights, and plain tables—not the welcoming kind of place you'd want to hang around for long. At the counter stood a few women whom Esparza called *ficheras,* whose company could be bought for a few drinks.

Outside, half a dozen prostitutes leaned against the walls. They weren't attractive, but they smelled so just-bathed clean that the aroma enveloped the men as they walked past. Frank tried to ignore the smell, looking at them in the same way he did every Mexican woman—as a potential victim. It could just as easily be their skulls in his hotel room.

Esparza told them that even though prostitution was dangerous, it was worth it. The women could earn a hundred dollars a night, while in the *maquilas* they took home maybe thirty dollars a week.

In the El Acueducto bar that evening, Barnes expressed his growing annoyance. The attorney general was giving him the runaround. He had canceled a second interview, scheduled for the following morning. Frank went up to Esparza, who was getting drinks at the bar.

"Doesn't the attorney general realize that this makes him look bad? I thought you wanted publicity in America. This isn't how you get it."

"I know. I'll call him again."

Before Esparza left, an interview had been arranged for the next day, but it was with the attorney general's deputy, Oscar Valadez.

||||||||||||||||||||||||||||||||||||||||||||||||||||

The room felt odd without the Girl from Chihuahua, as if one of the girls had gotten off the bus and her friends who were left behind were suddenly quiet.

Barnes shot some footage of Frank working. Frank walked around the table, considering what he had done so far. Each girl seemed to have an innocence. Or was he just imagining it? They didn't look like the *ficheras* and the prostitutes he'd seen at Lucy's, a possibility the authorities kept suggesting. They didn't look hard at all. Or was he just creating them that way?

To him they were four young women who felt good about themselves. The Girl Without a Lower Jaw was more of a loner than the others, more caught up in her own thoughts, more private, not as outgoing. The Girl with the Crooked Nose was warm and friendly, and she made you smile when she was around. The other two he was still getting to know.

||||||||||||||||||||||||||||||||||||||||||||||||||||

In bed he read Jan's latest fax, which had been put under his door. She wrote something to him almost every day. She told him about what she was doing, about the woman at work who was always arguing with her, about the cats Boy and Guy.

After he turned out the light, his eyes drifted to the heads in the darkness. He was caught by the way the second girl looked up—inquisitive, dreamy—while the girl to her left smiled tentatively. He

wondered if he hadn't distorted them by putting too strong an emo-
tion on each face. Variation was important, he was convinced, but
exaggerating something on a bust could be its downfall.

## "WE'LL TALK ABOUT THIS IN THE MORNING"

### Day 16

The first interview Barnes had the next day was with Steven
Slater. It still wasn't clear to Frank how the American fit into the
investigation. Not once had he seen him at the Fiscalía Mixta office.

Slater, who had previously worked as a security adviser to the
attorney general and, before that, in Las Vegas casinos, was over-
weight and glib. Barnes disliked the American, and very little came
out of the interview until the very end, when Slater made an unusually candid confession: If it hadn't been for Amnesty International
constantly harassing the government to do something about the
*feminicidios,* he said, they never would have brought in outside investigators like Ressler or Frank.

The admission confirmed what Amnesty had been saying all
along—that the Chihuahua government and the police didn't care
about the murders and that they had brought in international help
simply to reduce the pressure. Frank and Ressler were mere window
dressing—and now, by implication, so was Barnes.

The two men drove back to the Lucerna in silence. Later that morning Barnes had an interview with the assistant attorney general, and when he got back to the hotel, he and Frank met up in El Acueducto. After they each ordered a beer, Barnes said what they were both thinking.

"It doesn't take an expert to see that something's not right. I thought it would be great coming down here and having access to the cops through you. But whenever I'm with them, it's like we're in this cocoon. My gut is telling me that."

The interview with Slater was the turning point. Until then it was as if the two men had agreed to avoid discussing the problems and questions cropping up daily.

Frank knew that Barnes was right. He had tried to stay faithful to the police, not only because they had given him the five heads but also because he liked Esparza. Yet there were too many things that didn't make sense. In two weeks he'd picked up or overheard bits of information—maybe things he wasn't meant to hear, from the UN team or even from Esparza—about the police burning evidence, losing evidence, mixing up DNA samples, torturing suspects in the former police academy. Things in Mexico, he had suspected for quite a while, were very wrong.

"The murders seem too organized," Frank said. "When I saw all the crosses together that first time and realized that it meant the bodies were found together—when I heard that all the bodies were decomposed and skeletonized before they were found—I knew something was up.

"There's too much order and structure here. How come someone wouldn't stumble on those bodies when they were fresh? I figure it's probably because the police were keeping them away until the bodies had rotted. Maybe the cops, without even knowing it, were told to keep people away from the railway tracks and the desert area. How else would all those bodies get there and not be found for so long?"

"Frank," Barnes said, smiling slyly, "you don't sound like their publicist anymore. Maybe you should join Amnesty."

Frank didn't laugh. "I'm just trying to get these women identified."

Ever since Anna Duval, putting a name on a victim had always been the point of making faces. Sure, there was also the thrill of getting an ID, solving a puzzle, maybe even finding a murderer. In Juárez, there was all that, of course, but the stakes were much higher. Not only was he working outside the United States for the first time, but he had five shots at helping to solve one of the most shocking crimes in the world.

"Have they told you what they're going to use your busts for?" Barnes put it to him. "Have you even asked them? Are they going to put up flyers of them at the bus stops and ask people whether they have seen these women?"

Frank didn't know. He assumed it would be the same as in America. "They haven't told me."

"Maybe they won't," Barnes suggested. "Maybe what Slater said is true—that you're just being used."

"You too," Frank countered.

Barnes downed the rest of his beer. He was surprised by the turn of events in Juárez, but he also wasn't. Mexico was bringing back memories of something he'd witnessed in America in the 1970s, when he took a year off journalism to work as a special agent dealing with organized crime in New York.

"That experience taught me that corruption is everywhere and that no cops want to look into the lives of powerful people," he told Frank. "Today that's what the evidence room at the academy told me again. It seems like an investigation designed to fail—or at least never to succeed." He set his empty glass down on the table and stood up. "I've heard enough of the government's side of things. I want to speak to some of the murdered women's families now."

Barnes was meant to leave the following day. It was his birthday, his first in North America in seven years—he'd been in Peshawar the previous year, and Nigeria before that—and he had wanted to spend it with his family. But now all that had changed.

"I think I'm going to stay a few days extra," he said.

He found a waiter at the hotel named Carlos who was prepared to go with him to see some of the families of murdered girls and to be his translator. They arranged to go out to the barrios that afternoon.

⁌⁌⁌⁌⁌⁌⁌⁌⁌⁌⁌⁌⁌⁌⁌⁌⁌⁌⁌⁌⁌⁌⁌⁌⁌⁌⁌⁌⁌⁌⁌⁌⁌⁌⁌⁌⁌⁌⁌⁌⁌⁌

Frank returned to his room, but he couldn't work. Slater's words kept bothering him. He felt duped.

When Esparza came by that evening, Frank told him what Slater had said. He had been honest with the Mexican until now, and he didn't see any reason to change.

"It makes me feel a bit stupid," he said.

"What did Barnes say about it?" Esparza asked.

"He's angry. He feels we're being used. He wants to interview some of the families now."

Esparza immediately got agitated. Frank thought it was because of what Slater had said about Amnesty, but he was wrong.

"Why is he talking to the families?" Esparza asked.

Frank didn't understand. "He's a journalist. That's what he does."

"But that's not why we brought him down here."

"What do you mean?" Frank asked. "I thought you brought him down here to publicize the murders."

Esparza looked angry and began fidgeting with his keys. "We'll talk about this in the morning," he said, and left.

# THE BEST MARGARITAS IN MEXICO

### Day 17

Frank went downstairs to the lobby with Esparza. Several people from the attorney general's office were waiting for them, including the assistant attorney general, Oscar Valadez; the comptroller from Chihuahua City; another prosecutor; and the tall woman from Esparza's office, Angie.

Barnes joined them after a few minutes, and they all went into the hotel restaurant. As soon as two tables had been moved together to accommodate the group, they sat down, and a waiter took their orders for drinks.

Esparza was talking to the prosecutor and the comptroller in Spanish, and Frank could tell it was about the Slater interview. He heard him mention Barnes and how he wanted to interview the murdered women's families. The two men kept motioning to Valadez. "Tell him," they said. "Tell him."

When Esparza finally did, Valadez listened intently, his head nodding slowly as he took in what Esparza was saying.

Frank and Barnes were lighting up cigars they had bought at Sanborns when the assistant attorney general stood up and slammed his hands down on the table. Everyone stopped talking. Valadez said something in Spanish to Esparza, who turned to the two Americans.

"He has a suggestion," Esparza said. "He would like to take you to another restaurant, the governor's favorite."

Their drinks had arrived, and the waiters were about to take their orders for food. Frank and Barnes didn't understand what was going on, but they thought that, as the Mexicans' guests, they should follow the others. Without anyone paying for the drinks, they walked out of the hotel and drove several blocks to another restaurant.

By the time they got there, the prosecutor had left. After they took their seats, one of the men from the attorney general's office said that Frank and Barnes must try the margaritas—they were the best in Mexico—so they each ordered one while the others had beers or sodas. Before the drinks arrived, the man who recommended the margaritas went up to have a word with the maître d'.

Frank had hardly drunk his margarita when he started to feel sick. He thought perhaps he was having a bad reaction to an appetizer he'd eaten at Esparza's suggestion, a cheese-stuffed pepper. He went to the men's room and tried to throw up, but he couldn't.

Back at the table, he started to feel drowsy. Angie rubbed his arm, trying to make him feel better. He nodded off in the middle of the meal and woke up a half hour later. Only then did he notice that Barnes didn't look too well, either. After the meal, both men had to be helped out to the car.

At the Lucerna, Barnes said he was going to take a nap and would meet Frank in El Acueducto at eight. If he wasn't there, Frank should call him first thing in the morning. No sooner had Frank gotten to his room than he threw up and immediately felt better. He put on jeans and a T-shirt and returned to the busts.

Over the last two days he had been refining the faces less and less and was spending more time on the hair. He had changed the hairstyle on the second girl twice, tucking it behind one ear, parting it in the middle, but then returned to what he'd originally done.

Just before eight that night, he went down to El Acueducto to meet Barnes, who wasn't there. After Frank had a glass of Calafia, he went back to his room and worked on the busts until one A.M.

It was especially in those late-night hours when his room seemed to take on a life of its own. He saw images everywhere—in the folds of the curtains, in the patterns of the tiles in the bathroom. The armoire became a giant building, large and square like a factory, a *maquila*. He found faces and noses and eyes in everything.

## Day 18

Five hours later, he woke up to work. As arranged, he put a call through to Barnes at eight A.M. but there was no reply. He went for a swim and then ate breakfast. Back in the room, he contemplated what he had done the previous night. He was happy with the second girl's hair.

He circled the busts, touching them up in small, almost

unnoticeable ways—a crease inside an eye, a wipe with a stick across a cheek, deepening the line between the lips, flattening the earlobe.

Glenn Miller played, then Mahler.

Frank did some sit-ups and crunches, took a fifteen-minute nap, then told the bodyguard that he was going for a swim but sneaked out to Sanborns. At eight P.M. he went down to El Acueducto, where Jackie was on duty.

"Where is your friend?" she asked him.

"Who?" Frank asked. He had totally forgotten about Barnes. The last time he had seen him was right after the lunch where they had gotten sick.

"The journalist," she reminded him.

"You haven't seen him today?" Frank asked.

She shook her head.

"Maybe he's out working."

Before Frank left the bar, he saw Carlos, the waiter who was meant to be translating for Barnes. Frank returned to his room and tried calling Barnes again, but there was no answer. When he went to bed at midnight, he knew that he was ready to make plaster molds of the four heads.

### Day 19

The next morning Frank called Barnes's room a third time. His friend answered, sounding groggy.

"Where were you yesterday?" Frank asked. "I never saw you."

"What do you mean?" Barnes said.

"I never saw you yesterday."

There was a silence on the other end.

"Jesus. I think I've been asleep since I last saw you."

That meant he had been in bed for more than twenty-four hours. Barnes groaned. "Those were some margaritas!"

When they met for breakfast, Frank told Barnes that he was convinced they had been drugged. The journalist laughed.

"Think about it," Frank continued. "You can normally drink anyone under the table, even a cop, yet one margarita puts you out for an entire day? Impossible."

Going over the events at the restaurant, they realized there were plenty of signs that should have made them suspicious. The assistant attorney general's violent reaction to the disclosures about Slater and Barnes. The rapid, unexplained change of restaurants. The unexplained disappearance of the prosecutor. The mysterious man's recommendation to drink margaritas, followed by his chat with the maître d'.

"It could have been a message," Frank said.

Barnes agreed. If the Mexicans were scared of the victims' families implicating the police, maybe they wanted to stop Barnes from seeing and interviewing them. Which is exactly what they had achieved. They knew he was scheduled to leave that day and wouldn't be able to do any more interviews if he could somehow be kept out of the way.

Quickly downing his coffee, Barnes got up from his chair. "I've got to go interview some people."

Barnes left the Lucerna with Carlos the waiter. They first visited a woman who kept records of all the murdered women in Juárez, then they saw a representative of Amnesty. Using several names he'd been given—always just a name, and always a relative of a murder victim but never an address, because Anapra was not a place of addresses, and people were too suspicious to give him details—Barnes and Carlos drove into the labyrinthine shantytown.

Most people were scared to talk to him or even to give them directions. At first Barnes thought it might be a generic fear of strangers, something he'd seen before in third-world countries. Then he realized it might be a fear of reprisals, a reaction he'd become acquainted with while covering the Mafia.

The families who talked to him believed that the police were fabricating killers, such as the Egyptian Sharif and the two bus drivers, and that they had no intention of finding the real murderers. Some thought that the police themselves were the killers.

Barnes met the mothers of two of the murdered girls. One said that her daughter had disappeared the day before she was supposed to start a new job. She had left the house to buy something at the store and had run into the police, who had taken her away—all of this witnessed by a friend—and then her body had been found later on.

The second woman said that right after she had reported her daughter missing to the police, she had been stabbed. It was a warning not to take the case any further.

When Barnes got back to the hotel that night, he told Frank he needed another day to wrap things up. Frank was going to miss him. He didn't know whom he could believe or trust anymore.

After Barnes left the room, Frank took one last look at the clay busts and then signed his name on the back of each girl's shoulder.

# IN BIG TROUBLE

### Day 20

Early the next morning, his birthday, Barnes drove off with Carlos to do one last interview. An hour later, there was a knock at Frank's door. It was Esparza. "I need to talk to you," he said.

"I'll meet you downstairs later," Frank replied. He had in his hands one of the rubber molds and was holding it as gently as if it were a piece of diaphanous material. "I'm in the middle of something."

Esparza nodded and left. Frank went back to the bathroom. He had barely slept the previous night. After signing his name on the busts, he had started the molds. Into each clay bust he pushed an aluminum shim, which went over the top of the head, behind the ears, and down to the shoulders, resembling, once in place, an over-size Elizabethan collar.

He shellacked the clay surfaces to make them stronger, and over that he sprayed a releasing agent, Pol-Ease 2300. The synthetic rubber solution, which was applied next, came in two components, both in five-gallon containers. He mixed batches on the table, painting the backs of the heads first, until the coating was a quarter inch thick and looked like the opaque frosting on a cake.

As he waited for the rubber to dry, he lined the bathtub with trash bags and began mixing the plaster. The kind he had bought in El Paso was FGR95—gypsum reinforced with fiberglass—which took slightly longer to dry, about an hour, but was also stronger.

Wearing latex gloves, Frank took a bucket of plaster into the room and slathered it on top of the rubber coating. Once it had dried, he removed the shims and then laid each head's plaster side on the table, repeating the rubber-coating process on the front. Keeping the head faceup helped to avoid air bubbles, allowing the rubber to penetrate the inner parts of the nose and ears.

It was two A.M. by the time he'd finished putting the plaster on the fronts of the busts and left them to dry. The city was almost silent by then, except for the occasional sound of a car revving its engine or a siren. Several hours later, when Frank awoke, he pried apart the four mother molds with a screwdriver. Separating the two sides was difficult, no matter how many times he had done it before. In Philadelphia, Joan usually helped him. Straining his fingers and wrists, he soon broke into a sweat.

The pieces of plaster came off one at a time, and then he carefully tugged at the rubber inside. On two of the busts, the Girl Without a Lower Jaw in particular, pulling at the rubber distorted the clay underneath, even though there was releasing agent too. The distortion didn't matter, because he was finished with the clay now, and it was the rubber that held the imprint of the face.

Each sheet of rubber resembled a piece of thick plastic hide. Bits of clay stuck in most of the crevices, so Frank took the sheets to the bathtub to wash them with a nylon brush. It was then that Esparza had knocked at his door.

When the policeman left, Frank finished scrubbing, especially in the ears and the nasal areas. The dried rubber, which bore fingerprint-fine details of the clay bust, he gently laid inside the two portions of the mother mold, finally binding them back together with a luggage strap.

In the bathtub and on the bathroom floor, he had arranged four empty barrels. Into each one he placed a strapped mother mold, the neck opening facing upward. After each one was secure, he filled the mold to the brim with plaster. Then he washed himself, changed his T-shirt and jeans, and went down to the lobby.

Before Esparza even opened his mouth, Frank could tell that things between them had changed. It wasn't like his first two weeks at the Lucerna, when they had met to drink Calafia, talk about the day's events, and share a cheese platter.

"You guys are in big trouble," Esparza said.

Frank wasn't surprised, especially after the last three days.

"The attorney general wants to know where Barnes is. He knows that you know. And that's why he sent me over. I don't like getting in the middle of this, but he's really mad. And he's mad at you because you got Barnes down here."

Frank interrupted him. "You guys asked me to get some media down here to show that you're doing something on the murdered women. And that's what I did."

"Yes," said Esparza, "but Barnes has been talking to Amnesty and to some of the murdered women's mothers, and the attorney general does not want that."

"As I said before, that's his job," Frank said.

"Where is Barnes now?" Esparza asked.

Frank didn't know.

"A group of congressmen is visiting from the United States, and they heard that Barnes was here and went to see some of the families. And that you went with them."

Frank had seen in the paper that a seven-member American group led by Hilda Solis, a Democrat from California, had been in Chihuahua talking to laborers and activists, and had visited the cotton field.

"We thought you were on our side," Esparza continued.

Frank's first impulse was to defend himself. "You know I didn't go with Barnes. I was here at the hotel the whole of yesterday."

Esparza nodded. "I know you were here. But people are very angry with Barnes. They want him brought in for questioning." He said the police had put out an all-points bulletin for the journalist.

"That's crazy," Frank said. "They want to arrest him? But why?"

"They just want to talk to him."

One by one, Frank began splitting open the molds. He was glad that the work was mechanical now, because he found it hard to concentrate. His mind kept returning to the events of the previous forty-eight hours.

He had been pushing away little suspicions even before the incident with the margaritas. But now that he had decided to openly question the investigation, he had less and less faith in the team, in Esparza, and in his own effectiveness.

Almost from the very start, he had seen things that bothered him. The way Esparza was constantly interrupted by the attorney general, which meant he couldn't do his job properly. How Esparza called Amnesty "the enemy." How he never saw Slater participate in the investigation. Then there was also the deplorable headquarters of the Fiscalía Mixta, where nothing ever seemed to happen. And the lack of evidence, which, in any event, was usually mixed up. And the secrecy about the Girl from Chihuahua. Now there was the threat to arrest Barnes.

The thoughts swirled around in his head and confused him. He wanted to call Jan, to reassure himself somehow. Instead, he read her last fax, in which she talked about going to see a movie and visiting Vanessa in New York. Their granddaughter, Claire, had celebrated her third birthday, and they'd eaten cake. Thinking about his life in Philadelphia was easier than thinking about Mexico.

Frank went to the bathroom and took the fourth and last mother mold out of its bucket. He cracked it open and pulled off the plaster and the rubber lining. Each time he opened a casing, revealing the final sculpture, it was like seeing the girl for the first time as she emerged in white plaster. With the four busts lined up on the table, he went to bed.

He drifted in and out of sleep, dreaming about driving through the industrial zones, the cotton field, the barrios, and into the factory buildings. But the people in the dreams weren't Mexican; they were all characters from David Lynch's surreal, nightmarish movie *Eraserhead*. The white busts shone alabaster-like in the light coming through the window. The sight of them made him feel better.

## SEX

### Day 21

After filling any airholes with plaster, Frank started smoothing down the final plaster casts, first with a metal file and then with sandpaper. All that he needed to do was paint them.

Taking a break, he slipped past the guard and went down to Sanborns for some coffee. As he sat in a booth, he watched a pretty young girl behind the counter, thinking how she probably would not be the killer's type. Too much lipstick, skirt too fashionable.

It surprised him how fast his time in Mexico had gone. In less than three weeks, he had almost finished. That meant it had taken him just over four days for each head.

Shortly after Frank got back to his room, Esparza came by and asked after Barnes again. Frank was prepared for him this time. He said he hadn't seen Barnes that morning. "I think he's left already."

"What do you mean?"

"I think he's gone to Russia. Remember, when he arrived he told us he was doing a story in Russia next."

"So he's not even here?"

"I don't think so."

Frank hoped that Esparza wouldn't ask at the reception desk when he left the hotel. As far as he knew, Barnes was still out interviewing people.

||||||||||||||||||||||||||||||||||||||||||||||||||

Steven Slater came by that evening. He was upbeat, sounding like he wanted to make peace. Frank wondered if the American had been reprimanded for his remark about Amnesty. He asked Frank if he wanted to go out with them and have some fun. "We'll take care of you," he said. "You want to get laid? I know where we can go. I know a lot of women here. We want to make sure you're happy while you're here."

Frank shook his head. "I really want to get these busts finished."

"Come on. We've got connections. You like young women? We can get you young women."

Frank declined again. When Slater and Damian left, he couldn't stop thinking about what Slater had just said. The American had offered him sex with the kind of girls who were being murdered, perhaps in the very kind of place where the killings happened. The only thing more despicable was that the offer had come from a man who was meant to be solving their murders.

Frank went down to El Acueducto. On the way he bumped into a policeman whom he had seen before, a large man who always shook Frank's hand whenever he saw him. Frank thought once again, as he had before, how easily the policeman's big hands would fit around a woman's neck.

Jackie the barmaid told him that Barnes had left a message to call his room. Barnes said he was leaving in the next hour.

"Be careful," Frank said. "They want to arrest you and beat the shit out of you."

Barnes didn't reply for a moment. "I'll call you from New York."

## BURNT SIENNA AND RAW UMBER

### Day 22

Out of the tenth and last of his barrels Frank took several paint-brushes, a thick palette of paper sheets, and two dozen tubes of Liquitex acrylic paint. He got a small pail of water from the bath-room and set it down on a corner of the table.

Without thinking, he squeezed a line of Turner's Yellow and Titanium White on the top sheet of the palette, added a dab of Burnt Orange, and mixed them together. Those colors normally created the flesh tone for a Caucasian person, but to allow for a darker Mexican skin, he added some Burnt Sienna and Burnt Umber to one side. Last came a touch of green, Raw Umber.

Starting on the Girl Without a Lower Jaw, he quickly covered the face and then the shoulders with broad strokes. The wet paint picked up the light from the lamps in the room, and there was a gloss on her upper cheeks, shoulders, and at her throat. In the hot weather, the paint dried fast.

From the hairline up, he left the bust white, focusing on the ears. He tilted the bust back with his left hand to paint under the chin, occasionally dipping his brush in the water and going back to the palette for more color, gently swirling the acrylic paint each time. At each touch of the brush, the Girl Without a Lower Jaw became more human. He dried excess water from the brush with a paper towel and dabbed again at the paint. He dipped the tip of the brush in the Raw Umber and ran it over the girl's lips.

Tearing off the used top sheet from the palette, he squeezed some more Burnt Umber on a clean sheet. With a thinner brush, he ran a quick line over the girl's eyebrows, not the final line, just a trace to give a statement to her face.

Next came the eyes. Onto the sheet he put dabs of Unbleached Titanium and Titanium White and the smallest bit of Indigo Orange Red. As with the skin, he wanted the eyes to have a base. In the very center of the irises he put a tiny white dot and then left the eyes, as though he'd forgotten them. He applied some Burnt Orange to the lips, as well as touches of orange and white to the cheeks, like a makeup artist. His movements became smaller, more controlled.

The expressions were already on their faces, but in plaster and hard to see—the slight smirk, the suggestion of a smile, the open mouth of surprise—but the paint was bringing them out. He used Burnt Umber on the hair. Halfway through painting the Girl with the Crooked Nose, he felt there was something wrong about her lips. He added tiny pieces of clay, pressed them into the plaster with his thumbs, until they were no more than light brown smudges.

Then he went back to painting her.


## Day 23

There was a forensics conference in El Paso, and Frank needed to get away from painting the busts for a few hours, so he asked Hector to drive him across the border.

One of the delegates was an attractive, well-dressed woman from

Mexico City. She told Frank she was involved in the investigation of the murdered women but didn't say how. Whenever he asked, she evaded the question. Her name was Claudia.

# CLAUDIA

### Day 24

He was sitting by himself in the Lucerna restaurant that night. The next moment Claudia was next to him. "Mind if I join you for a drink?"

She sat down and ordered a glass of wine. "What are you doing tomorrow?" she asked.

"I'm finishing off painting the busts. Why?"

"I'd like to get together with you and take you out."

Frank was curious about who she was exactly. Esparza knew about her; he said she had been hanging around the former police academy. But he didn't care for her. He thought she might be working for the federal government. "I don't know why she was sent here," he told Frank. "Stay away from her."

But Frank liked Claudia. "Sure," he replied. "I'll go out with you, but I can't stay long because of the heads."

Day 25

Claudia picked him up, and they went to Frida's, an upscale restaurant on Triunfo de la República that was painted pink. The back wall of the restaurant was full of reproductions of Frida Kahlo's work, and the waiter gave them menus done in the style of her paintings. All of a sudden, Claudia lifted hers in front of her face.

"Don't let that man see me with you," she said, nodding to someone walking out of the restaurant. It was dark indoors, even in the daytime, so it was unlikely the man would see them.

"Why not?" Frank asked.

"He's my boss."

Frank slipped out of the seat and went to the men's room. When he came back, the man was gone. "What was that all about?"

"It is nothing," she said. "He doesn't know I'm here."

Frank didn't know whether he cared for any more secrecy. At the same time, he found Claudia attractive and mysterious precisely because she said so little about herself. He ordered seafood; anything without cheese. She asked him lots of questions. She wanted to know about sculpting. And Philadelphia. And hadn't she read somewhere that he had worked for the FBI?

After an hour he needed to get back to the busts. It was an urge that had started coming over him almost from the first week. If he was away from the heads for too long, he got anxious. As the days progressed and he got closer to finishing, the feeling got more intense.

"I really have to go," he said.

"Can I come up and see your work?" she asked.

A week earlier, he never would have let a stranger into his room to see the heads. Now he didn't care who saw them. What did he have to lose?

"Sure," he said.

When they got to Frank's room, she walked around the table, not saying anything at first, evaluating the girls.

"You should make the eyes bigger," she said. "Mexican women have bigger eyes."

Frank didn't reply, but she was wrong. It wasn't the eyes that were big but what went on around them that made them *seem* big—the eyebrows, the darkness of the pupils. Some eyes just looked bigger. It was like someone who came into the room with a red handkerchief sticking out of his back pocket. You couldn't help notice it.

Before she left his room, Claudia asked Frank to write down his personal details for her. "We are going to have you down here again," she said.

"Who is 'we'?" he asked.

The secrecy again.

"I can't tell you any more right now. I will call you."

The next day Frank was in Esparza's office at the former police academy. Claudia was there, but Frank didn't want Esparza to see that they were friendly. At one point she walked over to a secretary near Frank to collect some papers. She looked at him knowingly. As she passed him again, he slipped her the piece of paper with his information on it, making sure no one saw him. She walked to another part of the office, and the next time he looked for her, she was gone. It was the last time they met.

Day 26

When Frank finished painting, he put the heads to one side and started cleaning up the room and packing away his tools and clay and plaster. He had already peeled the clay off the skulls, sometimes using nail polish remover to get off the tissue markers that stuck to the bone. The skulls were back in their original boxes. He put all the trash in the bags with which he'd lined the bathtub. When he'd finished, the room was spotless. No one ever would have guessed that a sculptor had been there.

That afternoon, a Wednesday, he got Hector to drive him across the border to El Paso, where he mailed his barrels back to Philadelphia. A Mexican border official took several hours to go through them. Near where they were parked was a final reminder to Frank of why he was here, a large pink cross.

Back at the hotel that night, the room strangely bare of his equipment, Frank had no music to play because he'd sent his CDs and Walkman home. All at once he found himself worrying about leaving Mexico.

Slater had told him—but now he thought it might have been a warning—that no one was allowed to take more than ten thousand dollars out of the country. That was exactly what Frank had been paid for his work, a fact that Slater knew.

"You will be arrested if you have more than that," he said.

Frank didn't want to take a chance. Too many things had gone wrong, and he felt he was being watched. He would take two precautions. Instead of leaving on the weekend, as planned, he would go right after the press conference on Friday. The border guards wouldn't be looking for him.

He also hid away his money. He covered the notes in plastic, wrapping them up very tightly, and put them inside a piece of clay that he shoved deep into his bag.

That night he'd intended to place the four busts in cardboard boxes, to get them ready for the press conference. Instead he left them out on the table. He was used to having them there with him.

## THE GIRL WITH THE CROOKED NOSE

Esparza kept looking at the bust. He went up and studied her face. "Is that girl's nose really crooked like that?"

"Yes," Frank said.

They had hardly spoken in the last few days, even when Frank had gone with Esparza to the former police academy the time he'd seen Claudia. But Esparza was fascinated by the bust of the Girl with the Crooked Nose, the same way he had been with the Girl from Chihuahua.

He explained why. Several months earlier, a mother had come to the police to report her daughter missing. She had given them a photograph, so Esparza knew what the girl looked like. They had taken DNA from one of the skeletons that might have been her, but it had come back inconclusive.

Frank instinctively thought of the messy evidence room. How effective could a DNA test be of any bones recovered from there?

Esparza carried on. "We put her skull with the others we gave to you. We thought we would start from scratch on her. We didn't realize that she had a crooked nose, because there was no face. But it's her."

## The Last Day

The press conference was held in a small room at the former police academy. Frank was dressed in slacks and a black shirt. He was pensive, not smiling.

There was a screen at the front of the room, and on the plain brown table in front of it, he and Esparza had set up the four heads and, alongside them, their respective skulls. From left to right was the Girl Without a Lower Jaw, the Serious Girl, the Girl with the Crooked Nose, and the Girl Looking Up.

Just after midday people started to arrive. There were journalists from local papers and the *El Paso Times*. Assistant Attorney General Oscar Valadez spoke, and so did Esparza, who introduced Frank. Looking at the audience, Frank saw something he hadn't noticed before. People were snickering when Valadez or Esparza talked, as if they didn't believe a word either man said.

Otherwise, at least for Frank, it was much like the first press conference three weeks earlier, at which he had stood behind four skulls, one whiter than the others and without a lower jaw. Back then he'd been full of excitement and expectation, and now he felt a sense of disappointment and resignation.

Someone asked if he believed the police were doing a good job. Not knowing what to say, Frank looked over at Esparza. There were so many things he could have said about what was going wrong with the investigation—indeed, whether there was an investigation at all. But he wanted to give the people hope, even if it was just to let some families get closure.

"Yes," he said finally. "I think the police are doing something. Bob Ressler and I were brought down. They are at least trying."

One of the reporters said it had been suggested that Frank actually received photographs of several women before he started the busts, so he would know what to sculpt. Frank shook his head in dismay. Never in twenty-five years had he been accused of that. Clearly, the people saw him as a police patsy. They were probably snickering at him too.

He looked at the faces in front of him, searching for three people in particular—a father, a mother, and their daughter. Earlier that morning, on Esparza's invitation, they had come in for a special viewing of the heads.

The father had plaster smears on his jeans and shoes, as if he had come directly from his job at a cement factory. Following him were the mother and daughter, who looked just like each other. They both had crooked noses.

After they arrived, Esparza took them into his office, where he had the four heads lined up on his desk. Frank stood in the hallway watching them, as Esparza had instructed him to do. Both women walked up to the bust of the Girl with the Crooked Nose, not even noticing the three other girls.

The mother touched the girl's hair, which Frank had left loose, half covering her face, as if she were trying to hide an abnormality. They told Esparza that their daughter's ears had stuck out a little, and that was why she had worn her hair that way. But they stopped short of saying it was their daughter. The mother brought her hand up to her chin, a mannerism that Frank imagined the Girl with the Crooked Nose might have had.

"You recognize any of these four heads?" Esparza asked them pointedly.

"No," the mother quickly replied. Then she added: "But if you say this one is our daughter, we want the body and we want to bury her."

At the press conference, Frank finally spotted the family standing close together, almost giving one another comfort. All three of them had their eyes fixed on the same head.

# THE FUGITIVES

# CARRYING A GUN

<u>1986</u>

Frank walked to the courthouse at 601 Market Street one morning in early August. Two men led him to a back entrance, through a door that needed a code number punched in, and up to the sixth floor.

In a spacious room on the western side of the building sat a group of a dozen men with their jackets off, ties loose, pistols in their belts. It was the office of the U.S. Marshals, Eastern District of Pennsylvania.

The head of the group was a burly, friendly man named Tom Rapone, whom Frank had met through Fillinger. When two of Rapone's deputies had suggested that they use Frank on one of their cases, Rapone asked him to come in and give a presentation.

Until then Frank had worked only with the police and had sculpted only the dead. Much as he wanted to team up with other law-enforcement agencies, he'd had no luck. Jan's letters to the FBI, the CIA, and Interpol had brought him little response and no work.

Frank was convinced that if anyone would contact him, it would be the FBI. Krogman and Angel both worked with the agency, and Frank had visited its training academy in Quantico, Virginia, with his friend Don Cahill, a detective in Prince William County who was friendly with some of the agents.

Cahill, who had seen Frank's work and was sure he could be an asset, warned him that it wouldn't be easy selling his craft to the FBI. The agency could be "bureaucratic, one-way, uncooperative, and full of red tape." As they drove to Quantico, they once again discussed an idea they'd come up with to make Frank more attractive—the possibility of catching Carlos the Jackal.

The Venezuelan-born revolutionary had disappeared in 1976, and his ability to slip past the law had been highly publicized. Cahill was convinced that Frank could help capture Carlos by doing some composite sketches of how he might look numerous years after last being seen, and then doing a bust of him.

But the FBI wasn't interested. They had just invested in a new computer system for making three-dimensional scans of skulls and heads, and they believed that would gradually phase out the need for human artists.

The U.S. Marshals, meanwhile, couldn't have been more different in their approach. Frank felt it almost from the moment Rapone invited him down to 601 Market Street. In any case, he had been told that the deputies were more relaxed, open to suggestions, and weren't hamstrung by rules or supervisors. They were the anti-FBI.

It didn't bother them that they had never used someone like Frank, but there was still a problem to overcome: Frank had never done the kind of work the U.S. Marshals wanted him for. Everyone knew that he could put faces on the dead, but could he put one on a fugitive?

‖‖‖‖‖‖‖‖‖‖‖‖‖‖‖‖‖‖‖‖‖‖‖‖‖‖‖‖‖‖‖‖‖‖‖‖‖‖‖‖‖‖‖‖‖‖‖‖‖‖

Hans Vorhauer was one of the most wanted criminals in America. A known producer of bombs and methamphetamine, he was also suspected of being a contract killer, although it had never been proved. In 1972 he was sent to the State Correctional Institution at Graterford, the largest maximum-security prison in Pennsylvania, to serve several consecutive sentences for burglary, larceny, conspiracy, and armed robbery.

By the early 1980s, he had been assigned to work in the prison's carpentry shop. There he met an inmate named Robert Nauss, who had been convicted of murder, and the two hatched a plan to escape. An acquaintance on the outside ordered an armoire, in the base of which the two men built a hollow big enough to hide. If someone noticed the cavity, they didn't say anything. And just in case anyone questioned its cumbersome weight, they had stained the lightweight pine to look like oak. On November 17, 1983, the piece of furniture was transported out of the grounds, and with it Vorhauer and Nauss. After that they disappeared.

Three years later, Rapone took a special interest in the case. He had at one time been the warden of Graterford and knew both men. A task force was put together of sixteen people—U.S. Marshals, state troopers, policemen, and members of the district attorney's office—who were all deputized.

The most obvious of the two fugitives to pursue first was Vorhauer. Word on the street was that he'd been seen in Philadelphia, where his wife lived. Besides Phyllis Vorhauer, who worked at a local hospital, the deputies tailed some of Vorhauer's former associates.

The task force had a limited amount of time and money to find

Vorhauer, and no sooner had they begun than they realized they had a major problem. No one really knew who they were looking for.

Their last photograph of Vorhauer had been taken about fifteen years earlier, at the time of his incarceration. He was also known to be a master of disguises and used lots of aliases. For one of his robberies, he had posed as a policeman and probably would have gotten away with it if someone hadn't noticed that he had put on his sergeant stripes upside down, the German way (his father had been a member of the S.S. in Nazi Germany).

When Frank came down to the U.S. Marshals' office, he knew that he would be creating a bust not of the dead but of the living. Rapone didn't need him to imagine what Vorhauer's face might have looked like many years earlier but what it might have become.

|||||||||||||||||||||||||||||||||||||||||||||||||||||||||||||||

After giving a slide show of his usual suspects—Anna Duval, the Girl from North Leithgow Street, and Linda Keyes—Frank was taken around the marshals' office. At one point the deputies showed him photographs that they had taken during their stakeouts, more to explain what they did than because they expected him to find something. But he did.

From the pile Frank pulled out a photograph of a man with a brown beard and glasses standing outside a row house. Then he looked up at the two WANTED posters on the wall. One was of Nauss—in his thirties, long hair, a straggly beard. The other was of Vorhauer—fortyish, clean-shaven, with short light hair.

"That's your man," he said, looking at the clean-shaven man and then pointing at the bearded stranger outside the row house. "That's Vorhauer."

A deputy called Rapone over. "Hey, boss, he says this is our guy."

Rapone believed Frank. "He's been right under our noses!" Without a further thought, he asked Frank if he could start drawing them some sketches of Vorhauer right away. "We also have to get you deputized so that you can go around with us and learn how to shoot," he said. "We need your eyes with us."

"I know how to shoot," Frank said. "Been going to the range since I was a kid."

"Well, that won't take long, then."

Back at the studio, Frank put aside the head he was working on—a young man whose skeleton had been found in a cornfield outside Lancaster—and started sketching Vorhauer. Using two old photographs the marshals had given him, he did several drawings in charcoal and a few others with pastels.

Vorhauer's face was pitted with acne scars, although it was his eyes that Frank found himself drawn to. They were piercing and had a squint. Rapone told him they were icy blue, the coldest eyes he'd ever seen. "He's also got a laugh that makes the hair stand up on the back of your neck."

Frank's first sketches were photocopied and handed out to the deputies. Because Vorhauer was known to be a chameleon, they needed other incarnations of him—with and without a mustache, wearing a baseball cap, behind the window in a car, in the sun, in the shadows. The limitations of the drawings were obvious. Unlike a bust, two-dimensional images couldn't be rotated or looked at from different angles.

Within the first week Frank developed a friendship with one of the deputies, Paul Schneider, and started driving around with him. A bulldog of a man, Schneider was a detective from Upper Darby who treated all his cases with an intense tenacity. He hated to let anything go unsolved.

One day they headed out to Sixty-ninth Street, where someone resembling Vorhauer had been spotted. Frank asked Schneider whether he had pursued other fugitives. Schneider said he had.

"Do they all disguise themselves so carefully?"

The cop shook his head. "Sometimes they don't change anything about themselves. They're too vain, or they stick with a successful formula. They think it's lucky, or that it's because of their look that they haven't been caught. But Vorhauer—he changes all the time."

They reached Kensington and Allegheny avenues, an intersection from which a well-known gang in the 1960s had taken its name. Frank had even come across some of its members during his clubbing days with Jan at the Paris and the Randolph. But like North Leithgow Street, the area had changed dramatically in two decades. While the K&A Gang had a reputation for being local Robin Hoods who stole from the rich, the crime was now bigger and more violent, with Philadelphia becoming the methamphetamine center of America. And Vorhauer was known to be a producer of the drug.

Schneider parked on a corner and watched as cars pulled up. The driver sometimes got out and went to talk to someone else in a parked vehicle, both of them trying overly hard not to seem suspicious. At the same time, Frank could feel that he and Schneider were being looked at too, even though their car was unmarked. But the deputy wasn't bothered. He sat back and waited.

"You got to do what they don't expect you to do," he told Frank. "Throw out the line and wait for them to grab the bait."

That night several of the marshals masqueraded as sanitation workers to collect Phyllis Vorhauer's trash, which they sifted through for evidence. Frank rode next to the driver, with a sawed-off shotgun under the floor mat. The second night they went out, the truck got stuck turning a corner in the alley behind the house, and as Frank tried to direct the driver out of the jam, he was sure he saw curtains shifting in a window of the Vorhauer house.

By the third week Frank had done about fifteen sketches of Vorhauer and was refining the bust. In between, he carried on driving around with Schneider and even joined him on a visit to his friend Penny Wright, a psychic.

After the two men sat down with Wright, who was almost totally blind, she asked several questions and then told them three things about the case. One, a wife and husband were involved. Two, the person they were after would be captured in a place with a large pillar. And three, the suspect they apprehended after this one would have a bad stomach.

The final prediction put Schneider in especially high spirits, because he was sure she must mean Vorhauer's partner, Robert Nauss, who had been wounded in the stomach before being jailed.

Frank continued sketching Vorhauer, even if only to make a slight change to the wrinkles around his face or to his hairstyle. On learning that Vorhauer hung out at bars frequented by gays and transsexuals, where he looked for people to work for him, Frank guessed that the fugitive would take on some of their characteristics. In his very last drawing, he showed Vorhauer with hair that was closely cropped and bleached blond.

In early September the marshals' persistent tailing of Phyllis Vorhauer paid off. One morning, she didn't follow her normal route home from the hospital. She made countless turns and U-turns and went up side streets, clearly suspicious that she was being followed. Stopping outside a diner on Penrose Avenue, she went in. When she came out, she went not back to her car but into a Quality Inn across the street.

The deputies watched the hotel through the night, and once they were pretty sure that Vorhauer was also there, they called for backup. He had been caught in a similar situation once before and had shot his way out of it, and they didn't want that to happen again.

At ten A.M. the next morning, Vorhauer and his wife walked out of the hotel and were immediately surrounded by U.S. Marshals. Only as they were all driving out of the parking lot to leave did Schneider notice something for the first time—the Quality Inn was shaped like a pillar, just as Penny Wright had predicted.

Frank was working on Vorhauer's bust when Rapone called to tell him that the fugitive had been caught. He asked Frank to come down to 601 Market Street.

"I want you to be the one to take Vorhauer's photograph for them to use in the *Daily News* tomorrow," he said.

When Frank got to the marshals' office, Vorhauer didn't look at him once, not even while he was being photographed. Up close, Frank could see that his eyes were truly icy blue. His latest hairstyle, though, was totally new—it was cut very short and bleached blond.

# THE MAN IN THE CORNFIELD

That evening, after a short celebration at 601 Market Street, Paul Schneider was heading home when he made a detour to the studio.

"Great work, Frank."

"You too. You're the best cop I know."

Schneider smiled. "Says who? The visual detective?"

That was his nickname for Frank. They both laughed.

"Want to get a beer?" Schneider asked.

"No, I'm finishing this head. I want to paint it tonight."

Schneider knew the head well by now. He had seen it progress from day to day for the past three weeks, because Frank worked on it between doing sketches and the bust of Vorhauer.

The skull, which belonged to a white man in his twenties, had been discovered by a farmer plowing his fields in Paradise, Pennsylvania, about five miles from Lancaster. Being buried in a field full of manure had given the skull an awful smell, and nothing that Frank did seemed to stop it. He even boiled it in bleach, Biz, and Axion, while Jan kept burning incense and spraying deodorant.

Frank put the cleaned skull on the roof, thinking that drying it out might help. When he went up to fetch it several days later, Tom Rapone and his deputy, Allen Kurtz, were standing at the bottom of the ladder. "What you got in the bucket?" Rapone asked.

"A head," Frank said.

Rapone bent over to look at it but instantly recoiled. The stench seemed to have gotten worse. Even after it was covered in clay, which usually sealed a skull, the odor seeped out.

Over the next three weeks, Schneider watched the skull go through its metamorphosis: from bone to clay bust to plaster mold. He'd only seen Frank sketch an age progression, and he was curious to see how he sculpted a face onto a dead man. When he came by after Vorhauer's arrest, the bust was in plaster but still unpainted. The way Frank saw him, the Man in the Cornfield was young and good-looking, with hair hanging down to his shoulders.

"Now that you've found Vorhauer," Frank said, "wouldn't it be great if you could find this guy too."

Schneider thought Frank was making fun of him. He knew nothing about the Lancaster case. Even though the body had been found in Pennsylvania, the man could have come from anywhere. Frank might as well have asked him to look for a needle in a haystack.

"You know nothing about him, right?" Schneider asked.

"Nope, nothing."

"With thousands of missing people in the country—and thousands more we probably don't even know about—you want me to find this guy?"

Frank smiled, his silver incisor shining. "If anyone can," he said, "you can."

Schneider left the studio to go home for the day but decided at the last minute to swing by his office in Upper Darby. Because of his work with the U.S. Marshals, he hadn't been to the police station in several weeks, and he wanted to pick up his mail.

As soon as he walked into the station, a colleague called him over. An informant had just told him about a guy named Edward Myers, who he claimed had been killed by a biker gang and then buried in the mountains. Schneider was known to be an expert on biker gangs, so his colleague showed him a flyer with a photograph of Myers. "This is the guy," he said. "You know him?"

Schneider took a quick look at the picture. "Yeah," he said. "I saw him about fifteen minutes ago."

His colleague thought he was making a joke. "You just saw him? But he's supposed to be dead."

"Well, I don't know if he's dead or not," Schneider continued, "but I just saw his bust in Frank Bender's studio."

"What kind of drugs you on?"

"I'm telling you," Schneider said. "Bender did a facial reconstruction, and it's your guy. I'll call him."

Once Schneider had Frank on the phone, he told him he was sure he had found the victim. Schneider had been gone from the studio for less than an hour.

"What do you mean?" Frank asked.

"The guy in the cornfield."

Frank was quiet for a few moments. "You're kidding, right?"

"Nope," Schneider said. "I'm coming down to you with the flyer."

Back at the studio, Schneider showed Frank the photograph of Myers, and they held it up against the bust. The only thing wrong with the reconstruction was the hairstyle—it was shorter in the photograph.

When the teeth of the skull were compared to Myers's dental charts, the police knew they had him identified.

"I knew that you could do it," Frank told Schneider the day they drove the skull to the funeral home where the rest of Myers's body was lying, waiting to be buried.

The skull had started smelling again as soon as Frank had peeled the clay off of it, and the odor permeated the car. When they reached the funeral home, the man in charge said the rest of the skeleton stank so much that they had put loads of charcoal in the casket to try to stop the smell. "But it didn't help," he said. "We've never had a body like this one."

## SCRAPPLE

The quick capture of Vorhauer fired up the marshals. They were eager to make as swift an arrest of the man he'd escaped from Graterford Prison with—Robert Nauss.

Going after Vorhauer first had been a tactical decision, but Nauss was equally dangerous and ruthless. Originally from a well-to-do family, he had fallen in with the Warlocks, a biker gang involved in drugs and prostitution, and soon became one of its leaders. He was eventually tried for the murder of his girlfriend, Elizabeth Lande.

When Nauss went on trial, it came out that he had killed Lande in 1971 after she threatened to leave him. He strung her body up in his garage and even showed it to several people. One of them helped him bury her, although Nauss, fearing that his accomplice might tell on him, apparently went back to the burial place on his own, dug up the body, and cut it into pieces that he buried in different places.

Lande's body was never located, but Nauss was found guilty anyway, which made him the first person in Pennsylvania history to be sentenced for a murder with no eyewitness or body. Also convicted on counts of robbery, rape, extortion, and drug trafficking, he was sentenced to life imprisonment.

Tom Rapone wanted Frank to do not sketches this time but a sculpture. It had been four years since the two men escaped from prison in the pine armoire, and the last photograph of Nauss, which was also used in his WANTED poster, had been taken at the time of his incarceration, in 1977. The ten-year-old photograph showed the typical biker, with shoulder-length hair and a scraggly beard. Nauss was five feet nine and had brown eyes. At the time of the escape, he was thirty-five and weighed 190 pounds. He had several tattoos, most notably a large blue parrot on his upper right arm, as well as a girl and a swastika on his left forearm, and farther up the same arm, a skull and dagger with the phrase BORN TO LOSE.

Frank drove around with Paul Schneider for several days to try and learn something about bikers. Schneider was an expert on the Warlocks and the Pagans, which was why he had originally joined the task force.

Law enforcement had been cracking down on biker gangs since the 1970s, and many of their leaders had been jailed. Delaware County, lying between Philadelphia and Chester counties on the border of Delaware, was not only home to the Pagans' governing body, the Mother Club, but was also one of the last holdouts of the biker gangs in the country.

One day Frank went with Schneider to a White Tower hamburger joint off of I-95, where the bikers often hung out. A dozen motorcycles were parked outside when they pulled up, and Schneider got out to question some of the bikers. Frank, who seldom felt intimidated by anyone, grew uncomfortable as he stood alongside the cop. Three of the bikers wore bandannas, and all four had beards and tattoos.

Wanting to capture as many details of the men as possible, Frank went back to the car and did some quick sketches—the men on their bikes, drinking coffee, standing in small groups—constantly aware of them watching him from behind their sunglasses.

||||||||||||||||||||||||||||||||||||||||||||||||||||||||||

Frank never underestimated the significance of pure luck and good fortune. He only had to think, most recently, of how Paul Schneider had been shown a flyer of Edward Myers barely thirty minutes after seeing a bust of the Man in the Cornfield. Or how he himself, instead of starting the sculpture of Nauss, had gone to an annual conference of the American Academy of Forensic Sciences. If he hadn't, he never would have bumped into Richard Walter.

The conference was taking place in Philadelphia, at the Ben Franklin Hotel. Frank wasn't a big fan of the academy, and with good reason. According to its rules, he could address delegates, but, not being a college graduate, he couldn't become a member. He nevertheless liked going to any function where he could meet other forensic experts and talk about cases they were working on. You never knew what leads and ideas might come up.

And Frank was desperately in need of an idea. Creating Nauss's face was proving to be more guesswork than he'd anticipated. With Vorhauer, things had been a lot simpler. He'd joined the investigation when it was already in full swing, and was able to get away with doing sketches that he constantly updated as information came in. The bust of Vorhauer, though Frank finished it later on, hadn't figured in the case at all.

But with Nauss, the investigation was brand-new, there were no leads, and the marshals were waiting for his age-progression bust to let them know whom they should be looking for. The sketches of

Vorhauer had shown the fugitive in many possible guises, but the bust of Nauss would be a one-off.

All that Frank had to go on were some ten-year-old photographs. On a facial reconstruction, he would have had the skull as well as the critical input of forensic anthropologists and dentists and pathologists. But on a live person who hadn't been seen in years? Besides the normal signs of aging, he needed to know things about the fugitive that might have altered his appearance. Was he a poor eater? Did he exercise? Did he worry? Was there anyone, Frank wondered, who could tell him how Nauss might have changed in appearance?

To clear his head and maybe get some new perspective on the case, he went to the conference at the Ben Franklin. During a break, he was sitting in the hotel coffee shop with Betty Pat Gatliff, the forensic sculptor from Oklahoma whom he had come to know through their common pursuit and Krogman. She was telling him about a case from Florida she was working on where the victim's entire upper jaw and part of the nasal aperture were missing. Suddenly she broke off as a tall, thin, hawk-faced man walked by.

"Oh," she said, "I must introduce you to my friend Richard Walter."

Walter was a clinical psychologist who worked with the Department of Corrections in the largest indoor prison in the world, in Michigan. His patients were hard-bitten criminals, rapists, and murderers, a fact that he seemed to relish. A droll man with a sharp sense of humor and a precise way of talking, Walter did not suffer fools easily. Taking one look at Frank, who was dressed in jeans and a T-shirt when most of the other delegates were in suits and ties, he saw an easy target. But when Frank himself laughed at the snide remarks, Walter was caught off guard.

Frank, meanwhile, was making his own appraisal. He listened to Walter's low voice and studied pronunciation, and noticed the way he chain-smoked and his eyebrows went up at the sides when he talked. Whenever Walter made a deduction, which he did often, he prefaced it with the words "as a consequence, then" or "hence, then," making it sound like one word—"hencethen." To Frank, Walter was just so bizarre-looking, he had to be good at what he did.

"Why don't you join us?" Frank said, pulling out a chair.

The two men couldn't have been more different—one had completed only high school, was an artist and very sensual, had a cheerful disposition, and worried about his body; the other was an academic, a loner, and a cynic, and he chain-smoked. But they got along almost at once, and from that moment on Frank became the one person to call Walter by the unlikely-sounding nickname for someone so serious and sardonic—Rich.

Lighting up a cigarette, Walter told them that he was busy putting together a profile of Jack the Ripper for the hundredth anniversary of his killing spree. Frank, in turn, explained how he'd gotten involved with the Vorhauer and Nauss investigations.

Walter took short, deep drags of his cigarette as Frank told them about Nauss killing Lande, showing off the body, hiding it, and then cutting it up. Walter said it sounded like a power-assertive murder, and that he often dealt with bikers like Nauss at the prison where he worked.

"With someone like him," he carried on, "there's machismo, aggression, and an exaggerated sense of importance. Hencethen, he's probably very concerned about image. And it seems like he was desperately afraid of being seen as a pervert in any way. He was also probably very homophobic."

Frank was intrigued. He had never met anyone like Walter, some-one who could get into a killer's mind. He wanted Walter to share his theories with the U.S. Marshals.

"Maybe we can work together on this case, Rich," he said.

Walter wasn't sure if Frank was serious, but early the next morn-ing he got a call to tell him that Tom Rapone had agreed to a meet-ing. A few hours later, the three men met for breakfast at a diner in the city.

"You must try the scrapple," Frank said. "It's a Philadelphia tradition."

"What's that?" Walter said.

"Meat," Frank answered cryptically, his silver tooth shining.

Scrapple, a local dish made of minced scraps from the butcher that could include offal, was the last thing Frank could imagine Walter eating, but the prankster in him couldn't help playing a joke on the somber newcomer. When the order arrived, Walter took one look at it, pushed it away, and lit up a cigarette. Frank burst out laughing.

"This guy Nauss is bright," Walter began, often using the present tense, as if the fugitive were right there in the room with them. "He sees himself as better than the rabble, but he uses the rabble to get where he wants to be. He wanted to be a Mob guy."

After listening to Walter, Rapone said they should go down to 601 Market Street. There he introduced Walter to several deputies.

"Listen up," he called out.

As the men gathered around, Walter repeated his thoughts. On being shown some old photographs of Nauss, he noticed that the biker never wore a symmetrical-patterned shirt but one that was striped on one side and plain on the other. Like much of what Walter said, it could mean a lot or very little. But it was a possible clue that hadn't been there before.

Walter made several predictions. First, Nauss would return to the kind of middle-class lifestyle that he'd led when he was younger. Second, he would be clean-cut and would have a job. Third, he would live in suburbia.

"I think he'd have put on more muscle," he added to Frank, "and try to become a he-man."

Frank was surprised not only at the extent of Walter's predictions but at their precision. "You seem pretty sure about all this," he said.

"I've never been wrong since 1944," Walter replied.

Frank was curious. "What happened in 1944, Rich?"

"That's the year I was born."

|||||||||||||||||||||||||||||||||||||||||||||||||||||

When Frank finally got down to sculpting Nauss, he was equipped with not only what he'd learned from Walter but what he'd figured out during the pursuit of Vorhauer. Because finishing the earlier bust had been less important than finishing the sketches, he'd had time to make up some rules for sculpting an age progression. In a way, Vorhauer was to fugitives what Anna Duval had been to murder victims—a test cast.

After enlarging several photographs of the biker to life-size, he laid clear acetate paper over Nauss's face and traced it with waterproof black paint. As he added clay to the twisted aluminum sculpting armature, he kept comparing it to the tracings. He thought of them as X-rays. No matter how much the flesh over Nauss's skull might have changed, there were things about his head that would stay immutable. The nose could get bigger, the jowls could sag, the cheeks could inflate or collapse, but the bones underneath didn't. The width between the eyes stayed the same, as did the nasal aperture, the jaws.

During this time, the U.S. Marshals received a call from a man in Washington, D.C., named John Walsh. A businessman whose son had been kidnapped and murdered in 1981, Walsh had become a crusader for justice and, with his wife, had created the Center for Missing and Exploited Children in 1984.

Walsh had been approached by the newly established Fox television network to create three pilot shows for a program that was to be called *America's Most Wanted*. Fox had started broadcasting only in early 1986 and still reached less than a third of the households that could get the major networks.

The producers wanted to shoot something about Nauss, and the marshals quickly agreed. Not having much of a budget, *AMW* asked if the marshals could help with the reenactment. Several of the deputies, including Paul Schneider, played themselves and used their own cars.

As part of the segment, *AMW* also wanted to air Frank's bust. He was even asked if he too didn't want to play a role in the reenactment, although when they told him whom he'd be playing, he wasn't sure he should have accepted. It was Vorhauer.

"But I look nothing like him," he argued, pointing out that he had close-cropped hair and a goatee, while Vorhauer had thick hair and a pockmarked, clean-shaven face.

"You've got the same blue eyes," he was told. "That's good enough."

Frank finished the bust of Nauss in three weeks. Some of the deputies were taken aback when they saw it, in part because it was the first depiction of Nauss he had done for them. With Vorhauer, they had received a series of updated sketches almost daily. Now they had a single version of Nauss set in plaster.

The sculpture looked nothing like the man in the WANTED poster on the wall of 601 Market Street. Going on his own feelings and Richard Walter's profile, he had cut off Nauss's hair, shaved his beard, thickened his neck, and given him a plaid shirt. Instead of a murderous biker, Frank had created someone suburban and homely.

"But he is so different," Rapone said.

"You asked me what I think he'll look like, and this is it."

## THE SEVENTH BODY

The excitement that had built up around Vorhauer's capture and then carried on throughout the filming of the television segment about Nauss quickly died off. *AMW* was only going on the air in early 1988, which was still several months away, and the marshals had no substantial leads to follow up.

With the Nauss investigation running out of steam, the deputies started drifting back to their units. In the end there were just two of them left, one of whom was Paul Schneider, who didn't want to give up. He was the biker expert who had helped launch the investigation, but he couldn't justify staying on.

"We've got other cases calling us," he told Frank. "You can only do ones that are hot and ready to fly. And we don't have any latest tips here."

A few days later, he headed back to his police unit in Upper Darby.

||||||||||||||||||||||||||||||||||||||||||||||||||||||

With the fugitive work over, Frank got back to his photographic career, which he knew he had been neglecting. But he couldn't help it—playing detective was a lot more fun.

He had also been so busy riding around with Schneider, staking out Phyllis Vorhauer's house, acting in the *AMW* segment, sculpting Nauss, he had barely taken notice of a fact that once would have thrilled him. A number of his sculptures of murder victims had gotten quick IDs.

Yvonne Davi, or the Girl from Croydon/Bensalem, was followed by Diane Lewis, whose strangled decomposed body was found in North Huntingdon, Pennsylvania, in early 1987. David Lewis and his wife saw a flyer of Frank's bust in the Imperial Bar in McKeesport, about ten miles away from their home, and he was struck by the resemblance to his daughter. She was identified less than a day before she was to be buried as an unknown. Lewis, who was known for soliciting and running away from home, had left her family's McKeesport home in October 1986 and hadn't been seen again.

The next ID was of Valerie Jamison. In the summer of 1987, police went to an apartment in North Philadelphia that had recently been lived in by a twenty-eight-year-old named Harrison "Marty" Graham. A foul odor had been coming from the apartment for some time, and when the landlord went in, he traced it to a bedroom whose door was nailed shut. Looking through the keyhole, he saw a pair of woman's legs on the bed. The police broke into the room, which was covered in trash, and found a bloated body on the bed, another on a mattress next to the bed, and more decomposing humans underneath.

Altogether there were six bodies in the apartment, and a seventh was later found on the roof of a nearby house. One of the first people at the scene was the medical examiner's investigator Gene Suplee, who had investigated another serial killer in Philadelphia a few months earlier. Gary Heidnik had kidnapped and murdered several women.

"Heidnik went for the mentally challenged," Suplee told Frank, "Graham for the drug-challenged. He would take them up to his fleabag apartment, do what he wanted, have sex, and strangle them. He lived in a cesspool. We were in back of the building, and there were needles and syringes piled up several inches. I'd never seen anything like it."

Within hours of the bodies being found, all but one of them had been identified. Frank's bust of her was photographed and appeared in *The Philadelphia Inquirer* on November 10, 1987, thirteen weeks after she was found. He had given her short hair and slightly pursed lips, and he had put an earring found at the scene in her right ear.

A woman who saw the photographs was convinced it was her friend Valerie Jamison, whose family had recently reported her missing. Several people who knew Jamison said the bust looked nothing like her. But the tentative ID was enough.

The only available X-rays of Jamison were of her chest and lower back, which normally wouldn't have told them much. But the medical examiner noticed that one of her bottom ribs was shorter and fatter than on the other side. Victim number seven had the same abnormality.

In the same month, Robert Davis and his children identified the Girl in the Steamer Trunk as Aliyah Davis.

## ALLIE BOY'S BLUE LIP

The man on the phone identified himself as Bob Leschorn. He was a chief inspector with the U.S. Marshals and worked out of their headquarters in McLean, Virginia.

"I have heard of your work, Frank," he said. "And we need your help again."

Frank couldn't hide his excitement at hooking up with the marshals once more. As much as he liked working with Fillinger and the guys at the medical examiner's office, he never was allowed to get too involved in their investigations. On the Valerie Jamison case, he hadn't even seen the apartment where she'd been found. But the deputies took him on stakeouts, required him to carry a gun, taught him things about their detective work.

"I'll do anything to help," he said.

"My assistant will bring you to me," Leschorn said. Then he added, "And Frank, I'd like you not to mention this to anyone."

Several days later two deputies, Tom Conti and Steve Quinn, picked up Frank and drove him to the Philadelphia airport. Leschorn had intentionally not provided his flight details, just an estimated time of arrival, and the three men ended up waiting for him for several hours.

As Conti scanned the passengers, Frank spent the time trying to learn more about the case. But the two men were giving away nothing. Frank didn't mind, because it heightened the sense of cloak-and-dagger.

When Leschorn arrived, he greeted them, and they walked over to an airport restaurant and took a corner table in the back. Leschorn quickly got to the point. The fugitive they were after was Alphonse "Allie Boy" Persico, an underboss of the Colombo crime family who had served sixteen years in Sing Sing, a maximum-security prison in Ossining, New York, for second-degree murder. He had skipped bail of $250,000 in 1979 and hadn't been seen in eight years.

The FBI had been handling the case until recently. Unsure whether Persico was still in the country or even if he was alive, they handed his file over to the U.S. Marshals, who were better at dealing with fugitives.

The marshals had since learned that Persico was not only alive but quite possibly living in Florida or Connecticut, two states where organized crime was known to stash any of its people on the run.

Leschorn pulled out two three-by-five photographs of Persico that had been taken about twelve years earlier, one a full face, the other a profile. As with Vorhauer and Nauss, no newer photographs had been taken of him in prison. Frank noticed a bluish mark on Persico's lower lip and a pockmarked texture to part of his face.

"What happened there?" he asked.

"Someone threw acid at him when he was in Sing Sing," Leschorn replied. He asked if Frank could do a fully painted bust in ten days, and hardly waited for an answer. "We're spending a lot of money on this operation and need to act quickly."

Once again, he impressed upon Frank the secrecy of the project. Even among the marshals, no one was allowed to say Persico's name—they used a code word for him instead. Subpoenas were worded so broadly that he couldn't be identified.

"We don't want the police to know, or the FBI. Don't even mention it to deputy marshals who have nothing to do with the case. No one."

A waitress came up and asked if they needed anything else. The men went quiet all of a sudden, which made her suspicious. "What are you up to back here, anyway?" she asked.

Leschorn smiled. "We're tracking down a fugitive."

She laughed uncertainly and then moved on to the next table.

Frank went down to 601 Market Street to gather more information about Persico, although he was always careful to speak to only Quinn or Conti.

He learned that Persico liked good clothes, drank just one brand of Scotch, and ate certain kinds of food because of a bad stomach, which probably would have made him lose weight. Unable to ask Richard Walter if he had any thoughts about Persico, Frank had to go on that scant information.

If there were any visitors to the studio besides Quinn and Conti, he made sure to hide the bust. At the time he was hosting a Tuesday-night drawing class, where about eight people—including Berny Brownstein, who had an advertising agency, and the children's book illustrator Charles Santore—chipped in for a model to come pose for them. Instead of canceling the Tuesday session, Frank put Persico in the basement.

Jan and Vanessa saw the bust of the man with the badly textured skin but knew better than to ask Frank who it was. His habit of being secretive about his cases made them less inquisitive about this one. As for Joan, who was coming by more often to do his books, Frank made sure to hide it from her with trash bags.

"Who's that?" she asked, pointing to the hidden sculpture. "Fugitive or murder victim?"

"Oh, it's just clay," Frank said. "I'm keeping it wet."

Joan still didn't know that he used only oil-based clay that didn't need to constantly be kept moist.

Before completing the bust, Frank was asked to bring photographs of it down to 601 Market Street, where Quinn would show them to someone in the witness protection program who knew Persico.

After giving Quinn the photographs, Frank waited outside his office for forty-five minutes. He never saw anyone enter or leave except for several deputies. When Quinn came out, he was smiling. The bust was obviously going in the right direction.

On the eighth day, Frank had to show the bust to U.S. Marshals in New York City, where the Persico operation had its headquarters. He caught the train to Penn Station, carrying the bust in a special fiberglass-and-steel box that he had made especially for his heads.

The meeting with the marshals was quick, and they informed Frank they were happy with the bust. Refined but still in clay, it depicted an older, thinner Persico, respectable and perhaps even dapper.

When Frank told the marshals that he would be catching the train back to Philadelphia, they stopped him. It would be preferable if he flew back, they said. They didn't want to take any chances. Two deputies took him to the airport and led him through security, so he didn't have to open the box with the bust. Before putting him on the plane, the deputies got permission from the pilot for the box to come on board unopened and to be strapped in the seat next to Frank. In doing so, ironically, they attracted exactly the kind of attention they were trying to avoid.

Once the mold of Persico was painted, Frank took a series of photographs from all sides, with and without a mustache/glasses/baseball cap, as well as with different shirts of his own or that he'd bought from the Salvation Army.

Two deputies from New York picked up the bust and the photographs, copies of which were made and turned into a booklet that was handed out to everyone involved in the case. One of the deputies, Arthur Roderick, had already made plenty of headway. Going through thousands of licenses at the department of motor vehicles in Connecticut, he checked them for any males of similar height and weight to Persico, a similar birth date (one that Persico could easily remember), and surnames ending in a vowel. The number was narrowed down to 150.

One of those people lived at a small apartment complex in Hartford. Roderick showed the landlady some of the photographs, and she immediately recognized the bust. It was one of her tenants who called himself Al Longo.

Several deputies went up to Longo's apartment and knocked on the door. The person who answered was Persico. Roderick was shocked by his appearance. He had lost weight, his hair was a different color, and he had a mustache. He looked only slightly like the man on the WANTED poster, but very much like the bust.

Persico, who had been cooking a spaghetti dinner, accompanied the marshals without any argument.

||||||||||||||||||||||||||||||||||||||||||||||||||||||

Sitting at Day by Day several weeks later, Frank was having lunch with Bill Fleischer. Finally able to talk about the Persico case, Frank was explaining how he had to work from twelve-year-old photographs and only a few facts, such as Persico having a bad stomach, when he suddenly stopped. "Jesus," he said. "Penny Wright. That's exactly what she said would happen."

Fleischer had no idea what he was talking about.

Frank explained that Wright was a psychic whom Paul Schneider sometimes used. While they were pursuing Vorhauer, she had predicted that the next fugitive they would catch would have stomach problems. At the time Frank and Schneider had thought it would be Nauss. But it was Persico.

# THE MASTOID PROCESS

On Valentine's Day, 1988, *AMW* aired its segment on Robert Nauss. The episode was meant to have been the first of three that had been made, but when the producers learned that one of the other fugitives they had profiled was possibly in the Washington area, where *AMW*'s offices were based, that got priority.

Schneider called up Frank after the Nauss show. "I wish they could air it over and over again," he said. "That's the way to catch him, to get your bust as much exposure as possible."

He was right, but it would take two more airings and two more years for Nauss to turn up.

The lack of a capture didn't keep *AMW* from using age-progression sculptures again. In the early spring of 1989 a producer at the show, Michael Linder, contacted Frank about doing a bust that *AMW* would personally commission. When Frank heard the name of the fugitive—John Emil List—it immediately rang a bell.

Five years earlier, a detective friend had told Frank about a case—a brutal family murder—that had stumped the state police in New Jersey, as well as the FBI, for thirteen years. "I bet you could make a bust of the killer," he said, giving Frank the WANTED flyer of the man. "I'd like to introduce you to the captain in charge of the case."

The introduction never happened, but Frank took the WANTED flyer and stuck it on a wall of his studio. The flyer eventually got lost behind a myriad of postcards of naked girls on the beach at Saint-Tropez, photographs of body parts, and a newspaper ad for *A Nightmare on Elm Street*.

The case nevertheless lingered in the minds of law-enforcement officials, as *AMW*'s Linder found out. Several months before calling Frank, he had addressed the Eastern Armed Robbery Conference, where he was approached by a number of New Jersey policemen who asked if *AMW* could try to help find out where List was hiding. His disappearance had become both a legend and an irritation to police all along the East Coast.

The case sounded too big for *AMW,* and Linder had serious doubts about solving it, but the policemen kept encouraging him to reconsider. In spite of his deep reservations, he agreed to take it on. The show, which had gained popularity since the Nauss segment aired, was now being shown across America and was in the country's Top 50.

"Our ratings are up, and we can afford to take a chance," Linder told Frank. "We can help catch him."

"Well," Frank said, feeling cocky after the recent identification of Allie Boy Persico, "I can certainly show you what List looks like. But whether you catch him is another story."

"That's good enough for me," Linder replied.

Frank's success rate with fugitives was good—two out of three—so he was eager to take on another one. Because this one was for *AMW,* it meant that the U.S. Marshals wouldn't be directly involved. But he was sure he would come in contact with them or the FBI. He also liked the possibility of another quick ID, something he seemed to get more frequently with fugitives than with murder victims.

"What background have you got on List?" Frank asked Linder. "Give me everything you have. Photos, psychological profile, whatever."

Linder hesitated. "Well, I don't have much—several old photos and some newspaper articles. There's no psychological profile."

The photographs of List were front views only, and there was nothing taken from the side.

"I'll work with what you've got," Frank said, then looked at Linder through his eyebrows. "I like challenges."

In November 1971 John List murdered his wife, three teenage children—a daughter and two sons—and his eighty-five-year-old mother in Westfield, New Jersey. Neighbors assumed that the family was on vacation, since they saw no one going in or out and the lights in the eighteen-room Victorian house had been left on, although after a month they started burning out.

When the police came to check, they got through an unlatched window and discovered List's wife and children laid out on sleeping bags in the ballroom. The bloodstains showed that they had been dragged from other parts of the house. List's mother was found in the attic, where she had a room. All of them had been shot in the head, except the older son, who had numerous wounds in his face and chest.

Things had not been going well for the forty-six-year-old List for some time before he disappeared. A committed churchgoer, he believed that his family was slipping morally. His wife had stopped attending church with him, and his daughter was going to parties and smoking. He had also lost his job, although he never told anyone. Instead of going to work every day, he headed off to the park. He started collecting guns and hatching a plan to get rid of his family.

While his children were at school one day, he shot his wife at the kitchen table, then went to the attic and shot his mother. She was too large to bring downstairs, so he put her in a cupboard. He took his wife's body into the ballroom. He shot his children as they came home, first the younger boy and then the girl, both with just a few bullets. The older boy he shot ten times. He lined them up next to one another, covered their faces, left behind the guns he'd used, and wrote a letter to the pastor of his Lutheran church asking for forgiveness.

"This was too much," he wrote. ". . . At least I'm certain that all have gone to heaven now. It may seem cowardly to have always shot from behind but I didn't want any of them to know even at the last second that I had to do this to them. PS. Mother is in the hallway in the attic, third floor. She was too heavy to move. John."

List's car was found at JFK Airport in New York. It was thought that he might have killed himself, which often happens in family murders, but his body was never found.

||||||||||||||||||||||||||||||||||||||||||||||||||||

Almost eighteen years had passed since List's disappearance. If he were still alive, he would be sixty-four.

The photos of List that Frank received from *AMW* included the one used in the WANTED flyer on his wall. Frank remembered the man in it well: tie and jacket, straitlaced, thinning hair, glasses—in short, a neat, boring banker.

More so than with any other fugitive he had done, Frank wanted to find out as much as he could about List. Unlike Vorhauer, Nauss, and Persico, who were professional criminals, List was a man more like himself. But his being so low-profile also meant there was a lot less information to go on.

Frank spent a few days walking around the town of Westfield, and on Sundays he started attending church. He looked at what the men were wearing, how they reacted to their wives. Did they have eyewear, and if so, what kind? Which men were fleshier? How did they change as they got older? Did their eyes get baggy from age or weight or both? What about the curve of the mouth? Up or down? He stayed till the very end of each service, closely watching the men as they walked out.

List had undergone surgery on his mastoid process—the bony

protuberance behind the ear—so Frank contacted Scott Bartlett and Linton Whitaker, two first-class craniofacial surgeons at the University of Pennsylvania School of Medicine who had done extensive studies of facial aging.

Bartlett said that the surgery probably would have left a significant scar behind List's ear, although age and wrinkles could have made it less noticeable. After almost two decades, there would be significant changes to the eyelids, the brows, and soft tissue of the face. Bartlett also said there could have been changes to the bone. If List had lost many teeth, that would have shortened his face and, with the altered soft tissue, given him a very different look.

Frank guessed that List probably would have put on some weight because, even though he didn't smoke or drink and was an unexciting eater, he didn't exercise and was a meat-and-potatoes man.

Almost every day Frank called Richard Walter to exchange ideas. He had mentioned his criminologist friend to Linder, saying that if the FBI had no psychological profile on List, then Rich could do one for them. Linder agreed.

Walter came up to Philadelphia and stayed at a bed-and-breakfast next door to the meat market.

"I want to get in this man's shoes," Frank told him.

Walter asked for more details on the murder scene, facts that would have been in the papers but which Frank might have overlooked. How had the victims been shot? Had the bodies been moved, and if so, how? Walter classified the crime as an anger-retaliatory murder and said that List was the kind of man who went for stronger, older women whom he used to criticize himself so that he never had to accept responsibility for anything.

"It's always 'Oh, that bitch wife,' " he told Frank, once again mixing the present tense with the past. "These men can become quite pathological. In List's case, it seems he was also a snob. He was raised by a relatively strong mother. He feels part of the elite. He adopts a lifestyle bigger than he can afford.

"Hencethen, he becomes stuck in the mud. His gun collection increases, his isolation increases, he starts blaming his mother and wife for his ills. His children are starting to be successful, and he's somewhat jealous of that. His mother's in poor health, and he has access to her banking."

Walter was particularly interested in the fact that List had shot his older son so many times more than anyone else. "He showed his cold hard anger at the boy for having resisted. 'How dare you challenge me while I'm trying to kill you?' Then he eats lunch, cleans up, and naps. He lines up the bodies—a unique characteristic. People like him will not leave the bodies facing egress when they leave. They'll cover their faces. It was his accounting sense that drove him to line them up by age."

Walter was convinced that List had laid the blame for the killings on his victims. "He *had* to do it. He feels a great sense of relief after doing it. Then, an hour later, it'll be 'Oh, my wife is killed!' So he writes this note about how his daughter was becoming a sinner and he's sending them to heaven.

"He feels no guilt. He went to church, yes, but he was as Christian as I am Chinese. It's all bullshit. He has knowledge that he committed the murders, but they were justified. So what's the problem?"

Walter ended off, as he had with Nauss, by making several predictions. List would also backtrack. He would remarry, live in the suburbs, go to church, and be living less than three hundred miles from where the murders took place.

ɪɪɪɪɪɪɪɪɪɪɪɪɪɪɪɪɪɪɪɪɪɪɪɪɪɪɪɪɪɪɪɪɪɪɪɪɪɪɪɪɪɪɪɪɪɪɪɪɪ

The bust of List was the first one that Frank started moving around the meat market while he was still working on it. Instead of keeping it on his workbench, he transferred it to the front near the bay windows, went with it under the skylight, took it down to the pit. How would List change in different lighting and in the shadows? It was a crucial dimension of busts that sketches didn't have, much like a human being. A person seated at the counter of a dimly lit bar, for example, didn't look at all like the same person standing below a streetlamp. With a bust you could see those changes.

Relying on what he had learned from Walter and the two rhinoplasty doctors, Frank made List a man on whom life had taken its toll, even though the murderer didn't believe he was guilty of any crime. He would try to become a generic individual, not wanting to make any waves, yet he would want to remain intimidating enough that people didn't ask him questions about his past.

Frank made him not only older but fleshier, receded his hairline and made the hair thinner and grayer, gave his eyes more lines, pronounced his jowls, and imagined him paler. Instead of turning his lips up at the corners, as shown in the photographs, Frank turned them down. He sculpted on a shirt and a tie rather than put on real clothes, because he believed that particular uniform was an unchanging part of List's character. The neighbors had remarked that they never saw List without a tie, even when he mowed the lawn. Frank wanted that trait sealed in so that no one in the FBI or at the *AMW* studio could alter it.

Later that week Joan came around to help Frank make the mold. Ever since he'd sculpted the Girl with Hope the previous year, Joan had become more involved in the mold-making process. She was the only person besides Jan whom he felt comfortable having in the studio while he worked.

"What do you think of the lips?" he asked her, stepping away from the bust.

Lips were one of the first things Joan had asked him about. How did he determine how big or small they were, how narrow or fat? She knew that Frank worked less according to science than to art. He felt something was right or wrong even if the rules said otherwise. The Kollmann & Büchly charts were a guideline, and so was the rule about the eyes, but just a guideline.

As for the lips, he said, on a skull he could look at the depth of the gums—which often left a line on the teeth—and gauge them from that. But with a fugitive, lips were an estimation.

Looking at the bust of List, Joan thought the lips Frank had created worked with the rest of the image. After she had taken off her coat and put on an old T-shirt, she went down to the pit to get the two containers of rubber solution that they needed to mix.

Frank preferred latex, which he had used until Princess Doe, a teenage girl who was found beaten about the head and face with a blunt instrument in a cemetery in Blairsville, New Jersey. But latex was fragile, took a long time to dry, and required numerous coats, which could easily be ruined if one coat was applied before the previous one dried. When the price of latex went up in the 1980s, with the higher demand for condoms, Frank switched to synthetic rubber.

By that afternoon they were ready to crack open the plaster mother mold and remove the rubber coating the clay bust.

"Watch out when you take it off around the ears," Frank reminded Joan. "Also around List's mastoid scar and the jowls, where the detail is."

Once the plaster was poured into the mother mold and its rubber interior, all that remained to do besides paint the bust was to find the right pair of glasses. At an antiques store on Twenty-second Street that his friend Bill owned, Frank searched through a basket filled with glasses that had come from deceased estates. He wanted a pair that would give List an air of confidence and control, lending him an austere and authoritative facade that would intimidate people. But none of the glasses was right.

Frank asked Bill if he had any others.

"I've got three pairs of my own in the drawer here," he said.

One of them was just what Frank was looking for.

"Take them," Bill said. "I never wear them anyway."

<hr/>

*AMW* informed the FBI from early on that a bust of List was being done. Several agents visited the show every week, and even though the FBI wasn't directly involved, they asked Frank to let them see an early version of the bust.

On the way down to see the FBI in Washington, Frank was excited. It was the first meeting with him that they had requested. Ten years had passed since Jan had written to the agency, and it was five years since Frank and Don Cahill had visited Quantico with their plan of trying to catch Carlos the Jackal.

In Washington, Frank met with James O'Donnell, who worked in the division that handled computerized reconstructions, which the agency seemed to favor, and Richard Berry, who was head of the special projects unit. They were both unimpressed with what he'd done.

"I'm going to be honest with you," O'Donnell said. "We feel our computer is more accurate."

Frank looked at their image, which he thought lacked character and was almost cartoonlike. But he didn't say anything.

O'Donnell continued, "But we don't like to compete. We're not going to get in your way."

"If what you say makes sense," Frank said, "I'll think about it. Maybe I'll make the changes, maybe I won't."

Neither of them could specify what was wrong with the bust.

"Well," Frank said, "why don't we put both images on the show and let the end justify the means."

O'Donnell shook his head. "That's not the way we work."

The FBI contacted Linder about their reservations, but he said that the program would be aired only if Frank's bust was used.

|||||||||||||||||||||||||||||||||||||||||||||||||||||

The *AMW* episode about John Emil List was shown on May 21, 1989. An estimated fourteen million people tuned in, and more than three hundred calls came in from around the country. One of them was from a woman in Colorado who said the bust looked like her former neighbor Bob Clark, who had moved to Virginia.

The FBI followed up on the calls, and eleven days later, agents went to Clark's home, where his wife told them he was at the office. When the agents confronted Clark, he insisted they had the wrong man. But he had a mastoid scar and List's fingerprints.

List had remarried and worked as an accountant. He even regularly watched *AMW* but had missed most of the show that night because he'd been at church. Catching the tail end of the reenactment, he saw Frank's bust. Later on, he said he hadn't known there was technology to show how people would look when they aged.

The FBI told a Washington newspaper it was their computer-generated picture that had led to the arrest.

Frank immediately wanted to tell Walter the good news, but his friend was on a plane to Scotland.

"You were right, Rich," Frank said when he finally got Walter on the line. "List had remarried and was going to the Lutheran church again. And you know what? You said he'd live three hundred miles from where the murders took place. It was actually two hundred and forty miles."

# THE MEN WHO WOULD BE DETECTIVES

### Presidents' Day, 1990

To an outsider, the three of them must have looked like an odd trio. One of the men was dressed in jeans and a T-shirt; another had on a suit, his hair neatly swept back and his smile broad; and the third was emaciated and angular. One was an artist, one a customs agent and recently qualified polygraph expert, and one a criminal profiler.

As they took their seats at the Day by Day diner, you could almost guess what each of them would order from the menu. One looked like he ate sensibly, one enjoyed his food a bit too much, and the third didn't eat enough: Frank, Bill Fleischer, and Richard Walter.

Two of the men were members of the American Academy of

Forensic Sciences, although they had never met and were being introduced for the very first time by the one who wasn't an academy member. Walter was in town visiting, and Frank wanted him to meet Fleischer.

The men had barely ordered their food before they were talking about misdemeanors and murder. The subject today had come up many times before. Namely, why was solving a crime so hard, often unnecessarily so? For Frank, it all came down to egos. If more than one law-enforcement agency was involved in a case, that agency wanted the limelight at the end of an investigation. Individuals within the agencies did the same thing. Rather than disseminating what they knew, they hoarded it. Solving a case was no longer the primary goal.

Frank knew that he had been spoiled by the Philadelphia medical examiner's office, which worked closely with the police. It didn't matter who got the publicity at the end, so long as the victim was identified and the murderer found.

"It was great," Frank said, recalling his early days on Anna Duval and the Girl from North Leithgow Street. "The investigators shared information with the police, and it was like two investigations going on. But then there were cases like Princess Doe. It took so long to get anything done. I think there were detectives who screwed it up. We could have gotten her identified."

After Wendy brought them their food—a salade niçoise for Frank, a burger for Fleischer, and a coffee for Walter—Frank told them about his meeting with the FBI in Washington during the List case. Instead of offering help, the agents were antagonistic.

"I bet they even had a profile of List they didn't want to give me," Frank said.

As they began eating, it was quite obvious to them what the problem was—and the solution: people like themselves. Relaxing on their own at Day by Day, casually talking about a case, they could throw random thoughts at one another, no matter how different their backgrounds, and often come up with something totally new.

"We can put two and two together," Walter said, "and make the connections where they have always been but no one recognized them."

To make his point—a gory point, but no one seemed to mind mixing crime and cuisine—he told them about the Case of the Bloody Underwear.

A few years earlier, he had given a lecture to members of the Michigan police, one of whom talked to him afterward about an investigation that had them baffled. Several pairs of female panties had been found draped over the bushes in a park. They had been slit down the crotch, and it appeared as if the victim, or victims, had been wearing them at the time. There was also a teddy that had been gutted. Later, more slips were found, in the same condition and circumstances. All of them, plus the teddy, were inscribed with a letter J that had been written with a black Magic Marker. But no bodies ever turned up.

"He asked me what I thought," Walter continued. "I said maybe the bodies were in another location. They gave me pictures of the slips. One had been used as a jack-off rag. There wasn't much I could do with the information, but I thought I should keep it in my head."

A year later, he was at a conference in St. Louis. An FBI agent was talking to him about a case in Atlanta, more than five hundred miles away, where six women had been murdered and the killer had a slip fetish.

"I immediately said to him, 'What did the letter J mean?' He was stunned and asked me how I knew about that. After I told him, he said that J was the first letter of the killer's name. So it turned out that he had the bodies and someone else had the slips."

Walter paused to take a drag of his cigarette. "You see what sharing information can do."

Wendy was cleaning up the tables at the diner before closing up, and she told the men they'd have to leave soon. Walter stood up and got ready to go back to his hotel, but the other two stayed seated.

For some time now, Frank and Fleischer had been talking about the idea of creating a venue where people like themselves could meet, have lunch, and talk—not just about unsolved crimes but about anything—exactly the same way they did in the diner. They mentioned this to Walter, who thought they were crazy. "I don't organize anything," he said.

The men stood on the sidewalk outside the diner as night fell over the city and people headed down Sansom Street toward the subway. Fleischer offered to send out letters to two dozen people and ask if they were interested in the venture. There was a function room down in the Navy Yard where he worked that they could use for meetings.

"What are we going to call it?" Frank said.

The obvious choice was something like the Sherlock Holmes Club, but Fleischer had the name of another sleuth in mind: Eugène Vidocq. A Frenchman from the eighteenth century who had turned from a life of committing crimes—he'd been a thief, impostor, and murderer—to solving them, Vidocq had started the French Sûreté and, in some circles, was regarded as the world's first modern detective. He had become a friend of the writer Victor Hugo, whose character Jean Valjean bore more than a passing resemblance to

Vidocq, as did Auguste Dupin in Edgar Allan Poe's *The Murders in the Rue Morgue*.

A few weeks later, Fleischer contacted Frank and Walter to tell them that of the twenty-eight letters he'd sent out, only two people had declined. The first meeting of the Vidocq Society was about to take place.

## THE PARROT TATTOO

The capture of John List brought Frank more publicity than he'd ever had, and more forensic work.

*The New York Times* carried three photographs of List, one from 1971, one of Frank's bust, and one taken the day List was caught. The final two were almost identical, even down to the owlish-looking glasses he was wearing. *People* magazine carried a story on the arrest, and *The Philadelphia Inquirer* magazine, in a flattering article, described Frank as Mephistophelian. Betty Pat Gatliff wrote to congratulate him on his success. A staffer at *Time* magazine told him that during the week of List's capture, he was more famous than Ronald Reagan. The London paper *The Mail on Sunday* thought that if Frank could help catch a man who'd vanished for eighteen years, perhaps he could help them catch someone who had been missing for fifteen years, ever since allegedly murdering his children's nanny: Lord Lucan.

But perhaps the most unexpected attention Frank got was from the FBI. Despite their reservations about what he'd done with the bust of List, they called him in January 1990 and requested an age progression of Leo Joseph Koury, an underboss of a Lebanese crime family who had been on the run since 1979. Two months later, the FBI had Frank's bust, although how they used it didn't make sense to him. Several days before it was to be shown on *AMW*, a photograph of it appeared in *USA Today*.

"I wonder if that didn't alert Koury," Frank put it to Fleischer the next time they met for lunch at Seafood Unlimited, where they were talking about arrangements for the first meeting of the Vidocq Society. "Maybe he went into hiding when he saw it."

A few months later, Frank did his second commission for *AMW*, a woman named Florencia, or "Flo," Gooding, who was wanted in California and Connecticut for arson and attempted murder. The summer brought him more publicity, with the ID of the Girl with Hope, Rosella Atkinson, at the Mütter Museum.

In September Richard Walter invited Frank to talk at a forensics conference in Sydney, Australia, along with a criminal profiler from the FBI whom Frank knew about but had never met, Robert Ressler. Walter said it would be only the three of them speaking at the conference.

It was Frank's first long trip away from Jan. On the way there, he called her at every stop and told her how much he loved her. His calls didn't reflect what was happening at home—both of them knew that their marriage was on the rocks.

Frank was paying attention to his forensics career and the renown that came with it rather than to his photographic career. The sculpting jobs didn't bring in much money at all, and Jan was having to take on more jobs to make up for the shortfall. Something had to give.

|||||||||||||||||||||||||||||||||||||||||||||||||||||||||

The Australian conference lasted three days, but Frank lasted only one. He had warned Walter beforehand that he would make his speech, but then he was heading for the beach.

"It's just a bunch of fuddy-duddies at the conference," he said, never thinking of himself as one of them. He was happier with the cooler, hipper image of riding shotgun with the U.S. Marshals.

Down at Bondi Beach, he found a place to sit down, took off his shirt to get some sun, and then he watched the people. He greeted anyone who passed him—surfers, girls in bikinis, children, old women walking their dogs. They thought he was being friendly, which he was. Frank's best quality was his easygoing ability to talk to anyone, and people always left liking him.

But at the same time he was studying their faces, noticing how they were put together. He did the same thing at least once a day on South Street—drank his coffee on the bench outside the meat market and talked to passersby, examining the wide brow with the wide lips, the smile lines at the edge of the mouth and the eyes, the small nose that had obviously been worked on, the man with the feminine face. It was fun, but also it was work.

By the third day on Bondi, people were greeting him by name. They knew he was the guy from America who put faces on the dead. He was the man who'd helped catch John List. That afternoon he got back to the hotel room that he was sharing with Walter, and there was a message for him at the front desk.

"Your wife rang!!!" it read. "At 4.07 P.M. Conti from the marshals' office rang her to let you know they have caught Nauss. He apparently was living in suburbia with a wife and children and they knew nothing about him."

Frank contacted Walter at the conference and told him the news, saying that he needed to get back to the United States at once. If anyone understood, Walter did.

"Phone me with the details," he said.

"By the way, Rich," Frank said. "He was caught in Michigan."

It was exactly what Walter had predicted.

||||||||||||||||||||||||||||||||||||||||||||||||||||||

*AMW* aired the segment on Nauss a total of three times, the last of which had been only a few days before Frank and the others left for Australia. A viewer in a suburb of Detroit had contacted *AMW* and said there was a man resembling the bust who called himself Richard Ferrer and lived in Luna Pier, a small town on Lake Erie not far from Michigan's border with Ohio. Ferrer was a quiet family man with three boys and had a knack for doing carpentry jobs. He wore a baseball cap and long-sleeved shirts that covered his arms. When the marshals confronted him, he had—just like Frank's bust—short hair and a thick neck, and he was wearing a lumberjack shirt. He denied being Nauss, but under his long-sleeved right arm was the tattoo of a parrot.

By the time Nauss was flown back to Philadelphia, Frank had returned from Australia. Tom Rapone said that if Frank wanted to, he could come down to the holding cell and take the booking photograph, the same way he had with Vorhauer.

Frank grabbed his camera and rushed over. Unlike Vorhauer, who had avoided looking at him, Nauss was unusually friendly.

"Hey," he said to Frank, "you did that bust of me, right?"

"Yeah," Frank replied, surprised that Nauss would talk to him. He felt at ease enough to even joke with the murderer. "How does it feel to be immortalized?"

"I wish it was under better circumstances." He smiled and put his hand on Frank's shoulder. "Didn't you also play Vorhauer, my partner, on *AMW*?"

"You saw it?"

"Yes. But you're better-looking than him. He's ugly, isn't he?"

They both laughed.

Frank couldn't understand why Nauss was so casual for a man who was about to be locked up for the rest of his life. Paul Schneider, who had been brought in for the biker's arrest, said it wasn't uncommon. Nauss hadn't gone into prison mode yet, which was when he would shut down.

||||||||||||||||||||||||||||||||||||||||||||||||||||||||||||||

In the middle of 1991 the Vidocq Society held its fifth meeting. What had begun as a casual luncheon for members—many of whom were in law enforcement—to get together and socialize was quickly becoming more of a place to do detective work. Almost from the start they took on only cold cases, and not just any cold case but some of the oldest and most perplexing in the country.

At the latest meeting, which took place in a colonial tavern in the historic Society Hill section of the city, they discussed the forty-year-old Cleveland Torso Murders, in which at least a dozen homeless people had been killed and dismembered.

Including Frank, Fleischer, and Walter, there were now sixty-two members.

# CHEATING

After the capture of Nauss, Frank was on a high. Within a year List and Nauss had been caught, and Rosella Atkinson and Valerie Jamison had been identified. In April 1991 two men went on trial for the murder of Yvonne Davi, and there was talk of a television movie being made about Princess Doe.

In July Leo Joseph Koury's body was identified in a San Diego morgue. Even though the ID had nothing to do with Frank, the coincidence of the mobster's body turning up not long after the bust had appeared on *AMW* didn't do his reputation any harm.

*AMW* commissioned Frank to take on another seemingly impossible case that bore many similarities to List's. In early 1976 Brad Bishop—a tall, good-looking former army intelligence officer who worked for the State Department and had been stationed in Italy, Ethiopia, and Botswana—bludgeoned to death his wife, mother, and two young sons before driving their bodies from Bethesda, Maryland, to a forest in North Carolina, where he burned them. The bodies were found by a park ranger the next day, but by that time Bishop had disappeared. No trace of him was ever found.

Bishop's fluency in five languages made his flight to Europe not only easy but very likely. There had been two unconfirmed sightings of him, one in Stockholm in 1978 by a family member and one in Sorrento a year later by a former colleague.

Because Bishop had a distinct cleft in his chin, which he clearly would want to hide, Frank made the bust with a clip-on beard. Both versions were shown on *AMW* in early 1992.

In between creating faces of the occasional fugitive and murder victim, Frank spent his time going out to lunch with friends, having meetings with Fleischer, popping in on the investigators at the Philadelphia medical examiner's office, or visiting Fillinger, who had been elected coroner of Montgomery County. What he wasn't doing, though, was photography.

Unhappy with all the publicity he was getting for his forensic work, advertising agencies were loath to use him anymore. They also assumed that someone getting so much media coverage didn't need the work. The last major commercial job Frank received was, ironically, to do a series of busts for Blue Cross—although they weren't skulls but a telephone, a computer, the company logo, and a pair of hands shaking one another. After that the photographic work dried up.

Frank's fee per head was now a thousand dollars, but he had done only thirty-five in fifteen years. Forensics had taken up most of his time, but it paid the least of his bills. He and Jan were broke.

Jan was taking on more part-time jobs. Besides working at Strawbridge's, she had just started as a receptionist at a law firm. The money problems created more and more tension between them, and they were constantly fighting. They had sold Frank's van and his last motorcycle.

Jan saw changes in Frank that she didn't like. Gone was the naive, good-hearted amateur forensic artist dedicated to solving murders, the man prepared to work for nothing to identify Anna Duval or to use his own money to buy a wig for the Girl in the Sewer and for Linda Keyes. Now he was a showman and a show-off.

"Success is going to his head," she wrote in her diary after he returned from a two-day trip to the U.S. Marshals' headquarters in McLean, Virginia. "He keeps talking about himself."

What Jan didn't know was that he had also started having an affair.

Frank had cheated before. The women he painted or photographed—usually in the nude—often became friends he went on dates with and sometimes slept with.

Jan knew about the girlfriends, and they didn't bother her. At least she said they didn't. After all, that was how she herself had met him, and telling him to stop would be like telling him to stop being Frank. Anyway, his outsize libido was too much for her, and she was convinced that letting him sleep with someone else occasionally would keep everyone happy.

Even though he didn't think of it this way, the sexual act had also become an inextricable part of his forensics life. Remedy or not, lovemaking was certainly a fleshly comfort once he was done seeing the gore of a bloated body or working on the skull of a five-year-old beaten to death. What better way was there of countering the specter of death than with an act so full of life? So he started sleeping with several women on a regular basis.

But with Laura Shaughnessy, things were different.

Frank had met her through his friend Paula Lisak, who had rented the pit in the meat market in the early years. He and Shaughnessy immediately hit it off and arranged to go to the Franklin Institute to see a show on special effects. Wandering through the exhibits of mannequins from *Psycho* and miniature spaceships from *Star Wars,* Frank opened up to her about the problems he was having with Jan.

Afterward, Shaughnessy said she wasn't feeling well, and she asked to come back to the studio to lie down. That was the first time they slept together.

Frank started spending more and more time with Shaughnessy, meeting her friends and going out to Longport, New Jersey, to visit her family, who were wealthy and well connected and lived in a large compound.

Things with Jan only got worse.

"You're wasting your time with her," Shaughnessy told him. "You know that you guys don't get along. She has her nose in the air all the time, and she kind of ignores you and Vanessa."

Frank agreed with her. Jan did seem to be distant and self-centered. She never paid attention to his work. He responded by spending even less time with her. Finally, Jan couldn't take the tension anymore and confronted Frank in the bedroom one morning while he was still lying in bed.

"Are you fucking Laura Shaughnessy?" she screamed.

"Yes, I am," he said. He didn't care what happened. "Now can I go back to sleep?"

Jan sought advice from one of the lawyers where she worked about a divorce. But by this time the affair had already started to flag. Shaughnessy tried to control Frank, something he didn't like, and she was so bossy that he began calling her "Sarge." She wanted him to switch his accountant and not to use Joan anymore, and she tried to separate him from his friends. Being with her, ironically, made him realize why he had lasted twenty years with Jan. She let him be himself.

Frank had recently gotten a job from Interpol, his first from the international policing agency, to do a bust of Ira Einhorn. A leading member of the 1960s counterculture who mixed with people like Abbie Hoffman and Peter Gabriel, Einhorn had killed his girlfriend, Holly Maddux, in 1977 and kept her body in a trunk in his Philadelphia apartment for eighteen months. He fled before his trial in 1980 but had been seen several times in Ireland and Europe. After he kept eluding law-enforcement authorities, Interpol contacted Frank.

As soon as Frank was finished with the bust, he and Shaughnessy were planning a visit to her sister in France. Shaughnessy said that maybe it would also be a good time to break up with Jan. Instead Frank broke up with Shaughnessy and took Jan with him to Europe.

It was the first holiday the two of them had taken in a long time. They couldn't afford it, but they needed time together outside of Philadelphia. They spent a week in Paris before taking a train down to Milan, where Frank had been invited by the city's police force.

In between, they stopped off in Lyon to visit Interpol. Frank gave a slide presentation of his work and handed over two busts, one of Einhorn and the other of the family murderer Brad Bishop. Not long afterward, Einhorn's bust was aired on British television, but he wasn't found until years later.

## DIVING OFF PIER 40

A stark picture faced Frank back in Philadelphia on the return from Europe. He was almost bankrupt and had no work.

In Lyon and Milan, he had tried to get more forensic jobs, but nothing came of his presentations. Back home he called the medical examiner's office and the police departments he had worked for in Pennsylvania, New Jersey, and New York. None of them had a budget for outsiders to do facial reconstructions and all were being instructed to use their own artists, no matter how much better Frank might be. The successes of John List, Rosella Atkinson, and Robert Nauss were yesterday's news. A few years earlier, Frank had owned two properties, a van, several motorcycles; now he was on the verge of having to sell the meat market, and his means of transport was a bicycle.

One morning in midsummer, shortly after Jan had left for work, Frank took his heavy Schwinn cruiser and rode down Washington Avenue. He turned left when he reached the Delaware River, immediately slowing down to look over the railing. He kept his eye out for rusted bolts and pieces of metal that had washed up on the banks and could be used in his artwork.

At Pier 40, he saw Jim O'Donnell, who was in charge of the half-dozen tugs moored there. They had met when Frank photographed the *Tug McGraw* for Blue Cross a decade earlier but hadn't seen each other for a while.

"You still doing those faces?" O'Donnell called out.

"Yeah," Frank said.

"I read about you in the paper. You're famous."

Frank hated to admit the truth. He had no money, his marriage was still shaky, and they might have to sell their home. "Work's a bit slow," he said.

"Come and have lunch with me," O'Donnell insisted.

They went to Ila's, a bar near the river that was popular among longshoremen and dockworkers. After a couple of beers, Frank opened up about how bad things were going.

"Ever since List," he said, "my photographic work died."

"How many heads you done so far?" O'Donnell asked.

Frank never kept count. "Forty or so. But it doesn't pay."

The pier master stood up. "You're not going home today," he said. "You're coming to work for me."

The idea sounded crazy at first. Working on a boat wasn't something Frank had seen in his future. But he had nothing better to do, and it paid. He went back to Pier 40 with O'Donnell, who took him on a tour through one of the tugs. Frank had spent his two years in the navy in the engine room of the U.S.S. *Calcaterra,* which had a Fairbank's Morse opposed piston engine. So did the tug.

"Okay," Frank said, "I'll do it. I'll take the job."

"Good. You can start today," O'Donnell replied. "We're taking out a septic tank."

Though Frank was wearing a new pair of jeans, he knew he couldn't say no. He climbed belowdecks to where the welders were cutting through the framework so they could bring the septic tank onshore. As they shifted it around, urine and feces ran onto them.

By the time Frank rode home several hours later, his clothes were filthy. As he pedaled through the early-evening traffic, piss swished around in his shoes. He'd never felt more humiliated in his life. He was fifty years old and had reached an all-time low. His colleagues and friends were art professors, advertising executives, district attorneys, and chief pathologists, but he had lost all his photographic work, forensics didn't pay enough, and he'd been forced to take a job on a tug where he'd gotten covered in excrement.

"Jesus, Frank," Jan said when he got home. "You smell like a toilet."

He threw all his clothes into the washing machine, thinking about how much the day had turned out just like his first day at the medical examiner's office fifteen years earlier. It was a new juncture in his life, and he'd come home from the experience in smelly clothes. Except back then he'd been exhilarated; now he felt empty.

But the tugs were just what Frank needed.

He went down to Pier 40 once or twice a week, sometimes every day. He heaved lines, scraped bilges, and painted the decks. When the other tugs came back to shore, he threw out fenders and hooked up water lines and steam lines.

Not being a union member, he was allowed to work on the tugs only when they were docked. But sometimes O'Donnell sneaked him out on the water for special occasions, like when they guided the *QE2* into the harbor.

No matter how piecemeal or menial the work, Frank liked it. He was part of a group again, even though the hardscrabble sailors were nothing like the marshals or the investigators at the medical examiner's office. Sometimes they came back from sea missing a tooth or two, or with a face bruised from a fight. And they laughed at him for bringing his espresso maker to the kitchen and not drinking from their pot of coffee. Still, working in a team was the perfect antidote to being alone in the studio.

Joan brought Frank some potential work, a commission to sculpt a memorial to her brother-in-law, who had died in Vietnam and received the Congressional Medal of Honor posthumously. But Frank had to first meet the officer in charge. A fund-raiser where he would do this was to take place in New Jersey one Saturday afternoon. But several hours before Frank was scheduled to leave the meat market, O'Donnell called from Pier 40 in a panic.

"Frank," he said, "we have to put a commercial diver down under the boats, and I need you to work with him. He's got a pacemaker, and he's not that active. You'll just have to hand him tools and things."

Frank explained that he was already dressed in his suit for a special occasion and that he couldn't be late because he had to make a speech.

"That's fine," said O'Donnell. "Just wear your clothes down here and I'll give you something to put on top of them."

Frank couldn't say no. At Pier 40 he pulled on an overall while the diver jumped into the water.

"Just watch his bubbles," O'Donnell instructed him. "If you don't see them for a few minutes, let me know. That's when I'll be concerned."

Frank did as he was instructed, but then the bubbles disappeared. He got worried and called out to O'Donnell, who came over. "You'll have to go down, Frank," he said.

"But I'm wearing overalls and my clothes," Frank replied. "And I hate cold water."

"I'll give you a week's salary."

Frank took off his shoes and jumped in. As he hit the water, his body jolted from the cold. He took a deep breath and went underwater, but there was no visibility. He felt his way under the boat's hull, trying to guide himself along, his hands scraping the barnacles. Coming up for air, he swam from the midsection to the fantail. He finally found the rope that was tied to the diver and pulled on it, but the boat shifted and the rope caught his head, knocking him against the hull. After a moment of dizziness, he managed to surface. He finally reached the rudder and saw that the diver was fine.

When Frank climbed back on the pier, he was already late for the ceremony and shivering. O'Donnell offered to drive him to New Jersey. On the way there, Frank tried to remove the wet overall, but it stuck to him like a second skin, and his shoes made a squishing sound whenever he moved his feet. Dressed like that, he arrived at the fund-raiser and introduced himself to the audience, which included a colonel dressed in full uniform.

"Why are you late?" the colonel said to him. "You're all wet and dressed like that."

"Wait a minute," O'Donnell interrupted him. "We sent him down under the tug to save a man. Don't holler at him."

Frank got not only the commission but also a bonus for the dive.

At the end of 1992, Frank was asked by *People* magazine to re-create the face of a 5,300-year-old man whose frozen body had been found by hikers in the Alps a year earlier. He was also approached by the family of Camilla Lyman, an heiress and transsexual from Boston who had gone missing in 1987, to check whether a skull that had been found belonged to their relative. After projecting an outline of Camilla onto the skull, Frank concluded that it wasn't her. He made an age progression of George Strzelczyk, a rapist and child molester who had been on the run for five years, that was shown on the CBS program *How'd They Do That?*

Each case brought Frank publicity but no money. He was getting used to that, and even though he and Jan continued to fight about their income, they were getting on better than they had in a long time.

In early 1993 *Monster* opened at the Sonnabend gallery in New York. The exhibition included ten Bronze Age progressions that Frank had sculpted to show what children who had died in the Holocaust, in Cambodia's Khmer Rouge execution camps, and in the 1963 Birmingham, Alabama, fire bombings would look like if they had lived. The same week of the opening he went back to George Faraghan's studios on Arch Street, where he'd started out as a photographer, to look for work. They didn't have anything for him but said he should call again sometime.

## THE BOY IN THE BAG

### November 1994

The afternoon that Bill Fleischer arrived at Pier 40 to fetch him for their monthly lunch, Frank was coming up from a dive. He had gone down to look for damage on the rudder of one of the tugs, still using his customary diving outfit: jeans and Nikes, no Aqua-Lung.

Fleischer shook his head in dismay. When he had first found out about Frank's diving, he was appalled. He even tried to persuade O'Donnell not to let him do it.

"Frank's one of the world's best forensic artists. We don't want him drowning in the Delaware."

Frank couldn't tell whether Fleischer was being serious, but he told him to stop bringing up the subject in front of O'Donnell. "You're going to lose me good work," he said.

Fleischer was preparing to retire as a customs agent and become a private investigator. As they drove to Seafood Unlimited, he told Frank that maybe he would have some freelance photographic work for him in the near future. Frank had never done surveillance work before, but he was ready to give anything a try.

"By the way," Fleischer added as they sat down in the restaurant, "how's that case with the boy going?"

Five months earlier, the body of a four-year-old had been found in a duffel bag on a vacant lot on Lawrence Street, in Philadelphia, his skeletonized remains wrapped in sheets and a towel. The medical examiner had concluded that he'd been beaten to death. He had decomposed so badly that his leftover skin resembled molten wax. Because his body was dumped near the Ben Franklin Bridge and I-95, it was thought to have come from out of state.

This was the first job Frank had gotten from the Philadelphia medical examiner's office in a long time, and, ironically, it bore similarities to one of the first cases he'd ever done for them. Even several newspapers pointed out that the city hadn't seen a killing like this one since the Girl in the Steamer Trunk in 1982.

Frank quickly started having nightmares about the boy, so he started a download—his way of getting the ghastly images out of his system—and this one was the biggest he'd ever done. Usually he chose watercolors, but this time he took an old broken grandfather clock that he filled with photographs of the site where the body was found, and then he added a plaster version of the distorted clay bust. To the clock's door he affixed the child's toe tag.

Several months passed after he delivered the bust to the medical

268 | TED BOTHA

examiner's office, and he heard nothing from them about his remuneration. It was never easy asking to be paid for something that felt like it should be a service to society, but it was even harder when you had to beg. Each time he contacted them, the procurement officer told him that they couldn't afford to pay him.

"Ripped off by my own city," Frank concluded. His and Fleischer's food had just arrived at the table.

It seemed like the end of a very important part of his life—the very coroner's office that had gotten him started on the heads was now making it impossible for him to do any more for them. The last time he had visited the medical examiner's office, it was a place he no longer felt familiar with. Fillinger was now in Montgomery County, and Gerry White had taken a transfer to Kansas City. After asking for his money one final time, Frank had cycled away from the ugly gray building on University Avenue toward the Schuylkill River, sure he would never receive a skull from them again.

# MEXICO

# INTUITION

Everything about Mexico said to give it up—the warning e-mail, the margaritas, the messy evidence room at the Juárez police station, the secrecy over the Girl from Chihuahua, the incompetent local investigators, the juggernaut of an investigation—but Frank couldn't. He had the *feminicidios* under his skin.

Besides, challenge was the name of the game. In all his cases, he had almost come to expect obstacles and setbacks. It had been ten years since he'd worked on the Boy in the Bag, and even though he still hadn't been paid, he kept holding out for an ID, as he did for the Girl in the Sewer, Princess Doe, the Burnt Boy, and numerous other victims who sat on his shelves, looking down on him expectantly, reminding him that they still had no names. An incurable believer—some might say he had never lost his naïveté—he wasn't going to let a few challenges in Mexico get in his way. He felt he owed each of his victims more than just a sculpture.

After he'd been back in Philadelphia for a week, he called Esparza to find out if there had been any IDs. The Mexican was courteous but brief. There had been one ID so far, although it was one that

Frank least expected—the Girl Without a Lower Jaw. The family who came to see the Girl with the Crooked Nose, meanwhile, still refused to concede that it was her.

"What about the Girl from Chihuahua?"

"Nothing."

Frank didn't need to ask anything more about the investigation, because he already knew it was sinking. Shortly after he had left Juárez, Oscar Valadez, the assistant attorney general, publicly admitted that the police might have lost the tissue samples of all the women killed between 1993 and 1998. If so, their bodies would have to be exhumed for more samples. Frank knew that would never happen.

Thousands of people had marched in Mexico City, demanding that Vicente Fox find and punish the killers, whoever they were. The president, meeting with mothers in Chihuahua, told them he was taking more action. He had instructed the attorney general to establish a DNA bank to help identify the murdered women. He also appointed a special federal commissioner to monitor why the state investigation had gotten nowhere and a special federal prosecutor to lead her own team.

In a final twist that Frank learned from Bob Ressler, the American Slater had been taken off the investigation.

With the Chihuahua government and its police force under fire more than ever, it was unlikely that Frank would be asked to come down again. Which was why he was surprised when Bob Ressler called one day and suggested that they do exactly that—return to Mexico. Frank, gung ho as ever, quickly agreed.

They both arranged their flights, but a few days before leaving, Ressler called to say he couldn't go. Frank was disappointed about the cancellation and annoyed that he'd wasted hard-earned money on a ticket he wouldn't use.

But Ressler insisted that he go on his own. To Frank, that didn't seem like a good idea—only Ressler could organize more heads for him, and without the profiler he felt powerless in Mexico—but he had a ticket. That alone was a good enough excuse to return.

He flew into El Paso on the evening of November 28, and the policeman Hector picked him up at the airport. They drove to the former police academy, where Esparza was waiting.

The visit wasn't budgeted for, so a hotel was out of the question. It was arranged to put Frank up in the former police academy, although he was assured that this was better than it sounded. It was "a suite" that the attorney general sometimes used.

After a short walk down the corridor, its walls stained and its floor tiles broken, the barred windows looking out to the prison tower, Esparza and Frank reached a poorly furnished room. Even though it had a kitchen nook and a television, Frank couldn't see a high-powered state official spending a night there. But at least the bed wasn't a concrete slab like the one he'd been offered on his previous visit.

Esparza took him for a bite at a burrito place in town. Any tension between the two was gone. The Mexican seemed quieter and more subdued. Not only was the investigation going nowhere, but their budgets were being severely cut. The former police academy didn't have any heat for winter; policemen were no longer allowed to investigate cases outside of Juárez, and their cell phones had been taken away; and worst of all, less money was being allocated to the *feminicidios*.

Frank shook his head. Nothing had changed—indeed, it had

possibly gotten worse. In Slater's absence, Esparza had become the de facto head of the task force.

"If I don't come up with something by February—in less than three months—I will lose my job."

Frank liked Esparza, in spite of everything that had passed between them. Of all the people he had worked with in Mexico, Esparza at least seemed to want to bring an end to the *feminicidios*. That's why Frank decided to take a gamble and tell him who he thought was killing the women of Juárez.

‖‖‖‖‖‖‖‖‖‖‖‖‖‖‖‖‖‖‖‖‖‖‖‖‖‖‖‖‖‖‖‖‖‖‖‖‖‖‖‖‖‖‖‖

People called it intuition, a special gift, a sixth sense, even genius. Frank himself didn't have a name for it.

In October 1977 he had walked into a room full of corpses, ventured a guess about what a decaying woman looked like, and discovered that he had a talent for something he'd never anticipated in his wildest dreams. Indeed, a more unlikely match was hardly thinkable. Until that moment he had been building a career based almost entirely on creating images of perfection—the naked female form and glossy ads. But here he was confronting violent death, decomposed and rotting bodies, and grisly skeletons, and then being asked to imagine them as healthy, living beings.

The juxtaposition of beauty and life with decay and death never struck him as odd. What began as a challenge with case number 5233 quickly became something that he wanted and needed to do. Only later did it occur to him that forensics was satisfying certain basic urges within him. He was sculpting for justice, helping to bring closure to a case, but most of all, creating art that had a purpose.

Along the way, he made up rules where there weren't any. What few conventions existed—whether it was for tissue thicknesses or the prominence of an eyeball—he used only some of the time. The rest came from something inside him—instinct, gut feeling, some primeval flair—that proved right so many times people started giving it a name.

Perhaps it was inevitable then that the same inexplicable qualities he called on to imagine a face for a murder victim, he would start using to imagine the murder itself. In a way, he couldn't help it. By the time he had completed a bust—working alone in his studio for days on end, focusing solely on one victim—he thought about the person in life and went through countless scenarios of how she or he might have died.

At his lunches with Fleischer and Walter, he started getting a chance to talk about his theories and to hear about the cases they were working on. It was precisely this kind of information swapping, theorizing, and crime-talking that had led them to start the Vidocq Society.

Fourteen years had passed since the creation of Vidocq, which had taken on some weighty cases, ranging from Frank's own Girl in the Well and JonBenét Ramsey to Princess Doe and even the Boy in the Box, a Wilton Krogman case from 1957 that had captured the country's attention at the time. Of the more than one hundred unsolved murders the society had tackled, in one fifth of them a murderer had been found, even though Vidocq couldn't pursue the matter any further. That was up to law enforcement.

For Frank, all the listening to evidence given by dozens of policemen and people presenting cold cases over the years, as well as the assumptions, suppositions, scenarios, and hypotheses posed by countless forensic experts, was like a crash course in detective work. It honed his instinct. If he smelled a rat, he said so.

At one point, he even went so far as to accuse a man he knew of being involved in the death of his girlfriend. The woman's body had been found with a gunshot wound to the head. The man had spoken to Frank about the case, asking him to get Vidocq involved, but Frank slowly became convinced that the man had something to do with the woman's death and wanted to use Frank and Vidocq to steer attention away from himself. The case was never resolved.

Sometimes Frank was way off the mark, asking questions in the Vidocq meetings that not only seemed irrelevant but sounded like they came from an amateur who had strayed into a meeting of professionals ("Did you consider the policeman?" "Did you notice that the grass around the weapon was bent at a forty-five-degree angle?"). But sometimes he was right. Whether or not his theory sounded stupid and crazy, he was never scared to say who he thought had pulled the trigger.

IIIIIIIIIIIIIIIIIIIIIIIIIIIIIIIIIIIIIIIIIIIIIIIIIIII

Esparza waited for Frank to talk.

"This may sound crazy," Frank began.

"No, go ahead and tell me. Who do you suspect?"

A growing number of theories had already surfaced about who had killed the women of Juárez, some of them more bizarre than others. A recent report in *The Village Voice* had listed most of them, except for the seemingly outrageous idea of snuff films made for the Asian market. It could be, the paper said, an international organ-trafficking ring, Satanists, organized crime, serial killers from the United States, a group of local serial killers, the Mexican government, or the state police.

Frank believed it was an evil alliance between organized crime and the state police, which made it that much harder to tell Esparza, himself a state policeman. Frank explained how he had come to this conclusion.

"I think the police rape and kill the women to prove themselves to the drug cartel," he said. "That's how they show their loyalty. Let's face it—the cartel isn't going to use a policeman unless he proves himself."

Esparza waited a few moments and then leaned conspiratorially across the table. "This is highly confidential," he said in a low voice, "but we arrested several policemen who regularly travel between Juárez and Chihuahua on suspicion of raping women in the desert. But they never killed them."

During another investigation, the police were doing surveillance when they accidentally came across a police officer at a sex party with young women. The officer asked Esparza not to tell anyone about it and to forget the incident.

"At the time I blew it off. He's just our colleague getting laid with all these women. But now that I think about it, and the people he was with, I think you're right." He paused. "But we can't tell anyone."

Esparza said he would talk to Angie about the allegation, but they shouldn't tell the attorney general yet.

After dinner, as they headed back to the former police academy, Esparza drove past some of the *maquilas*. Even at night the huge, characterless factories seemed to cast a dark shadow over everything around them. A woman was walking on her own along the wall in front of one unlit *maquila*. "This is how they get abducted," Esparza said.

He slowed down and made sure that she got to her bus stop, where they waited until the bus arrived. As they sat there, Frank asked Esparza if there had been any more updates on the five heads.

"No," he said.

Frank was still curious about why the Girl from Chihuahua had been kept a secret; he was sure that by now more about her was being made public. Esparza's reply caught him totally off guard.

"Oh, we found her," he said. "She's still alive."

"You *found* her?" Frank said. "But I worked from her skull. How could she still be alive?"

Esparza shrugged. At that moment, the bus arrived and picked up the woman who was waiting, so Esparza started the car.

"Then who was the girl I worked on?" Frank asked.

Esparza shook his head.

The excitement that Frank had felt only moments ago, when Esparza agreed that his theory about the killers could be right, was suddenly gone. Never in all his time of sculpting the heads of murder victims had a person turned up alive after he'd been given their skull. All his doubts and suspicions about Mexico returned—it was impossible to understand the place.

That night, as he lay in bed in the modest apartment in the former police academy, he couldn't sleep. This trip was so pitiful compared to the last one—no heads, no media, no Hotel Lucerna, no paycheck.

Perhaps it hadn't been wise of him to have confessed his suspicions to Esparza about his colleague possibly being a murderer. Here Frank was, miles from town, all on his own, without Ressler or any contract with the Chihuahua government, in the middle of a police facility now used as a prison where they were said to torture people.

His timing couldn't have been worse.

|||||||||||||||||||||||||||||||||||||||||||||||||||||||||||||||||||||||

Even before Esparza canceled their breakfast date the next morning—once again the attorney general wanted him in Chihuahua—Frank knew that he needed to leave Mexico as soon as possible. Hector took him to a taco stand for something to eat.

"I'm just getting in your way here," Frank said. Hiding his concerns about Mexico and what he'd told Esparza, he tried to sound upbeat. "I can see Manuel wants to get on with the investigation. I should just go home."

Hector agreed that it wasn't the best time to be in Juárez.

Back at the former police academy, Frank called Esparza and told him that he was going home. He lied, saying that he'd already changed his flight to an earlier one, even though the airlines were booked up for the Thanksgiving weekend. But he wanted to get out of the country.

Hector drove him across the border to the airport in El Paso. After waving goodbye, Frank waited a few moments and then took a cab to the train station and bought a ticket on Amtrak.

All the way back to Philadelphia, he felt relieved to be out of Mexico. But he couldn't stop thinking about what he'd left behind, a crime unsolved, thwarted by people, politics, drugs, the government, the police, anything and anyone you could think of. And yet . . . He'd had setbacks before, more times than he cared to remember, but he had never let them stand in his way. Why should

Mexico be any different? By the time his train arrived at Thirtieth Street Station two days later, he was already trying to figure out ways of getting back to Juárez.

# APPROACHING VIDOCQ

Frank had an idea.

If Esparza couldn't get the investigation moving in Mexico, maybe Frank could do it in the United States. He started making calls to whomever he knew in the media and law enforcement. Somebody would be interested in the Mexican murders, he felt absolutely sure.

He wasn't even deterred by the fact that the previous time he had phoned the media, from Juárez, he had gotten a resounding no, or by Ed Barnes's bad experience. (Barnes's short two-part segment on the *feminicidios* aired on Fox in late 2003.)

But no one was interested. All the shows replied the same way they had before. *60 Minutes* wanted to do a piece on Frank, but not on Juárez. A contact at the FBI said they couldn't help because Mexico wasn't within the agency's jurisdiction.

Then Frank thought of Vidocq. The Mexican murders were exactly the kind of crime the society had been created for: several years old, unsolved and seemingly unsolvable, and caught up in law-enforcement red tape and bungling. Being taken on by Vidocq would also guarantee publicity for the crime outside of Mexico, which, Frank believed, was crucial.

Vidocq was quite famous by now. Danny DeVito was trying to make a movie about it, and *Harper's* had just published a long article titled "Watching the Detectives: The Vidocq Society's Tale of Ratiocination." Members included not only the obvious people in law enforcement (polygraph experts, district attorneys, and members of the FBI, IRS, and DEA) but also the up-and-coming ones (forensic hypnotists, ritual-murder and handwriting experts, and a bloodstain-pattern analyst). There was even a professor of English.

But Vidocq had also become a lot more bureaucratic, with a media officer and a rigorous selection process. Out of hundreds of requests submitted for consideration, only a few were taken on. The cases had to be murders, at least two years old, and presented by a law-enforcement officer or an investigator "with standing."

The most obvious problem with the *feminicidios* was that the murders were taking place in Mexico. With so many unsolved crimes inside America, why look elsewhere?

Frank approached Fleischer and Walter with his idea. Eighty-two forensic experts would, without a doubt, shed some new light on the murders. Frank's five heads would also be publicized in America, giving millions of Mexicans around the country a chance to see and possibly identify them. Neither of Frank's colleagues thought his suggestion would get through the Vidocq selection process, and a formal request was never made.

Walter, however, had his own thoughts about the murders. Could they possibly be recreational killings? In the more traditional murders, which were often driven by passion or greed, there was usually a link between the murderer and the victim. But more and more modern-day killers killed someone—anyone—simply because they could. And when they got away with it once, they did it again. With no link between the two people, which was quite likely the case in Juárez, solving the crime was even harder, if not impossible.

||||||||||||||||||||||||||||||||||||||||||||||||||||||

Bob Ressler believed Frank was asking for trouble by wanting to return to Mexico.

"You're putting your life in danger," he said, adding that Frank was foolish to have been so candid with Esparza. "Now you can't go back."

Ressler, who was still owed thousands of dollars by the Chihuahua government for his work, also seemed to have given up on the case. "It's not good down there now," he said.

And he was right.

Esparza's February 2004 deadline had passed. In March—the same month the partially clad body of a woman was found along a road in Anapra, and a month after three other bodies were found around Juárez—the attorney general who had employed Frank and Ressler to come to Mexico, Jesús Jose Solís Silva, resigned amid allegations that he had provided protection to the Juárez drug cartel. Seventeen state police officials were implicated in the drug-related murders of a dozen men found buried in the backyard of a house in the city. Not long after that, eighty-one officials investigating the *feminicidios,* or just under half the total, were themselves under investigation.

"I heard that one of them might be Esparza," Ressler said. "It looks like the *federales* have taken over the case. It is unlikely that the two of us will ever be asked back."

# A MIRACLE IN EL PASO

April 2004

When the phone rang early one Saturday morning, Frank thought the call might be about mummies.

For the past few weeks, he had been communicating with Jonathan Elias, an Egyptologist involved in a project at the pyramids of Akhmim, a town on the Nile several hundred miles south of Cairo that had once been a prominent center for trade and religion.

In 1884, however, the Egyptian government was so cash-strapped that it sold off many of the Akhmim mummies to museums around the world. Elias's mission over a century later was to bring them back together and to do a reconstruction of what the Ptolemaic community might have looked like.

Re-creations of mummies had been done before, but never in a systematic way or of one population. In the early 1970s Richard Neave, a medical artist at the University of Manchester, reconstructed the faces of two brothers found in the rock tombs of Rifeh, their bodies dating back to 1900 B.C. (The Akhmim mummies came from about 300 B.C.)

Neave, like other British forensic artists who came after him, was part of what had become known as the European or Russian school. They followed the technique developed by Gerasimov, first creating the muscles and glands of the face with clay and then covering them with a thin layer that would be the skin. The American school paid more attention to the tissue charts and the final appearance of the face.

Frank's work, while American in technique—people talked of the anthropometric versus anatomical schools—reminded Elias of Gerasimov's style in its outcome. Frank gave more character to each face, which was one of the reasons why Elias liked his work and thought of him for Akhmim.

For Frank, the Egyptian project couldn't have come at a better time. A return to Mexico was growing more unlikely by the day. The mummies, meanwhile, could mean the beginning of a long relationship and numerous heads—an entire community, in fact. For the first time in his sculpting career, Frank could make a somewhat regular income from skulls.

So when the phone rang that Saturday morning, he jumped out of bed to answer it. Instead of Elias, it was a woman whose voice Frank didn't recognize right away. She said she was calling from El Paso and her name was Michelle Cromer.

Cromer was an advertising executive whom Frank had met briefly while sculpting the five heads in Juárez. A friend of hers who had photographed some of Frank's busts in the past, Arne Svenson, told her about him, and they arranged to have lunch at Maria Chuchena's.

Until that meeting, Cromer had known little about what was going on in Juárez, even though she lived right across the river. A pretty auburn-haired woman with lots of drive, Cromer had numerous interests—she'd written children's books and was finishing off a manuscript about coping with death. The two of them hadn't talked in several months. "How are things going with Mexico?" she asked.

Frank told her he was not a part of the investigation anymore, if there even was one still. The state police who had employed him had been taken off the case and had been replaced by the *federales*. He no longer had any connections in Mexico.

But Cromer, it so happened, did. She knew people in both the American and Mexican governments, and by the end of the conversation, she had offered to help. "Let me see what I can do," she said.

Frank immediately called Ressler to tell him about the conversation. Ressler was surprised that a civilian thought she could do something to help, although he didn't think she could. Neither did Cromer's friends.

"You're a white girl from El Paso who speaks bad Spanish," one friend said. "How are you going to do it? It'll take you two years to organize something."

It took Cromer four weeks.

From her luxurious home in the hills overlooking downtown El Paso, Cromer could see much of Juárez and the mountains behind it. As a place, it figured in her life daily. But until she met Frank, she knew very little about the *feminicidios*.

The more Cromer researched the murders, after learning a bit about them from Frank at Maria Chuchena's, the more she was struck by the ambivalence and lack of compassion around her, not only in El Paso but also among the wealthy people of Juárez. The murders were a problem that concerned the poor people of the barrios, and everyone else just wanted them to disappear.

Cromer quickly formulated a plan of action. She created a not-for-profit organization that she named after the pink crosses, and placed it under the auspices of her church, St. Mark's, so it wouldn't become a political football when she began raising money. The mission statement for Pink Crosses said that it aimed to "bring comfort and closure to the families of the murdered girls in Juárez through the use of forensic identification." At the top of the page was a drawing of the crosses done by Frank, whose forensic work the letter briefly explained.

Cromer targeted local churches and companies, especially women-owned companies, as well as the Oprah Winfrey Foundation, the Rotary Club, and Violence Against Women. She sent out a hundred letters to people she knew, asking for donations, and she held a fund-raiser. She met with several American politicians, including Karl Rove, chief strategist for George W. Bush; Congressman Silvestre Reyes; Texas governor Rick Perry; and El Paso mayor Joe Wardy. From each meeting she came away empty-handed—no help, no money.

The response from Mexico was better. The assistant attorney general, Sergio Camarillo Martínez, met Cromer at an office he kept in El Paso. She told him about Pink Crosses and brought up the possibility of Frank returning to Mexico, but this time under the protection of the *federales*.

Camarillo told her that the political climate in Mexico was shifting, and bringing Frank down might be a good idea. The two arranged to meet again, in Juárez, on April 19. At that meeting, Camarillo wanted to know how much the venture would cost, but Cromer said that Pink Crosses would cover all the expenses. All he had to do was agree to it.

Not only did Camarillo agree, but he offered to provide federal bodyguards to protect Frank. Cromer left the office encouraged, and felt so confident that things were moving in the right direction that she asked if she could see some of the sites where the murdered women had been found. The Mexicans said she couldn't—it was unsafe.

Cromer checked out several hotels for Frank to stay in. The Lucerna was too expensive, so she settled on the Lincoln Holiday Inn, a Mexican Moorish-style building near the Rio Grande Mall. Not only was it affordable but it was also near the American consulate and the border. If anything went wrong, she wanted Frank to be able to get out of Mexico fast.

# THE EXPLOSION

Cromer wanted Frank in Mexico by May 10, 2004. But less than three weeks before, on April 23, he got an urgent request to fly to Puerto Rico. Luis Vasquez, a detective in San Juan, needed a face put on a skull that had been found in a remote area and had a bullet hole in the temple. "We'd like you down here right away," Vasquez said.

Frank's loyalty lay with the *feminicidios,* so he called Cromer, who called Camarillo. The assistant attorney general said it would be fine if Frank postponed his trip for a few weeks. After all, Cromer was paying.

Frank flew to San Juan on May 3, accompanied by a reporter and a cameraman from *60 Minutes*. The Puerto Rico story had come up while he was still trying to sell the show the idea of Mexico. The cameraman wanted to do Mexico, but the producer of the segment didn't. He also had high expectations for the shoot.

He told Frank that *60 Minutes* had recently done a piece on Puerto Rico that hadn't worked out, and he hoped this one would. Frank didn't say anything to discourage him. He knew that a head could take years to identify after it was sculpted—the Boy in the Bag was still nameless; the Girl in the Sewer he'd done twenty years ago—if it was identified at all.

Frank shipped all his equipment to San Juan a few days before he flew out with the team of two from *60 Minutes*. Early on the first morning after they arrived, they were taken to a federal building in Old San Juan. Frank's equipment was waiting for him, and it wasn't long before Vasquez was there with the skull. Everything went without a hitch.

Even so, the job reminded him of Mexico, not only because it was outside the United States, in a place where everyone spoke Spanish, but also because he was being used for the same reason—to get some good publicity for the authorities. In this instance, they wanted to show the public that they were doing something about drug trafficking.

The murdered man's skeleton, Vasquez explained, had been found three years earlier, in 2001. The location, in the mountainous region of central Puerto Rico, was close to where a prisoner had confessed to leaving the body of a man he'd killed. They wanted to know if it was the same person.

As the *60 Minutes* camera rolled, Frank began the sculpture. It was the first time ever that he was being filmed for the entire creation of a bust. He had always needed to be alone, especially during the refining. Whether it was because there was a camera in the room, or because Frank felt an urgency to finish quickly so he could get home to prepare for Mexico, he finished the bust in record time.

At eleven A.M., two hours after he had left the room, Vasquez came back to see if Frank wanted to go to lunch or have it brought in. He saw the bust. "You're done!" he said in disbelief.

"Well, in about thirty minutes I will be," Frank replied. "Then I still have to cast and paint it."

Vasquez wanted to call in the media.

"But it's still in clay," Frank countered.

"We should get a picture of him out there for people to see."

After several newspapers had come by and taken photographs of the clay bust, it was too late in the day for Frank to carry on. By the next morning the police had gotten a tentative ID from the woman who had first reported the man missing.

"Well," said Vasquez, "now you can carry on making the mold and painting him."

"No," Frank corrected him. "I can't."

Vasquez asked why not.

"Because a tentative ID was made of the clay bust. If I change him, this model won't be admissible in court. We now possibly know the color of his hair and his eyes. That would be tampering with evidence."

Vasquez was insistent. "But it would be good to have a painted bust."

"We can do that later," Frank said, "after the trial."

Frank was booked for three more days at his hotel in Miramar. Rather than stay and do nothing, he told Vasquez he would prefer to go home to prepare for Mexico. He left Puerto Rico on May 6.

In the three days that Frank had been gone, there had been a terrible accident in Mexico. A plane had exploded after taking off from Juárez, and on it were seven federal agents investigating the drug cartel. The assistant attorney general, Sergio Camarillo, was meant to have been on it too, but his pregnant wife had gone into premature labor, and he had stayed behind to be with her.

When Frank called Cromer, she said they might have to postpone his trip. A meeting she had scheduled with Camarillo had been canceled after the crash. A few days later, though, she called again to tell Frank that Camarillo was more adamant than ever that he should come down.

"I don't like to be intimidated," he told her. "I want Bender down here right now."

Within a few days everything was organized. Cromer hadn't raised enough money, but she was going to fund Frank herself in the meantime. He would fly to El Paso in mid-June, and it was hoped that he could finish the job by July 4. That was the weekend there was to be a general election.

Once again there would be five heads for him.

## ◼ COMING BACK ALIVE

Frank didn't normally get scared, but the plane explosion rattled him.

Even Joan refused to go to Mexico. When he asked if she wanted to join him—things would go faster if she was there to help with the molds—she didn't even have to think about it. "Nothing personal, Frank," she said, "but I don't want to die."

Jan was of two minds. She didn't like Frank being in Mexico at all. If the cautionary e-mail she'd received wasn't enough, seven agents being blown up was. But she hadn't seen him so committed to solving a crime since Anna Duval.

Frank tried to find out from the FBI and the U.S. Marshals if it was safe to go to Mexico. Getting no answers from them, he contacted Jim Sullivan, an agent at Interpol whose name he had been given. He filled Sullivan in on some background of the case.

"Who's Michelle Cromer?" Sullivan asked.

Frank wasn't sure what to say. He didn't really know. "But she's gotten the okay from the Mexican government."

"These are Mexicans you're doing busts of?" Sullivan asked.

"Yeah, but there might be Americans among them. No one knows."

Frank told Sullivan about the plane blast. "Camarillo was supposed to have been on the plane but wasn't."

"How convenient," Sullivan said.

Frank didn't know what to make of the remark. Should he suspect Camarillo too?

"Why can't you do the heads in Philadelphia?" Sullivan asked.

Cromer had asked the Mexicans about this possibility, but on Frank's urging, Camarillo had said no. He had told her that he wanted Frank in Mexico and would have the best bodyguards to look after him.

"The attorney general felt they could better protect me down there," Frank said.

Sullivan laughed. "And he just had seven agents blown up?"

"He also said he didn't want the heads to get lost."

The unspoken reason why the Mexicans wanted Frank not only to start his work immediately but also to do it in Mexico, and not in the United States, was the election. The *feminicidios* were a contentious topic. The president had met some of the mothers, and there had been several marches demanding government action. Frank had been used for publicity by the Chihuahua government, and in Puerto Rico, so why not by the Mexican government? He didn't care, so long as he got there and could work on the women. Whatever it took to get back to Juárez, he would do it.

"I just would like to know who the players are," Frank told Sullivan. "And what are my chances of coming back alive? I know there's no hundred percent guarantee for anything you do in Mexico. I just don't want to be set up because of what I found out last time I went down. Is there any way you can help me with this?"

"I'd be happy to make inquiries," Sullivan said.

As part of Interpol procedure, Frank had to get one of his contacts at the U.S. Marshals to make a formal request to the international agency. When Sullivan called back a few days later, he said that it all seemed to be aboveboard. He was concerned, however, that Frank had mentioned his suspicions about the police being involved in the murders. He wanted any information about the case that Frank could give him on his return.

"And let me know how you make out."

Throughout his maneuverings to get back to Mexico, Frank made sure to relate his every move to the profiler Bob Ressler. Even though his friend was no longer directly involved, he had taken Frank down there in the first place. Ressler remained convinced that Frank was making a mistake going back to Mexico. But Frank was undaunted.

"I need the money," he reminded Ressler. "And I really want to get some more IDs."

# THE IDs

# JACQUELINE GOUGH

<u>1995</u>

A crew from the Fox television show *Sightings* was setting up
their cameras and lights in the meat market. Near the front of the
studio was the bust they had come to do a segment on—the Girl
with Hope, Rosella Atkinson.

"Everyone loves this story," Frank told the producer, and picked
up the plaster sculpture.

There was a knock at the front door. Frank thought it might be
Jan, who had left for work half an hour earlier, but he opened the
door to a handsome black woman in her late thirties. "I'm Virginia
Hill," she said.

Hill was a detective who worked on cold cases involving children,
some of whom had been missing for a long time. She had a reputation for being someone who didn't easily give up on a case—a female
version of the tenacious Paul Schneider. "The buck stops with me,"
she told Frank.

Hill had been instructed by her lieutenant to go to the studio
with flyers of some of the missing children, and to try and get them

filmed for the *Sightings* show. She introduced herself to the television crew and then wandered around the studio, finally landing up at the shelves that were lined with dozens of Frank's heads. One of the first ones she noticed was the Boy in the Bag, which she remembered seeing a story about in the paper recently.

Between Aliyah Davis and the Girl in the Sewer and Linda Keyes, Hill was struck by another bust, a white girl with a thin face and straggly blond hair. Hill studied the features for several moments. "Excuse me," she said, trying to get Frank's attention. The producer heard her first. "I think I know this girl. She looks like one of the girls in my files."

Frank came over. "That's the Girl from North Leithgow Street," he said. "She was found in a basement."

Hill had a fourteen-year-old case that she had reopened several years earlier, involving a girl who had gone missing in West Philadelphia. Frank brought her the *Daily News* story of the bust that had appeared at the time, in 1981, which was also fourteen years earlier. It said that the girl had vanished on about September 30 from Lehigh and Fourth streets, also West Philadelphia.

As Hill read the article and looked at the bust, she became more and more convinced that it was a missing girl named Jacqueline Gough. Even though Gough had brown hair—not blond, like the bust's—the similarity in the faces was undeniable. And so were the circumstances under which Gough had last been seen.

The night she had disappeared, she and a girlfriend had been together near the very same spot mentioned in the newspaper story, Lehigh and Fourth. They had met a Hispanic man and smoked some pot with him, and then he and Gough had left. The man had told Gough's friend to wait there, but Gough never returned.

"Perhaps the police questioned the guy and there was an investigation," Hill told Frank, "but I can't find much on the case."

All Hill found, in fact, was what she called a "dummy report," a single page that had been created for administrative purposes. Any other evidence there might have been, including a picture of Frank's bust, was gone, either lost or destroyed.

At the time when Hill took on the case, she called up Gough's mother, whose surname was Davis, to find out if her daughter had ever turned up. Davis said no one had contacted her about the case for years, and she'd been hoping Jacqueline would return one day. For that reason she'd never moved.

Hill started her own investigation and hit a lot of dead ends, but something about the case made her persevere. Sometimes she found herself so obsessed by Gough that she had to take a break and focus on other missing children.

Hill asked Frank to give her a photograph of the bust to take with her, then headed back to the office to call Gough's mother. Davis, who owned a bar on Frankford Avenue, wasn't there, but Hill got her other daughter, Lisa.

"I'm going to send you a picture," Hill said.

She hoped that it would be less of a shock if a family member showed Davis the photograph of the bust. For two weeks Hill heard nothing, so she called the family again. This time she got Davis herself, who said she knew nothing about a bust or a photograph.

"I will send you another one," Hill said.

When Davis got the photograph, she was sure it was her daughter. There weren't any dental records for Gough, so it seemed they would have to exhume her body to get DNA samples. In the end, that wasn't necessary.

On finding out that there was a possible ID, Gerry White, the investigator at the medical examiner's office who had worked on the case, contacted Haskell Askin. The forensic dentist was known to sometimes keep evidence from various cases, and he had in fact kept several teeth from the Girl from North Leithgow Street.

With Davis and a tooth from the skeleton, Hill needed only one more element in order to carry out a DNA test—Jacqueline Gough's father. Davis had never told the man that she'd had his child, and when Hill went to his last known address, she found out that he was dead. The hospital, however, had kept a tissue sample from him that could be used. The DNA test proved that the Girl from North Leithgow Street was indeed Jacqueline Gough.

A few weeks later, Frank, Hill, and White went to Gough's burial at a funeral home on Frankford Avenue. It had been almost fifteen years since Frank had given her a face.

# EDWARD SOLLY

## 2001

The scaffolding inside the Merriam Theater on Broad Street, in Philadelphia's Center City, was flimsy and precarious. It rose up about four floors, at the top of which was a single plank without a railing, where Frank and Joan were perched, making a mold of a damaged cornice.

That morning they had climbed up the scaffolding inside the 1918 building with two five-gallon containers of synthetic rubber. Unlike some of the other jobs they had done, at the Taj Mahal casino in Atlantic City and at the Edwin Forrest mansion farther up Broad Street, this one required them to make the mold on-site.

The procedure wasn't too different from making a bust, only a few hundred times larger. Onto the limestone surface they smeared a thick smooth layer of Vaseline, then eight layers of rubber, each of which took about an hour to dry.

The next morning they would have to create a mother mold out of fiberglass, which, when dried, they would remove and lower to the ground by rope. It was hard, dangerous work, but both of them liked it and it paid well.

For the past year Frank and Joan had been making molds for the Edon Corporation, one of the country's largest producers of fiberglass architectural products. Through an artist friend, Frank had met the CEO, Ed Axel, who liked his sculptures. Axel's mold maker was on holiday, and he needed a pineapple sculpted for a hotel in Boston. "You do that for me, and I'll start hiring you on other projects," he said.

The pineapple led to cornices, balustrades, and columns, as well as some medallions for a hospital foyer and a miniature of the Empire State Building. Joan, who had been working on the molds with Frank ever since John List in 1989, became his partner in the business. They split the money, and she made them a business card that said BENDER/CRESCENZ—MOLDMAKERS FOR THE STARS.

The fact that forensics didn't pay wasn't news to Frank, but he refused to give up the busts. His only recourse was to find other jobs, any kind of job, that would allow him to keep doing them.

By the time he took on the architectural work for Edon, he was still going down to the tugs on Pier 40—although not as often as before—and was doing surveillance work for Bill Fleischer, who was now working as a private investigator.

One of the jobs took Frank out to photograph a scrap yard that was being used to hide waste trucks from Fleischer's client. Frank had to take pictures from a helicopter, so Joan came along for the ride. The pilot had removed Frank's door so that he could lean out with his camera, and at one stage he was so far out Joan was holding him by his belt. Suddenly she noticed that several men on the ground had drawn their guns and were pointing them up at the chopper.

"Hey, Frank," she said, "don't those guys have guns aimed at us?"

Frank had been so intent on shooting the stolen vehicles, he hadn't noticed them. Quickly pulling himself back into his seat, he told the pilot to get them the hell out of there.

Companies in the entertainment industry cottoned on to Frank's age progressions and thought it would be fun to see how famous people looked when they got older. A syndicated magazine group asked him what JonBenét Ramsey would have looked like as a twenty-year-old, although they didn't like Frank turning her into a hardened young woman. A Japanese television station got him to put twenty years onto Masahiro Nakai, a popular singer in a boy band, and the image was then unveiled on a live show.

By the late 1990s forensics had become not only more popular among the public but more organized among law enforcement. Many of the agencies who had once used Frank were being specifically instructed to rely on their own artists and laboratories rather than outsiders. Some of them even had their own sculptors.

But work still trickled in. Frank got the head of a man whose burnt body was left in a Dumpster behind a Caldor store in Willingboro, New Jersey; a white woman found in Hazleton, Pennsylvania; a well-dressed white man—tan slacks, Italian calfskin belt, gold chain and cross—who had been shot execution-style in the head several times in Somerset, Pennsylvania, four years before his skeleton was found; and a white woman with the name "Benji" tattooed above her right ankle who had turned up in a landfill site in Schuylkill County, more than a hundred miles from Philadelphia, even though the receipts in her pocket were from the city.

Frank also received a gruesome case the likes of which he hadn't seen since going into the storage room with Bart Zandel in 1977. Pieces of a woman's upper torso had been found in a suitcase on the banks of Valley Creek, near Downington, Pennsylvania. Six months later, two legs thought to be hers were found in Core Creek Park, over fifty miles away. Police received more than two hundred tips, all of which led nowhere, before they thought of having a bust made.

In March 2000, Louis Rice, head of the Drug Enforcement Agency's office in New York, approached Frank when it was learned that the fugitive Frank Matthews might be in Philadelphia. A New York drug czar who had vanished more than a quarter century earlier, Matthews had lived a showy life with fancy cars, big apartments, and lots of girlfriends. In 1972 he was arrested, released on bail of more than two million dollars, and then fled a year later.

Matthews was Frank's fortieth bust.

When Frank got home from the Merriam Theater, covered in plaster from the cornice job, there was a message from Dennis Matulewicz, a U.S. Marshal he had worked with on Robert Nauss. A case had recently come to them from the FBI that was more than thirty years old.

"It might be less cold than we think," Matulewicz said.

Frank hadn't been asked to do a bust for the marshals since Nauss in 1987. This fugitive's name was Edward Solly.

In 1969, the twenty-four-year-old Solly beat his girlfriend's two-year-old son to death during a drunken rage because he didn't like the way he was being looked at. The child's screams caused the neighbors to call the police, but he died before they got there, and by that time Solly was gone.

Days later, he turned himself in and was tried in New Jersey and sentenced to twenty years in prison. With the help of a letter-writing campaign to the prison authorities by his mother, Edna Bolt, who said he was being mistreated, Solly was transferred to a medium-security prison. In 1974, accompanied by a social worker to allegedly visit a sick relative, Solly slipped out the back door and was never seen again.

Whenever the FBI went to question Bolt, who had steadfastly maintained that she didn't know where her son was, she became hostile. To the agents, that meant Solly was alive and well—and his mother knew where he was.

It was after Bolt died that the marshals took over the case. They gave Frank several photographs of Solly that had been taken twenty-seven years earlier, when he was a good-looking young man.

Frank first did some sketches, which were distributed among the marshals, and then a bust.

If Frank's involvement was minimal until then—no driving around in sanitation trucks, as with the Vorhauer case, and little actual contact with the marshals—it became even more so. The investigation's focus shifted farther south. When Bolt's daughter, who had been kept away from agents when her mother was alive, was questioned, she told the marshals that Solly was in Florida.

Marshals started closing in on a man who called himself Vinny Taylor. The real Taylor, who had been a member of the 1960s doo-wop group Sha Na Na, had actually died in 1974, the same year Solly escaped. Solly had taken over not only Taylor's name but his career as a singer. He used the stage name Danny Catalano—or Danny C—and even had his own website, which included photographs of him posing with local policemen and politicians. He got married and bought a house on the waterfront in St. Petersburg.

Some fans who heard Solly sing complained about him to the remaining members of the original Sha Na Na, who threatened to sue him. The marshals found Danny C's website, and they compared photographs of him to Frank's bust.

Danny C was tracked down to a waterfront compound in St. Petersburg. On the property was a van that had an advertisement for www.shananadannyc.com on the side. At ten o'clock on the night of May 10, 2001, marshals saw someone fitting Solly's description fishing off a pier near Danny C's home. When he finally went into the van, six of them closed in and arrested him.

# LOREAN QUINCY WEAVER

The two skulls couldn't have been more different.

They were found two thousand miles apart, one white male and one possibly black female, and fifteen years had elapsed between their murders. But they arrived at the studio within months of each other and were quite unlike any other skulls Frank had ever received.

The first came from Missouri. A laborer standing at a truck stop outside the sleepy town of Kearney was kicking mindlessly at an old plastic bucket when it split open. Inside he found a piece of concrete, at the bottom of which he noticed a glint of metal. Taking a closer look, he saw that it came from a gold filling in a tooth, which was still lodged in an upper jaw.

The crime laboratory hoped that the concrete, once broken open, might bear an imprint of the dead person's face, which would help with an ID. However, the head was not only missing its lower jaw but had been wrapped in material first.

One of the investigators at the Kansas City medical examiner's office was Frank's old friend Gerry White, who had transferred from Philadelphia. Frank had done three other skulls for White in the past few years—a young African-American girl named Precious Doe and two homeless people. He flew to Missouri to pick up the latest skull.

The lack of a lower jaw didn't bother Frank; he had worked on the half-burnt skull of Wanda Jacobs and the Girl with the Shattered Skull. He firmly believed that the form of the head would guide him. But it was the second skull that he received, only months later, that had him doubting how far he could take this theory.

|||||||||||||||||||||||||||||||||||||||||||||||||||||||

The police in Manlius, a town ten miles east of Syracuse, New York, had come to a dead end on a case, in spite of a particularly thorough investigation. They had even looked in nests near the murder scene to find evidence that birds might have carried away.

The victim was a girl who, even though she'd been murdered in the 1980s, was discovered many years later, by which time animals had savaged the body and dragged off some of the bones. A hunter had come across her remains in a remote wooded area in 1997. A tax stamp on a pack of cigarettes and a zipper on a disintegrated pair of jeans helped police determine that she had been murdered about ten years earlier. But by 2001 they had run out of leads.

One of the detectives, Keith Hall, and his wife were watching television one night when they saw a repeat episode of John List on *AMW*. Hall immediately thought that Frank could help reignite the Manlius case by getting the girl identified.

The victim was in her twenties and possibly African-American. When Hall explained this over the phone, Frank wasn't sure why her race couldn't be specified. He assumed it was because there were too few bones or she was a racial mix. When he got photographs of the skull from Hall several days later, he saw why. She had almost no facial bones.

There were no orbits, no nasal aperture, and no upper jaw. From the hairline all the way out to the temples and down to the lower jaw—nothing. It looked like a coconut that had its front third lopped off. On the Man in Concrete from Missouri, there'd been no lower jaw; on this one that's all there was. Almost every one of the twenty-one tissue-thickness points would have to be guessed.

Frank called Hall. "This is impossible," he said.

The two men had developed a good rapport by now, and Frank liked the detective.

"If anyone can do the impossible," Hall insisted, "you can. I saw what you did with List."

Frank had a weakness for two things in his forensics work, neither of which was a very good reason to take on a case. He liked a challenge, and especially if it was for someone who believed in him. Hall kept telling Frank he could do it, the same way Doc Fillinger and Tom Rapone had done with Anna Duval and Robert Nauss. If inexplicable faith in his talent had been justified before, why shouldn't he take on the impossible for Hall too?

Frank asked the detective if he had any other information on the girl. It was suspected, Hall said, that she had been a prostitute. A clampdown by police in Syracuse at the time had led some prostitutes to move to nearby Manlius and to Rochester, which was ninety miles west. For Frank that was still very little to go on to imagine a face. "Send me the skull," he said.

In the meantime, Frank showed Hall's photographs to several pathologists at the Philadelphia medical examiner's office, anthropologists, and colleagues at the Smithsonian. All of them were convinced that he was crazy to even try a reconstruction.

When the skull arrived, he took it out of its cardboard box and put it on his workbench, where it stayed for several weeks. Its condition was worse than he had imagined. The occipital bone on the back of the skull was intact, as were the parietal bones on the sides and some of the frontal bone at the top of the forehead, but there was absolutely nothing in between, just a gaping hole.

The physical presence of the skull also made the task that much more daunting. With Wanda Jacobs and the Man in Concrete, there had been more than 50 percent of the skull to work with. But where did he start when there were no facial features at all?

Frank called Hall and repeated his conclusion that it was impossible. But Hall wouldn't hear of it—Frank was his last chance. "You can do it," he said.

Frank made the detective an offer. He would sculpt a face but would not accept payment unless an ID was made. Hall had nothing to lose.

Frank left the skull for a few more days and continued with a sculpting commission he had received from Howard University in Washington, D.C. The art department had approached him several months earlier about creating a memorial to African-American slaves. It was to be erected in New York City at the African Burial Ground, the site of an eighteenth-century cemetery that had been unearthed in 1991, when the foundation of a new federal building in Lower Manhattan was being dug.

Out of the numerous skulls and bones from the excavation that were being evaluated by the Department of Sociology and Anthropology at Howard, Frank selected three to include in his sculpture: an old woman without any teeth, her skull almost paper-thin; a strong young man with big, long bones; and a younger woman who was thought to have been rebellious because she had been shot in the back. The skulls were so fragile that instead of risking Krazy Glue to attach the tissue markers, Frank used soft clay.

The Girl from Manlius arrived when he was well into refining the slave sculpture, which was going to be called *Unearthed*. Even though he had agreed to take on the project for Detective Hall, he still had no idea where to start affixing the clay. He didn't even have a clue as to what race the faceless girl was.

In the studio at the same time were two other adult skulls, one black and one white, from two different police departments. The busts were completed, but the skulls hadn't been picked up yet. Frank studied them for clues, although he wasn't sure what he was looking for.

Several days passed before he noticed that on both skulls, the butterfly-wing-shaped sphenoid bone, which was at the back of the cranium to the rear of the eye, seemed to be almost the same breadth as the nasal aperture. If that held true for other people, Frank thought, he might have a nose.

He called Mark Mack, a physical anthropologist at Howard who was involved with the *Unearthed* project, and told him about the Girl from Manlius, adding that she was possibly African-American. Would Mack test his theory out on some of the skulls at Howard? Later that day Mack called back with his assessment. "You might be onto something," he said. "In some cases there was perhaps only one millimeter of difference."

At last Frank had a point at which to start. He layered clay into the cavity of the face, then created a maxilla that correlated in size to the lower jaw. If there was an underbite, he couldn't tell. Using the middle six teeth, he had the width of the mouth. Above the maxilla, he marked off a nasal aperture that was based on the size of the sphenoid bone, shaped a nose with wings at the aperture's widest points, then added the orbits.

It looked nothing like any of the other busts he had done, but he had started. Never before had he felt it so vital to work as fast as possible. He had always believed that the face was an interconnected whole—eyes, ears, lips, nose, each taking its shape from the other— and for that to happen with a skull on which there was nowhere to start, he knew that once he had his first clue, he had to work without stopping.

Jan hardly spoke to him for two days. It was one of the few times when she watched him work—staring across the pit from the table in the kitchen—as his hands played over the skull as if it were a musical instrument.

When the Girl from Manlius was finished, she was predominantly African-American but had skin with a lighter tone. Her nose was broad and flat, her ears small, her lips fairly wide with an indent in the upper lip. Her black hair was pulled back into a bun, and her shoulders were left bare and without a shirt or jewelry.

Frank gave the bust to the Manlius police, and then the case went cold.

||||||||||||||||||||||||||||||||||||||||||||||||||||||||

One year later, the kind of coincidence that Paul Schneider would have appreciated took place. It was almost as good as the Man in the Cornfield.

A policeman who had been involved in the Manlius case from the start was a handsome young recruit named Thaddeus Maine. More than a year after Frank had done the bust, Maine, who was

312 | TED BOTHA

on light duty because of an injury, was asked to shred the files of cases that had gone cold.

Known to be a good investigator, he was asked by one of his superiors to check for any possible leads in several of the cases before shredding them. One of them dealt with the Girl from Manlius. Maine was also instructed not to tell anyone about what he was doing.

He remembered the Manlius case well—as a young cop five years earlier, he had stood guard over the scene of the crime—and he had even stuck a photograph of Frank's bust on his office wall.

After talking to people on farms near where the body was found, he realized that he was onto something. Dozens of phone calls turned into hundreds as he tried to track down itinerant laborers who had worked in the area fifteen years earlier. One name kept coming up: Roland Patnode.

An American Indian who moved around a lot, Patnode had been sent to jail for second-degree manslaughter after killing a transvestite prostitute, David McLaughlin, in October 1986. At the time, Patnode was ruled out as a suspect in the killing of the Girl from Manlius because he was thought to have already been in jail. But what if the Girl from Manlius had been killed before McLaughlin?

Maine learned that several people, most of them prostitutes, had approached the Syracuse police about Patnode, and linked him to several girls they worked with, including one named Lorean Quincy Weaver. But their evidence wasn't considered substantial enough. In late 1986 the police in Rochester received a missing persons report about a twenty-five-year-old who had been jailed previously for prostitution. Her name was Lorean Quincy Weaver. Maine started linking the names Patnode and Weaver. He spoke to Weaver's family and got a mug shot of her from the Rochester police.

Even though there had been some initial communication between the Syracuse and Rochester police departments, a possible connection between Weaver and the Girl from Manlius was never made. Not even Maine had connected the dots yet. Among all the evidence he had collected so far, he had a skeleton in a remote wooded area near Manlius, a missing girl in Rochester, and Patnode, who had since disappeared while he was out on parole. Maine still needed something to link the three.

Sitting at his desk one day, the policeman noticed a photograph that he'd tacked to his wall more than a year earlier but had forgotten about: Frank's bust of the Girl from Manlius. Maine had put it there more as a keepsake than as evidence. He'd never really had any of Hall's faith in Frank, and he didn't believe a reconstruction of a skull without a face could work.

He quickly dug the mug shot of Weaver out of his file. She was wearing a tight sleeveless shirt and hoop earrings. She had short hair that wasn't pulled back into a bun, and she didn't have a nose-lip furrow, but he was almost sure that she was the girl in the bust.

Maine's knees started shaking. If she was in fact Weaver, then he knew not only the dead girl's identity but also quite possibly who had killed her. He ran out into the hallway and bumped into two officers, neither of whom knew about his assignment.

When he told them what he'd been doing, they asked why he was reopening case files instead of shredding them. He held up the two photographs.

"Yes," the first officer said, looking at Frank's bust, "we've seen this one a hundred times."

"Well," Maine said, "this is her."

Maine could see that both men, on looking more closely at the two photos, were struck by the resemblance the same way he had been.

"I think she was killed by a guy called Patnode," Maine added. He briefly explained how he had come to his conclusions. The officers told him to go back to his desk, not to talk to anyone, and they went away for half an hour. When they came back, they took him off light duty.

Now assigned to the case full-time, Maine wasn't allowed to approach Patnode's family but tracked down a former girlfriend of his who was prepared to talk. She said she hadn't seen Patnode for a while but had heard that he was living on a reservation in Canada.

Maine had already arranged for DNA of the Girl from Manlius's skeleton to be taken and for the Office of International Affairs to consider extraditing Patnode, should the DNA test prove conclusive. The skeleton was indeed Weaver's, and Patnode was finally apprehended in December 2002.

Frank knew about none of this. From his side, in fact, the case seemed to be falling apart. Not even involving Vidocq had helped move the investigation forward. Keith Hall, the man who had gotten Frank interested in the case, had since left the Manlius police force for personal reasons. When Frank received word that the case was close to being solved, there seemed to be the kind of internal battle developing that he had become all too familiar with. Various people were trying to take credit for the success. He had no idea what role his bust had played.

Frank finally heard Maine's story at the twenty-first annual Manlius Police Benevolent Association Awards dinner in March 2003, where the two of them were among numerous people being honored for their contribution to the case. Frank told the audience that if it hadn't been for Hall's faith in him, he wouldn't have gotten involved.

Four months later, Bob Ressler called Frank about going to Mexico.

# MEXICO

# CODE WORD: "CHRISTMAS"

### Day 1–2

On June 7, 2004, Frank flew down to El Paso and spent the night at Michelle Cromer's house. The following morning, a Tuesday, he had breakfast with the assistant attorney general, Sergio Camarillo Martínez, and his aide Jonathan Arroyo, who then drove Frank across the border to Juárez.

It was only a ten-minute drive from Cromer's house and over the Cordovas-Americas Bridge to Frank's hotel, but it took an entire day for customs to clear his fifteen barrels of equipment. Having a high-ranking Mexican government official in the car should have helped, but it didn't.

Less than a mile from the border, they pulled in at the pink Lincoln Holiday Inn. The generic two-story hotel was nothing like the Lucerna. That wasn't the only change since Frank last worked in Mexico. It was clear that the investigation no longer lay in the hands of the state but was with the *federales*. Arroyo, who was filling Esparza's role, looked less casual and more like a businessman—trim, dressed in a smart suit—and spoke perfect English.

The two men went up to Frank's room. In the room next door were four bodyguards from Mexico City who had been assigned to protect him.

"They will stay with you at all times," Arroyo said. "They have to do what you want to do. Even if you go jogging, they'll jog with you."

The bodyguards—close-cropped hair, tough-looking, in their twenties—wore blue fatigues with the insignia AFI, the brand-new FBI-like Federal Agency of Investigation. Frank recalled that it was seven AFI agents who had died in the Juárez plane explosion. Each of the men carried an M16 semiautomatic rifle and had a handgun in his belt.

After being introduced to them—Frank remembered only one name, Francisco, but he was sure all their names were fake anyway—he was instructed to keep the blinds drawn at all times. If he bumped into Esparza, he could tell him about working for the *federales,* but he couldn't talk to him alone; the bodyguards had to be there too.

"What did you think of him?" Arroyo added, almost as an afterthought. "Esparza, I mean."

Frank still had a soft spot for his old colleague. "He was as honest as you can find down here," he said, unsure if Arroyo would be insulted by his candor.

When Arroyo left, Frank started to feel the excitement that came with every new case, this one in particular. He had thought that he would never get back to Mexico, but here he was, and the investigation seemed to have renewed life. Everything he had seen so far—the *federales,* Arroyo, the bodyguards—made the operation seem slicker, more organized. Under these conditions, he could easily see himself finishing his work in three weeks and getting out of Mexico before the election on the July 4 weekend.

Cromer was more cautious about the situation. The drug trade continued, people were still being shot and killed in town, and the bodies of several murdered women had been found only a few months earlier. For this reason she arranged to call Frank every day to check up on him. If he needed to get out of Mexico fast, they had a code word—"Christmas."

## Day 3

By Wednesday, June 9, the problems began.

When the bodyguards took Frank to see Dr. Sánchez—the coroner was the only person Frank had worked with who was still on the case—she told him that her reports weren't ready. He wouldn't get the skulls until Friday. That would put him two full days behind schedule. Frank called Cromer, who said she would contact Camarillo about the delay.

Frank went for a swim in the meantime. The bodyguards followed him down to the hotel pool, concealing their Uzis under towels, and sat on deck chairs around him when he got out of the water.

After he returned to his room, he got a call from the lobby. It was Esparza.

"I would like to talk," he said.

Frank told him that he could meet only if the bodyguards came along. Not liking that, Esparza left.

Day 4

By Thursday, it had been arranged for Frank to get the skulls. Camarillo himself came across the border from El Paso with several agents, picked up five skulls from Sánchez, and delivered them to the hotel. Then he drove back to El Paso.

Each head was in a brown paper bag with the same thing written on the side: *L'Antropologia forense Zona Norte. Craneo.* They were numbered 191/01 to 195/01.

Frank was used to the procedure by now, and it went quickly. He took photographs of the bags, together and separately, then removed the contents and arranged the skulls on a chest of drawers.

Accompanying each one was a report in Spanish. He could barely understand what they said, but it was a lot more than he had received the previous time, when any information had been communicated to him verbally. He asked Arroyo to translate the important facts, such as age, race, height, and any notable features.

He knew by this stage that the facts were probably wrong anyway. The skulls would have to tell him where to go.

# CASE NUMBER 193/01

With the tissue-thickness markers attached, Frank once again photographed the skulls in front of their brown paper bags. There were no obvious asymmetries, no lower jaws missing. The only thing that stood out on the five skulls was that case number 193/01 seemed especially large for a woman.

He paged through the reports, not really expecting to find anything, but then he noticed several words about 193/01 that troubled him. He knocked on the door to the room next to his.

"I have to go see Dr. Sánchez," he told the bodyguards. "I need some more information."

Arroyo came by and took Frank to the coroner's office, where he asked Sánchez if he could see anything that had come with the bodies—hair, clothing, jewelry. He was led through to the evidence room, where he was shown a few items of clothing that had been found with two of the five girls. He checked the report he'd been given against what was in front of him. "Something isn't right here," he said. "I think two of the bodies are mixed up."

One of the reports noted that 193/01 had been found with a petite size 30 bra. Going by the size of her head, though, she must have been a very large person. Sánchez checked and said that Frank was right. So, either the evidence was wrong or the skull had been put with the wrong body. And if it had, then another head was also with the wrong body.

The discovery was significant. It meant that even though the players had changed—no longer was it the state police involved but the *federales*—the problems hadn't. Before leaving the coroner's office, Frank was informed that at least one other head that he'd been given was with the wrong body.

Back at the Holiday Inn, Frank got his nightly call from Michelle Cromer, who had bad news. After all her money-gathering efforts, there was only enough to pay him for three heads, not five. What she didn't tell him was that she and her husband, Barry, had put up more than 80 percent of the funds.

Frank chose two heads—one of them was the second head that had been misidentified, although he kept working on 193/01—and, after storing them back in their paper bags, put them in his cupboard.

Now only three skulls were left on the table. By the time he went to bed, the tissue markers were in place on 193/01, and he had already started adding clay to the other two.

## Day 5

On Friday, when Arroyo came around, as he did most days, two of the skulls were well on their way to becoming faces—eyes in place, even—but 193/01 still had only tissue markers attached.

Frank had left it that way until he could point out something to Arroyo. "I think she was black," he said.

"No," Arroyo said, "I don't think so. Maybe she's Indian, from our mountains."

"No," Frank said, "she's black."

"What kind of black?"

"African-American black."

Frank had other news. "I think the skeleton could also be a male." The mandible and cranium, besides being large, were fairly thick.

"How's that possible?" Arroyo asked.

"Maybe it was a male dressed up as a female. That would explain the small bra."

Sánchez was asked to come over and see the skull. She agreed that it could be from a black person, but she wasn't sure about Frank's theory that it could be a male. Frank suggested to Arroyo that they get another opinion on the pubic symphysis, the cartilaginous joint located above the vulva or penis, to make sure what sex it was.

But then he remembered that would be pointless, because no one was sure whether they even had the correct body.

After Arroyo and Sánchez left, Frank started layering clay onto the third skull, to bring it up to the same point as the other two. The hotel room was hot and had no fan or air-conditioning, which made the clay pliable, the way he liked it.

He worked until seven that night, and then went down to the pool for a swim. The bodyguards followed him, their Uzis secreted under their towels once again, although this time a few of them jumped in the pool with him.

Frank hadn't been back in the room for an hour before he started getting a severe headache. He couldn't work, so he asked the bodyguards to take him out somewhere. When he told them where he wanted to go—a strip joint—they looked surprised. He didn't have the language or the energy to explain why. Part of him was curious about the sordid underbelly of Juárez life, the social conditions that had contributed to the murders. But part of him, the Frank who was a sculptor, who loved women and cheated on Jan, also wanted an up-close look at the prostitutes, the *ficheras,* and the dancers.

They drove to a club on 5 de Febrero. There was no sign outside telling them to check their guns, and they weren't frisked as they went in. The club was empty, large, and too bright.

Frank ordered a Coke. A woman, one of several walking around the club in a short skirt, came over to him. He stared at her straight in the eyes, studying her face, and all at once he was reminded of the days when he was in art classes with Tony Greenwood.

*Look. And then look. And then look again.*

He could smell her cheap perfume, and he found himself turned on at the same time as feeling nauseated. Another girl who was rubbing up against him couldn't have been more than a teenager, maybe fifteen or sixteen. His immediate thought was how little she would be able to struggle with a big pair of hands around her throat.

At that moment he got an urge to escape, to return to the heads, as if they were a safe haven. He told Francisco he wanted to leave.

### Day 6

Frank's headache was so bad during the night that he could hardly sleep. He went to lunch with Arroyo, and tears were running down his face from the pain. When Arroyo asked him what was wrong, he said he was fine. He didn't want anything to get in the way of the job, or for the Mexicans to think he couldn't finish it.

He called Cromer and asked if her husband could send him something for the pain. By this stage, he'd realized it was a gum infection that had probably gone into his sinuses. He'd had dental work done just before leaving Philadelphia, and the water in the pool and his room had created an infection. The water was so dirty, the clothes he washed in the bathtub smelled half an hour after he put them on, and he had to flush the toilet every hour because the water began to stink.

|||||||||||||||||||||||||||||||||||||||||||||||||||||||||||||

Arroyo brought some Cipro and Aleve from El Paso, but neither helped. Frank called Jan and asked her to get their doctor in Philadelphia to send more painkillers.

## Day 7

Frank desperately needed to get out of his room. The combination of his headache, the bodyguards next door, and the blinds drawn all day long made the room feel like it was closing in on him.

He tried to focus on the busts, but his mind kept wandering to the same questions over and over again. Did he have the right information on each victim? Was the right skull with the right body? Were things being kept from him that he should know? Why was the bra petite? Was 193/01 a man?

When Sánchez brought him hair samples for the three skulls, they didn't seem to match what Frank had. There was curly hair for a girl he thought would have had straight hair. That only led to more questions, many of which had begun during his previous sculpting trip to Mexico.

Once again he thought about how the bodies had been found in clusters—along the railway tracks, at the cotton field, and in the hills behind the city—and how all of them were in a similar state of decomposition. He started seeing the faces of the women everywhere he turned, in the folds of his curtains, in the patterns on the bathroom tiles, in the reflections in the pool.

But this time something about the questions and images was different. Whereas in the past he had accepted them as part of the creative process, just like the nightmares, now they made him feel unlike he'd ever felt on a case. He had become withdrawn and annoyed, and he felt very alone.

No case had ever been so confusing—possibly by design—equal parts conundrum and roller coaster. It defied logic, and maybe it was meant to. Questions had outnumbered answers from the start, and their number had only increased since then. Answers were either elusive or nonexistent.

Suspects kept growing in number too. Each time a finger was pointed in one direction—at the Egyptian, at the bus drivers, at one serial killer, at many serial killers, at an American, at drug traffickers, at the police—someone pointed it somewhere new. Law enforcement, meanwhile, couldn't have been doing less to solve anything.

It was a terrible thing to say, but Frank almost wished for the simplicity of a single serial killer, or even several of them. The alternative was, he feared, something much worse. The serial killer could be anyone, everyone, society itself. Except for the women protesting, everyone else seemed willing to tolerate the hundreds of murders, make excuses for them, wish them to disappear. And as time passed and nothing was done, the victims would be forgotten and the only things to remain of them would be the memories held by their families, the fast-fading pink crosses, and fewer than ten plaster sculptures that had been commissioned for reasons he didn't fully comprehend.

As a constant reminder to Frank that things in Juárez were neither normal nor safe, Francisco and the three other bodyguards were with him all the time. Their presence made him and everyone else nervous. If a waiter knocked at his door with a glass of wine or a sandwich, all four jumped out to see who it was. Whenever the staff came by after that, they were on edge. Frank felt an urgent need to get away from the bodyguards, to walk on his own from one side of Juárez to the other, to be free in the town, but he couldn't.

Francisco offered to take Frank to their favorite restaurant, Barriga's. But Frank wanted to go somewhere else, to do something they didn't usually do, far away from the routine of Juárez. He suggested eating Chinese. One of the bodyguards said he knew a place called the Mandarin Palace, although a second bodyguard didn't think that was a good idea. But all five of them piled into their Jeep Cherokee and drove down Constitución and into Vicente Guerrero.

They pulled up at the Mandarin Palace. While they ate their food, a big, burly man sitting in the back kept watching them. He came up as they were leaving and demanded to know what they were doing there.

"He's a policeman," Francisco whispered to Frank.

For the first time since he'd come down, Frank saw the two sides of the law physically facing off against each other—the state police versus the *federales*—and he was on a different side now. The clash between law-enforcement agencies in America usually had to do with ego and wanting to take credit for a crime's resolution, but here it was something deeper, angrier, unfathomable. How did you solve a crime with that internal war going on?

The policeman asked them to provide some identification. By this stage, they were all standing outside. Each of the bodyguards took out his identification card and held it up on a different side of the policeman's face, one to the right, one to the left, and one in front, to block his view. At the same time, Francisco motioned for Frank to get in the Jeep. The policeman backed down.

"That restaurant is owned by the cartel," Francisco told him after they left. "They don't like *federales* coming in."

# UNDER THE COVERS

## Day 8

It was one of those gorgeous days in El Paso that Michelle Cromer loved—crisp and clear, with a never-ending sky—when she drove across the border to visit Frank. She parked at the Holiday Inn and went up to his room.

For the past week, they had spoken only on the phone, and it would be her first time seeing the busts. It was also her first direct contact with the murdered girls for whom she had started the Pink Crosses foundation.

As she walked into his darkened room, Frank had clay in his hands and was working on the head of the large black woman. The other two were already more refined. One had shoulder-length hair with a middle parting and the other had her head tilted a bit to the right, her hair parted just off center and pulled back over her ears. Frank was creating a braid for the third.

Cromer hadn't emotionally prepared herself for what she would see. Frank started explaining what he was doing, but she wasn't listening. As soon as she saw the busts, she felt like crying. Knowing what was going on in Juárez was very different from seeing the evidence up close. At this moment the only thing that separated her physically from the dead women was a thin layer of clay. Seeing the faces, she immediately pictured people she knew, someone's daughter, sister, mother.

Cromer suggested they move downstairs to the coffee shop. "I think it's safer to talk there or in the parking lot," she said once they'd stepped out into the hallway. "The room might be bugged."

Frank, who had been keeping a tape recording of the events in Juárez, started doing it under the bedcovers from that night.

## Day 9

On June 15, Arroyo drove Frank to El Paso to buy synthetic rubber. The consignment he'd ordered from Philadelphia hadn't arrived. The bodyguards followed them in their car, then waited at the Cordovas Bridge until they got back that afternoon.

Frank began painting rubber on the clay after he got back to his room. Esparza called him again, but they just talked briefly.

Frank took more tablets for his headache, but they didn't help. Whenever he worked, he didn't feel the pain as much, so he tried not to stop. Before he went to bed, he layered the plaster mother molds on top of the dried rubber coatings.

## Day 10

It was Frank's birthday—he was sixty-three.

After he pulled apart the mother molds and poured a newly made batch of plaster into the inverted casings in the bathtub, he went to see a movie with the bodyguards, *The Day After.* One bodyguard sat on either side of him, one in front, and one behind.

Frank called Bob Ressler from under the bedcovers that night. Ressler said recent news reports had also disclosed that three women in Las Cruces, New Mexico, were murdered in the same way as victims of the *feminicidios* over the past three years.

"The same as in Juárez," he said. "They have just put up a pink cross in America."

Jan called Frank for his birthday, and he told her that he was almost done with the heads. She had read on the Internet that day about more killings in Mexico, but maybe that had to do with the upcoming election. "The tension is even getting to us here," she said.

Frank told her that he was fine and that the bodyguards were with him all the time. He didn't mention that he was talking to her from under his bedcovers.

"And I've got a mission—I'm going to finish these heads."

# BAD WATER

### Day 11

The next day he sanded and filed the plaster busts by hand and with his electric rotary tool. Afterward he began painting them.

At ten that night he went next door to see the bodyguards, only to find Francisco with his gun drawn and pointing it in front of him at the door to the hallway. One of the other bodyguards motioned Frank to back off.

Instead of making him feel more secure, they were scaring him. What were they after? Or whom? Was it the election? The drug cartel? Were there people with other agendas whom he'd never even considered?

He returned to his room. A few minutes later, he went back to the bodyguards' room, but they were gone. He hadn't even heard them leave, they'd been so quiet. They had never left him on his own before. Someone must be out there, he thought, or they wouldn't have disappeared like that. Fifteen minutes later, they returned. They said nothing.

### Day 12

The first thing Frank noticed when he woke up was that the busts had turned yellow. The bad water was affecting the plaster mixture, and as it dried out, the paint changed color.

He called up the factory where he had bought the FGR95, and they said the discoloration might well happen with the wrong water. There was nothing that could be done about it at this stage.

## The Last Day

Frank packed up his equipment and was ready for it to be picked up and taken across to El Paso. He put the cleaned skulls back in their brown paper bags, the way they had arrived.

The three busts were on the chest of drawers, exactly where he had photographed the skulls eight days earlier. It had taken him just over a week to finish them, and tomorrow they would be gone. There would be no press conference, no public statement. This was his final night with them. At that moment he realized that he had given none of them a name.

To the left was the girl with her hair parted in the middle—she could have been any age from twelve to sixteen—her nose wider than that of the girl on the far right. In the middle was the girl with the large head, 193/01. She had full lips and eyes that looked larger than the girls' on either side of her, but that could have been just the makeup Frank had added. Her hair was pulled back and braided.

The last girl, the one with her head tilted to one side, looked as if she were thinking about some small trifle, daydreaming, wondering about something that had happened to her that day, or maybe she was even contemplating why her bus hadn't arrived yet.

# POSTMORTEM

## ANNA DUVAL

When Duval's killer was found, he was already in jail for a more high-profile murder. John Martini, said to be a hit man working for Tony Provenzano, had kidnapped and killed New Jersey businessman Irving Flax in 1989, for which he was sentenced to death.

In his statement to police, Martini claimed that it wasn't he who had killed Duval but an off-duty cop he had paid to do the job. Both of them met her at the airport (it turned out that she'd had financial dealings with Martini in the past), and while Martini was driving, the policeman, who was sitting in the backseat, shot her. Martini was tried for Duval's murder in 2004. His last plea to overturn his death penalty was refused in 2005.

Curiously, at the same time Frank was sculpting Duval, his friend Marguerite Ferrari asked if she could do a life-size portrait of him. Not long afterward she got a chance to show the painting at a gallery in Phoenix, Arizona—the same place, it so happened, where Duval had lived.

Months later, Ferrari got a call from a dealer in bric-a-brac who said she had the painting of Frank. Would Ferrari like to buy it?

"But it's supposed to be at a gallery in Phoenix," Ferrari said.

When she called the gallery, they admitted that it had been stolen. The woman, who got Frank's number from Ferrari, called him one night to ask if he wanted to buy the painting for a hundred and fifty dollars. He asked her where she lived.

"Old Bridge," she said.

The name sounded familiar. Only after he hung up did he realize that it was the same part of New Jersey that the Italian men who'd arrived at his studio when he was sculpting Duval had come from. Frank told the Philadelphia police, who contacted their colleagues in Old Bridge. They didn't sound like they would do anything about it, so Frank drove up to see the woman himself.

A teenager answered the door and said that the woman was out and had instructed her not to let anyone in. Frank wanted to get in to make sure the painting was actually there, so he told the girl he had come to buy a painting of himself.

"Yes," the girl said, recognizing Frank, "it's in the living room."

Finally, she let Frank in. The painting was leaning against the living room wall. Later that day Frank returned with the Old Bridge police, and the owner was at home. The police told Frank to pay her for the painting, and even though he refused at first—"I don't buy stolen art," he said—he had no choice. He gave the woman a check but canceled it a few hours later.

Frank never figured out whether it was just a coincidence—Old Bridge, Phoenix, Anna Duval, the men with Italian names, the painting—but he did hear later on that acquiring a painting of someone in this way was known as a Spanish Vendetta.

## HALBERT FILLINGER

Fillinger died in June 2006, at the age of seventy-nine, after having performed, by modest estimates, more than fifty thousand autopsies.

## THE GIRL FROM NORTH LEITHGOW STREET

The murderer of Jacqueline Gough has not been found.

## PRINCESS DOE

On July 15, 1982, the partially clothed body of a teenage girl was found in a remote corner of a cemetery in Blairsville, New Jersey. An autopsy was done by the medical examiner in Newark. The girl was just over five feet tall and was thought to have been dead for one to three weeks. She had pierced ears but no surgical scars, birthmarks, or tattoos. She had been beaten repeatedly about the head and face with a blunt instrument.

There were several leads that suggested the case could be solved quickly, and even Haskell Askin, who was usually called in later to confirm a possible ID through dental X-rays, was asked to come in and see the body within the first twenty-four hours. But the leads went nowhere, which was when Frank was asked to create a bust.

He was told that the girl probably had an androgynous face, with the heavy, rugged bones of a Western European, probably a German. Going solely from the skull, in fact, her sex might have been difficult to determine.

For the first time since Frank had been doing reconstructions, a skull came to him with conditions. It was considered too fragile for him to sculpt directly onto the bone. Instead of taking measurements, as he had with Anna Duval, he photographed the skull from all sides with a zoom lens and used fluorescent lighting to eliminate shadows. Once he had enlarged the shots to life-size, he made a tracing that he placed over the bust as he sculpted, making sure he always stayed within the contours of the skull. It was a procedure he would use later on for fugitives.

The flyer for Princess Doe showed four photographs of the bust—from the front and various side angles. She was dressed in a V-neck pullover like the one the girl had been wearing when she died, and around her neck was a cross on a gold chain that had been found tangled in her hair. She was buried in January 1983.

In 1985 a Warren County prosecutor held a press conference to say that there could be a link between Princess Doe and a California runaway named Diane Dye, who had last been seen in December 1981, seven months before the body of Princess Doe was found. At least one dental expert made a connection between the two, but his evidence was then refuted by several others, including Haskell Askin.

For Frank, it was one of the most ego-driven cases he had ever worked on; numerous people were trying to get credit for a break in the case. But it never came. Even Eric Kranz, the detective who had put the case on the map and gave her the name Princess Doe, was charged with official misconduct, which was never proved, and he resigned.

On September 22, 1999, the body of Princess Doe was exhumed from the Cedar Ridge Cemetery so that DNA samples could be taken. The body remains unidentified.

## HASKELL ASKIN

Askin, who has worked as both a general dentist since 1959 and a forensic dentist since 1967, was one of two hundred dentists who searched through the wreckage of the World Trade Center for evidence of the victims of 9/11. As a WTC tour commander, he was responsible for certifying dental identifications. He also appeared at the trial of Jesse Timmendequas, who was tried and convicted for the rape and murder of seven-year-old Megan Kanka in 1994. The doctor testified that the teeth marks in Timmendequas's hand belonged to the young girl, evidence that contributed to his conviction.

The Princess Doe case is the one Askin most wants to see solved before he retires.

## YVONNE DAVI

In 1991 a man named Michael Dirago, a drug dealer who was Davi's boyfriend, went on trial in New Jersey for her death. It came out that after Davi threatened to leave Dirago, she got in a car with him and Robert Ferrante, who told her they were going to Atlantic City. When she realized they were heading in another direction, she began struggling, and Dirago shot her twice. They dumped the body across the state line, in Pennsylvania.

## DIANE LEWIS

Following the murder of Lewis, police arrested James Kruczek, who apparently bragged to a friend that he had killed a prostitute and showed him the corpse in November 1986, six months before the bust was recognized by Lewis's father. At his trial, Kruczek was found not guilty.

## THE MAN IN THE CORNFIELD

In 1993, seven years after Edward Myers was identified, the police went back to the last person he was seen with. David Stanley, who had worked with Myers in a furniture warehouse in Havertown, Pennsylvania, was initially a suspect, but there was no connection between him and the gun that shot the victim. When the link was made at last, Stanley admitted that he had killed Myers over a debt, driven the body to Lancaster County, and buried it there.

## ALPHONSE "ALLIE BOY" PERSICO

Persico was tried and sentenced to twenty-five years in prison. He was sent to Springfield Penitentiary, Missouri. A month later, in December 1987, he died from cancer of the larynx.

## THE GIRL ON ROUTE 309

The badly decomposed body of a woman was found off Route 309 in Montgomery County, Pennsylvania, in November 1988. The body was clad in a blue-and-white-printed cotton outfit. She was a black female in her mid-thirties whose hair was tied up in a bun, and she was over six feet tall. There was a red pair of jogging pants tied around her face and head, although the cause of death could not be determined by the pathologist. A local detective carried around a photograph of Frank's bust and regularly asked people he stopped if they knew her. In May 1989, someone he pulled over for a minor traffic violation did. He said she often went to a nearby church, and her name was Debra Wiggins. A few months later, police arrested Charles Matiland for her murder.

## THE GIRL WITH HOPE AND GRETCHEN WORDEN

If anyone wanted closure on the Rosella Atkinson case, it was Gretchen Worden, curator of the Mütter Museum. Whenever she saw Frank, she asked if an arrest had been made.

One day in the summer of 2004, Frank bumped into Worden, who, as usual, asked about the Atkinson case. Frank commented on how well Worden looked, but he didn't realize she was very ill. She died the next week.

A year later, a wing of the museum was being dedicated to Worden at a function, which was to take place at six in the evening. Three hours earlier, Frank got a call from the Philadelphia police. He was told that a man had walked into the station and confessed to killing Atkinson.

Until then the police had no idea how the girl had died. They had questioned the killer before, a man named Brian Hall, but had nothing on him. On giving himself in to police, Hall admitted that he had met Atkinson in a bar and they'd had sex on the football field. He had woken up afterward and found he was missing some money, thought she had stolen it, and had throttled her. He told the police that he kept seeing Atkinson's face, an image that he had seen broadcast on television after she was identified.

At the very same time that Worden's wing was being dedicated, an item on the six o'clock news said that Atkinson's murderer had confessed. It was announced at the dedication.

Hall was found guilty of third-degree murder in January 2007.

## TONY GREENWOOD

When Frank heard the news that his friend and former art teacher Tony Greenwood had shot himself, he wanted to see the body for himself. He felt like he owed it to the man who had helped him when he was starting out in forensics. He went down to the morgue to try and find the body.

Frank had never seen anyone he knew dead at the medical examiner's office—at least not on purpose. Once he was down visiting Doc Fillinger when he noticed a body on one of the gurneys that had tattoos he was convinced he recognized. On looking closer, he realized it was a guy named Billy, whom he and Jan had known during their wild clubbing days. Working as a bouncer many years later, Billy had been fatally stabbed when he got in between two women having a fight.

Greenwood's body had already left the medical examiner's office by the time Frank got there, although the investigators showed him photographs of how his friend had been found. Frank recognized the yellow shirt that Greenwood was wearing, although now it was covered in blood.

## JOHN LIST

Tried in Elizabeth, New Jersey, in 1990, List was sentenced to five consecutive life terms.

## BRAD BISHOP

The *AMW* segment on family murderer Bishop was shown at least eight times over the next decade, but he remains at large. In 1992 the *Daily Mail* of London quoted an inspector at Scotland Yard saying that Bishop—who, besides his distinctive cleft chin, is said to have a surgical scar on his back—was thought to be in Spain.

## GEORGE STRZELCZYK

Wanted for child molestation, he was caught in Phoenix, Arizona, in 1995. His bust had been shown on the CBS show *How'd They Do That?*

## DR. HUDOCK

George Hudock died in October 2005 at the age of seventy-seven. He averaged more than fifty autopsies a year since 1969. Frank never met him again after they cut off the head in Wilkes-Barre together.

## THE GIRL WITH THE GREEN EYES

In 2002 *National Geographic* wanted to track down the young girl with green eyes who had been one of their most famous covers; the shot was taken in Afghanistan by Steve McCurry in 1985. A magazine crew went back to the Pakistani refugee camp where she'd lived, and found a man who said she was still alive and lived in the Tora Bora region of Afghanistan. Her name was Sharbat Gula. In order to make sure it was her, they did an iris scan of her and got Frank to do an age-progression bust.

## THE BOY IN THE BAG

In February 2005 the uncle of a boy named Jerrell Willis, who had been missing since 1994, was looking on the website of the National Center for Missing and Exploited Children when he saw the sculpture of the Boy in the Bag. He contacted the Philadelphia police, who arrested Willis's mother, Alicia Robinson, and her husband, Lawrence Robinson, who was Jerrell's stepfather. At their trial, it came out that they had beaten the boy to death, carried the body from Camden by bus, and dumped it in Philadelphia.

The uncle said he noticed a family resemblance in the bust, especially around the boy's mouth and forehead. The medical examiner never called to tell Frank about the discovery, although Gene Suplee, one of the investigators, phoned to congratulate him.

Frank still hasn't been paid for this work.

## FLO GOODING

Wanted in Connecticut and California on charges of arson and attempted murder in 1981, the bust of Florencia, or Flo, Gooding was shown on *AMW* in 1990. She was caught the following year.

## IRA EINHORN

In 1993 Einhorn was convicted in absentia for the murder of Holly Maddux and sentenced to life. In 1997, after sixteen years of stakeouts and near misses, law-enforcement agents found Einhorn living under the name of Eugene Mallon in the remote French village of Champagne-Mouton. He challenged his extradition and was returned to the United States only in July 2001. Frank's bust of Einhorn is in the École Nationale Supérieure de la Police in St.-Cyr, France.

### FRANK MATTHEWS

The case against drug kingpin Matthews is still open. Frank thinks that if Matthews isn't dead, he is in a witness protection program.

### JAMES KILGORE

In 2001 an FBI agent in San Francisco contacted Frank to do an age-progression bust of Kilgore, the last fugitive member of the Symbionese Liberation Army, which abducted heiress Patty Hearst in 1974 and took over the Hibernia Bank in San Francisco a year later.

In August 2002 Kilgore was arrested in South Africa, where he was living, and extradited to the United States to stand trial. The agent told Frank the FBI would not release details of how Kilgore was identified, but the bust was very helpful getting the fugitive identified. The FBI thanked Frank on its website.

### THE MAN IN CONCRETE

In January 2001 an antiques dealer named Gregory May went missing from his home in Bellevue, Iowa. His adult children, Don and Shannon, reported his disappearance to police. May's house was empty, his phone had been disconnected, and his antiques, said to be worth a quarter of a million dollars, were gone.

Three months later, his car was found abandoned a hundred miles away, in Illinois, with May's wallet still inside. When Don May heard from one of his father's colleagues that the antiques were being sold at an auction in Arizona, the police went to Flagstaff. A longtime friend of May's, Doug DeBruin, and his girlfriend, Julie Miller, insisted the antiques were theirs. A trace of May's blood was found on DeBruin's jacket, and both of them were arrested. Miller told investigators that DeBruin had strangled May and dismembered the body with a chain saw and spread it around the countryside as they sold off parts of his collection.

Four hundred miles away, in Kearney, Missouri, the skull embedded in concrete was found seven months after May's death. Once Frank had done the bust, it sat on a desk in the Kearney police station, and a photograph was posted on the department's website.

In early 2005 a woman named Ellen Leach was going through the Doe Network on the Internet when she saw Frank's reconstruction and matched it with the missing persons photograph of Greg May. His children were struck by the accuracy of the bust, particularly some features that were hardest to guess from a skull—the ears, jawline, hair, and lips. It was barely a week before DeBruin and Miller were to go on trial without a body.

In May 2005 DeBruin was sentenced to life imprisonment for first-degree murder, which was upheld by the Iowa Appeals Court in October 2006.

Ellen Leach contacted Frank in January 2006 about another one of his sculptures on the Doe Network—the woman whose remains were found in a landfill in Schuylkill County, Pennsylavnia, in 1999. She remains unidentified.

## THE MAN IN THE DUMPSTER

The body was found in January 1995 in a Dumpster behind a Caldor store in Willingboro, New Jersey. It belonged to a white male between five-four and five-eight, between the ages of forty-five and seventy-five. He had a set of upper dentures and seven lower natural teeth.

A year later, the Vidocq Society was working on a case that had been brought to them from New Jersey. One day Frank and several other members joined the police to walk through a wooded area outside Trenton and look for a body. When they broke for lunch, Frank sat across the table from a detective from Willingboro.

"You did a helluva case on that guy they found in the Dumpster," the detective said to Frank.

One of the detective's colleagues had been sitting on the toilet reading a report from MAGLOCLEN (the Mid-Atlantic Great Lakes Organized Crime Law Enforcement Network) when he recognized a photograph of the bust as a missing person named Fundador Otero. The sixty-eight-year-old was reported missing in January 1995.

No one had ever bothered to tell Frank about the match.

## EDWARD SOLLY

Solly was sent to jail but was released early for time served and good behavior. He will be on parole until 2011.

## THADDEUS MAINE

The young detective who was instrumental in recognizing the Girl from Manlius as Lorean Quincy Weaver resigned after the case and is no longer a policeman.

## THE MAN IN PUERTO RICO

In August 2004 Frank was asked by Detective Vasquez to return to Puerto Rico for the trial of Xavier Rodriguez, who was accused of killing the man whose body was found in the mountains. The victim was known by the nickname Blue.

After arriving in San Juan, Frank was repeatedly told that the prosecutor would fill him in on the case, which he knew nothing about, except that it had to do with drug trafficking. In the end, Frank turned out to be the only expert witness. When he asked why, Vasquez told him that it wasn't the kind of case people liked to get involved in. It was too dangerous.

On being asked by the defense what made him an expert in identifying people, Frank pulled out a dozen photographs of IDs that he'd made. Only at the end of the trial did he find out that Rodriguez was a hit man for the drug cartel and was already serving thirty years. He got another twenty years for killing Blue.

That night a hotel worker came to Frank's room and said she wanted to turn down his bed. She was blond, which Frank thought was odd for a Puerto Rican. Or maybe he was still feeling edgy from his trip to Mexico. Just to be safe, he didn't let her in.

## THE GIRL WITHOUT A LOWER JAW

She was identified as Veronica Martinez Hernandez.

## CASE NUMBER 193/01

Not long after Frank left Mexico for the final time, photographs of the last three busts were lying on Michelle Cromer's dining table. A Mexican woman working for her at the time saw them and said that one of them reminded her of her friend's daughter, who was missing. The photograph was of case number 193/01, the girl with the large head.

"Tell your friend to give DNA to the *federales*," Cromer insisted.

The woman's friend went to see the *federales*, gave DNA, and they found out that it was her daughter. She wasn't black, and her hair was straighter.

Her name was Mayra Juliana Reyes Solís.

## THE GIRL WITH THE CROOKED NOSE

Several days after Frank got back to Philadelphia, the fifteen barrels of equipment arrived, and he started unpacking them. He put away the paints and the clay. He had more clay now than he wanted. When would he ever do five heads at once again, he wondered. Maybe for the Egyptian job.

That reminded him to call Jonathan Elias, who wanted him to start doing work on the first mummy from Akhmim. Her name was Neced.

Once he'd finished unpacking, Frank went down to the pit and brought up a barrel from his first sculpting trip to Mexico. In it was something he'd taken—stolen, in fact: one of the mother molds from the five heads.

Even though the Mexicans had made him return everything that he'd made, he hadn't. With all the secrecy about the Girl from Chihuahua and the confusion about how many heads he was doing, four or five, no one had realized that he'd given back one fewer mother mold than he should have. Frank had left so quickly after the press conference that no one had time to notice.

He put the barrel on the floor of the studio and took out the mother mold, which he'd wrapped in trash bags. As Guy lay on the love seat and Boy watched him from the workbench, Frank went to the kitchen to mix plaster. It hadn't been easy getting the mold home, but he'd known from the very start that he wanted a copy of the girl. It was his gift to himself.

She was the first of the Mexican girls whose face he could picture in his head, with her slightly misshapen features. She still had no name, but he was so familiar with the asymmetry, the cockeyed smile, and the crooked nose, he felt as if he knew her.

# AFTERWORD

In April 2007 a member of the FBI addressing the Academy of Forensic Sciences said that after years of trying to use computers to create facial reconstructions, the agency had concluded that human re-creations were more effective.

In July 2006 the Mexican government quietly announced that it was closing its investigation into the *feminicidios* and returning the cases to the state of Chihuahua. There was no serial killer involved, the government decided, so there was no federal offense.

In August the second bus driver arrested in 2001 for the cotton field murders, Victor García Uribe, was released from jail. The first one had died in prison. The same month, police in Denver arrested Edgar Álvarez Cruz on suspicion of killing ten of the murder victims, although doubt was cast on his arrest almost from the moment he was transferred to El Paso. Oscar Maynez, a former medical examiner in Chihuahua, said that achieving any conviction would be difficult because of "the incompetence of investigators."

In February 2007 workmen began clearing a portion of the cotton field to make way for a new commercial zone.

In late 2007 I went to Juárez armed with a single black-and-white photograph of the victim I have always thought of as the Girl with the Crooked Nose. Three years earlier, Frank had received three photographs from the Mexican investigators, saying that they were of the three girls who had been identified through his work.

While two of the photographs had names attached to them—Veronica Martinez Hernandez and Mayra Juliana Reyes Solís—the one suspected of being the Girl with the Crooked Nose did not. I assumed that it was because her "family"—the father who had turned up at Esparza's office in his splattered work pants, and the mother and daughter with their similarly crooked noses—had steadfastly refused to admit it was her or to have DNA tests done in order to prove it.

I was well into researching the book about Frank before he dug out the black-and-white photograph to show me. By that time, I had already come to know the victim only as the Girl with the Crooked Nose, and the only face she had for me was the one in plaster he'd given her. Like Frank, though, I had developed an inexplicable fondness for her. Now I was confronted with a real person.

The young woman casually posing in the photograph was quite beautiful, with lively eyes and a captivating smile that tilted down a bit on one side. Her hair hung loose over her ears, as Frank had predicted it would, and her nose had a slight curve to the right, imperceptible enough to be almost unnoticeable. You would have to know that it was there to look for it. Finally seeing who the Girl with the Crooked Nose was felt both shocking and exhilarating.

I hoped that someone in Juárez would recognize the photograph and that I would be able to give her a name and to interview her family. But no one knew who she was. Everyone involved with the *feminicidios* that I talked to just shook their heads when they saw her photograph. I shouldn't have been surprised, but it seemed that she had slipped through the cracks, of which there are many in Mexico, that exist between what the police know and the public don't.

I found this both frustrating and yet sadly apt. In the end, the Girl with the Crooked Nose could or could not be dead, and she could or could not have been identified by Frank's bust. It depends on how you read the often confounding facts. More than likely, though, she is one of the many murdered women of Juárez who remains unnamed and, except for her family, has been almost forgotten.

# ACKNOWLEDGMENTS

Many writers dream of a character like Frank Bender walking into their lives. Colorful, kind, unique, unassuming, gentle, stubborn, sexual, frustrating, inquisitive, happy-go-lucky, misunderstood, fearless—he was a complex man, and yet a very simple one. Some people just didn't get him, while many others adored him. They also knew something many others didn't: Frank was an unsung hero. But just as he was closing in on the fame (and perhaps some money to go with it) that had so stubbornly eluded him for the thirty-five years that he had worked in forensics, he died.

On July 28, 2011, at the age of seventy, Frank passed away at his studio/home after fighting a more than yearlong battle with plural mesothelioma that he probably contracted during his time in the navy. To the end he stayed true to the man so many of us had come to know, spontaneous, seemingly never without a mischievous grin, rarely showing that there were plenty of things in life to get him down.

Only fifteen months earlier, his wife Jan had died of cancer too, at the age of sixty one. In late 2006, Jan had been given six months to live, which meant she wouldn't live to see the original publication of *The Girl with the Crooked Nose*. It was a terrible blow, for if anyone had fought for Frank to achieve recognition through all the years, it was Jan. When she first learned of her illness and had to undergo chemotherapy, the residents of South Street saw Jan and Frank every evening walking hand-in-hand in the twilight. Frank stood by her bed feeding her morphine to ease the pain, until something miraculous happened—the cancer disappeared, at least temporarily. In the end, Jan was at all the book readings looking not only healthy but radiant. Her Frank had got his due. No matter what highs and lows they had been through, they were still smitten with each other. Theirs was a love as simple, and as complex, as Frank himself. You could try to explain it, but few would understand.

I will be forever grateful to Frank and Jan for opening their fascinating home, their very deep closets, and their immense trove of video and newspaper clippings of Frank's work. I am also deeply indebted to Frank and Jan's daughters, Lisa Brauner and Vanessa Bender, as well as to Joan Crescenz, especially for her thorough organization of Frank's files. I was also fortunate to have met the legendary pathologist Halbert Fillinger only weeks before he died, and to have heard some of his remarkable stories.

As always, a very special thank-you to my agent, Luke Janklow, and to Claire Dippel, the kind of warm, encouraging person every writer wants and hopes to have on their side. My appreciation also goes to Will Murphy.

While I was writing the book, numerous other people also helped me to understand two subjects that were relatively unknown to me—forensic sculpture, and the widespread murders of young women in Juárez and Chihuahua. Without their help or encouragement I would have been quite lost. The following people I list not in order of importance but at random: former police detective and U.S. deputy marshal Paul Schneider; U.S. Marshal Arthur Roderick; Dr. Stanley Rhine, at the University of New Mexico; Stephanie Dimadio, former anthropologist at the Museum of Natural History in Washington, D.C., who gave me technical and grammatical advice; John Ferrone, who always has positive words to say; my friends Sue and Scott Graham, in Durango, Colorado, for setting me right medically and encouraging me; New York police detective Keith Hall; Michelle Cromer, in El Paso, for opening her house to me and for playing an unheralded role in trying to solve the murders in Juárez; the photographer Arne Svenson; the criminal profiler Robert Ressler; Cynthia Bejaran, associate professor of criminology at the University of New Mexico, who has helped spearhead a campaign to show that the killing of women in Juárez could happen anywhere in the world; Rupert Knox at Amnesty International in London; the Egyptologist Jonathan Elias, who is involved in the project at Akhmim; Gene Suplee at the Philadelphia medical examiner's office, and Gerry White at the Kansas City medical examiner's office; former Philadelphia police detective Larry Grace; journalist Ed Barnes, for his memories of trying to investigate the baffling story in Juárez; Dr. Haskell Askin, in New Jersey; Virginia Hill; Bill Fleischer, cofounder of the Vidocq Society and former U.S. Customs agent; Richard Walter, cofounder of Vidocq and criminal profiler; Caroline Wilkinson, at the University of Dundee's Department of Physical Anthropology in Scotland; Louie Gilot, at the *El Paso Times,* and Sandra Rodriguez, at *El Diario,* for taking me around Juárez and sharing their opinions on the *feminicidios.*

I would also like to thank the women of Juárez whose lives have been forever changed and exposed by the *feminicidios*. Some of them—in particular, the mothers of numerous girls who disappeared or were found murdered—continue to fight for justice, even at the cost of being harassed and intimidated.